THE DAY HUEY LONG WAS SHOT

THE DAY

HUEY LONG

WAS SHOT

September 8, 1935

By DAVID H. ZINMAN

Center for Louisiana Studies
University of Louisiana at Lafayette
Lafayette, Louisiana

First published in the United States by Ivan Obolensky, Inc. and simultaneously in the Dominion of Canada by George J. McLeod Limited, Toronto.

Zinman, David (David H.)
    The Day Huey Long Was Shot, September 8, 1935/by David H. Zinman. Originally published: New York: Obolensky, 1963. Reprint, updated with added chapter, published: Jackson: University Press of Mississippi, 1993.
    First printing by the Center for Louisiana Studies, University of Louisiana at Lafayette, June 1997.
    Second printing, June 2001.
    Third printing, January 2004.
    Fourth printing, July 2005.

Illustration: "The Shooting of Huey Long,"
by John McCrady, 1939.
Courtesy of Mr. and Mrs. Keith C. Marshall

Library of Congress Catalog Number: 97-66906
ISBN Number: 1-887366-12-1

Published by the Center for Louisiana Studies
P.O. Box 40831
University of Louisiana at Lafayette 70504-0831

To my Father

Dictators ride to and fro upon tigers
which they dare not dismount.
And the tigers are getting hungry.
                    —Winston Churchill

    O they say he was a crook
        But he gave us free school book
    Now tell me why is it that they kill Huey Long?
        Now he's dead and in his grave
    But we riding on his pave
        Tell me why is it that they kill Huey Long?
                            —Cajun ballad

Contents

Introduction and Acknowledgments   xi

Prologue   1

The Kingfish's Sunday   13

The Doctor's Sunday (Part One)   49

The Doctor's Sunday (Part Two)   71

Death Casts Its Shadow   97

Blood on the Capitol Floor   111

Unto Dust   137

Between Life and Death   165

The Inquest   195

Aftermath (Part One)   225

Aftermath (Part Two)   247

Conclusion   277

Fifty-Six Years Later   291

Appendixes   335

Bibliography   355

Index   357

Introduction and Acknowledgments

Late in the summer of 1960, I went to the New Orleans Public Library to begin research on an Associated Press feature on the slaying of Huey Long. The story was to be pegged to the 25th anniversary of the Kingfish's assassination.

I was surprised to find that, although a flock of writers had done books on Huey, no one had written one on the slaying itself or on the enigmatic Dr. Carl Weiss, Long's alleged killer. In fact, virtually nothing had appeared about the young doctor in the newspapers or magazines beyond the bare facts of his career. In many cases, the "facts" were wrong. There was little that told what kind of person Weiss was or how the tragedy had affected his wife and family in the years that followed. Beyond frantic newspaper interviews right after the slaying, no publication had printed the Weiss family's explanation for the doctor's actions. In the ensuing years, no biographers and only one reporter—Westbrook Pegler—had even attempted to query the family. Apparently, few of Huey's biographers took great interest in the slaying—judging from the little space most gave it in their books. Since some of the facts seemed sketchy or missing, many of them wrote around the shooting. None made any attempt to clear up the mysteries that still cloud the assassination.

A reporter's stint in New Orleans led irresistibly to these mysteries. This book is an attempt to fill the gaps in this lurid double slaying, which is still being discussed in Louisiana. The author, who is not a native of the State, approached the subject free from political partisanship.

(I wrote those lines in 1963. Three decades later, I was surprised to see the controversy renew in all its fury. A team of forensic scientists unearthed Weiss's body, and the exhumation led indirectly to the discovery of long-missing evidence. That dramatic development brought the Louisiana State Police back into the case. This new edition updates the story with the independent findings of the scientists and the police.)

I make grateful acknowledgment to: Dr. Carl Weiss's family, who broke a silence of over a quarter of a century to tell in detail its side of the story. The author also acknowledges with appreciation the hours that Senator Russell Long, Huey's son, gave up one evening to discuss the events. Prior to each interview, the author made no expression to the Weiss family or to Senator Long— or to any interviewee—as to the position the book would finally take in the controversial slaying. No position was reached until all the research was completed.

For getting me back on the track when I went off the rails, I owe thanks to Ken Davis, my boss at the Associated Press Bureau in New Orleans where I worked when I wrote this book; and for their help in personal interviews or correspondence, I thank: Quincy Ewing, Ed Desobry, J. Alan Coogan, C. E. Frampton, Chief Justice John B. Fournet, Murphy Roden, Elliott Coleman, Sen. Allen J. Ellender, Seymour Weiss, C.P. Liter, Margaret Dixon, A. Veazie Pavy, former Governor Richard Leche, Dr. W.H. Cook, Dr. Joseph Sabatier Jr., Dr. Frank L. Loria, Dr. John Archinard, Mrs. R.B. Fitzgerald, Mrs. Paul Bateman, Theoda Carriere, Mrs. Jewel O. Chapman, Rt. Rev. Msgr. H.P. Lohmann, Bishop Louis A. Caillouet, the Rev. Sam Ray Hill, Judge James P. O'Connor, District Attorney Sargent Pitcher Jr., Ken Dixon, Harnett Kane, J. Huntington Odom, Jack Unbehagan, James Petrie, Emile Bourg, Hugh S. Fullerton, and the Louisiana Tourist Bureau and Department of Commerce and Industry. Thanks also to Drew Pearson for permission to quote from his column, "Surgery, Gynecology and Obstetrics," and to my wife, Sara, who supported me in all my research and encouraged me to follow the case down through the years.

The author also expreses his appreciation to the following for letting him use their resources: the William B. Wisdom collection of Huey Long materials in the Howard Tilton Memorial Library at Tulane University; the New Orleans Public Library; and the microfilm libraries of the New Orleans *Times-Picayune* and *States-*

Item, the Baton Rouge *Morning Advocate* and *State-Times*, and the Opelousas *Daily World.*

Also for helping me on the new chapter, I thank: Charles East, Carolyn Bennett, Ed Tunstall, Louis Milliner, Lester Bernstein, Philippe Y. Sanborne, Virginia R. Smith, Detective Lt. Scott A. Wanlass and Sgt. John Feil of the Nassau (N.Y.) County Police department, and Capt. Ronnie B. Jones, Lt. Don Moreau, and Patrick Lane of the Louisiana State Police.

I am especially grateful to Seetha Srinivasan of the University Press of Mississippi who gave new life to this book. For extending that life, I am indebted to the late Glenn Conrad, former director of the Center for Louisiana Studies at the University of Louisiana at Lafayette.

David Zinman is a graduate of Columbia and the Columbia Graduate School of Journalism. He worked as a reporter for the Associated Press bureau in New Orleans and Long Island *Newsday* for most of his newspaper career. Zinman wrote *The Day Huey Long Was Shot* in 1963. The book, which has been used as a supplementary text at Louisiana State University and has never been out of print, was the basis for *Who Killed the Kingfish*, a drama Zinman wrote with Michael Wynne of Alexandria, La. The play had its world premiere at LSU in 2005.

Prologue

We have lived long but this is the noblest work of our lives. It will transform vast solitudes into thriving districts. The United States takes rank this day among the first powers of the earth. The instruments which we have just signed will cause no tears to be shed. They prepare ages of happiness for innumerable generations of human creatures.

—Quotation from the Louisiana Purchase, carved into the main entrance of the Louisiana Capitol.

That fateful night, September 8, 1935, the uncertain light of a quarter-moon illuminated a sultry and sweltering Louisiana.

On the still Cajun bayous and swamp wildernesses of the coastal South, where mail is brought in by boat and children go to school by boat and French is still spoken (in a dialect no Frenchman would recognize), families in wooden cabins wash dinner dishes of gumbo and jambalaya and crawfish and shrimp and cornbread and cracklin's and potlikker and sweet 'taters and catfish and red beans and rice and black, black coffee. And not far away, near New Iberia, Lafayette, Crowley, and Lake Charles, the shadows of great oil wells play lacelike patterns on fields of sugar cane and strawberries and rice. And to the east, in New Orleans (where half a million people mask and dance in the street on *Mardi gras*), old Creole families—aristocratic descendants of French and Spanish settlers—attend Mass in ancient St. Louis Cathedral, next to the site of the Louisiana Purchase. And close by, on Basin Street, the ghosted laughter of easy women echoes in memory from what once were sportin' houses, and blacks loll in the limp Mississippi River breezes under the rustling willow trees of the levee, and corseted tourist ladies down one last pastry at Antoine's, and a jazz band belts out "Saints" in a Bourbon Street tonk. And newsboys hawking the *Times-Picayune* in the French Quarter shout, "Huey Long Steamrolls 39 Bills Through Committee."

This is south Louisiana. This is New Orleans. Life is gay. Life is carefree. The living is easy. The people are Catholic. The traditions are Latin.

North and central Louisiana is another country. The names are Anglo-Saxon and the manners and morals are Anglo-Saxon. Much of it is hillbilly land, land of the "red necks" and the "pea pickers" and the "flop hats." Here amidst the rolling country are Shreveport, Monroe, and Alexandria. It's Hard-Shell Baptist land. Life is hard. Life is serious. The Red, Black, Ouachita and Mississippi Rivers flow swiftly to the warm Gulf of Mexico. The rivers run through flat bottom-land and red-dirt hills and forests of scrub oak and pine gum and walnut and, in wet places, a fair grade of cypress. And the timbermen and cattlemen and cotton farmers, free for a day from scratching out a living, praise the Lord in Bible meetings. And descendants of slave-holding families sip after-dinner liqueur in sad, fading, ante-bellum mansions and tune in Jack Benny on the radio.

Somewhere not quite halfway between these two sections of Louisiana, these two worlds, the moon shines on the skyscraper Capitol in Baton Rouge. Two men are drawing together to meet their fate in the same way. They are a politician, Huey Pierce Long, dictator of a political empire unique in American history; and a physician, Dr. Carl Austin Weiss, a young ear, nose and throat specialist.

Long and Weiss. They are as different as opposite directions. Long, 42, is the ruthless, flamboyant demagogue—unmistakable in a crowd, magnetic, a man whose uncompromising politics has spawned the admiration or hostility of millions. Dr. Weiss, 29, is a retiring, scholarly, professional man—a quiet man, devoted to his family, his practice, and his religion. As far as anyone knows, they had never met. They met that night.

Strangely, the towering Capitol was to play a key part in the drama. It was only three years old that year. Louisianians still marveled over it. There was nothing in Dixie to match it. Thrusting up from flat marshlands, the building—tallest in the South—reared its 34-story shaft into the sky like a giant beacon, a colossus of the bayou land. Rivermen saw it in the distance as they hauled cargo up the Mississippi River. Farmers spotted it as their horse-drawn wagons pulled their crops up dusty roads into the Capital. State legislators walked in its shadow as they dashed down for one of Huey's hurriedly called special sessions. It reminded them of Huey. And that was as it should have been. Huey had built it. Engineers had said a skyscraper couldn't go up on swampland. But Huey had said, "Find a way!" They had found a way. It had taken only a little over a year to construct, and had cost only five million dollars.

Curiously, Huey and Mark Twain were of like mind in their feelings about the former Capitol. Of all things, it looked like a small medieval castle. The four-story building—it was the Statehouse when Huey became Governor in 1928—was an eclectic hodgepodge of Norman and Moorish architecture. It had turrets, stained glass, and arched windows. Mark Twain had called it "the monstrosity on the Mississippi." All it needed, he had said, was a "stick of dynamite."

Long agreed. To Huey, who had seen the great skylines of Eastern cities, the Capitol looked like a gingerbread pip-squeak. "I'm *sui generis*," Huey said. A class to himself. He wanted his Capitol to be unique, too. It was.

For some, the building inspired a stately respect. Visiting back-country folks talked in whispers, pussy-footed about as they would in a shrine. Others saw no reason for a skyscraper in tableflat Louisiana. They thought the building showy, pretentious.

"It's the richest thing in its line after the barbershop in the St. Regis," A. J. Liebling wrote in the *New Yorker*. "Huey's Silo," brother Earl Long dubbed it.

When it was finished, the soaring, 450-foot building contained over 30 varieties of marble from all over the world. It had floors of polished lava quarried from Italy's Vesuvius, white marble statues of Louisiana's early explorers, and two-ton bronze chandeliers. It rose in the midst of 27 landscaped acres transformed out of a swamp. When Huey strutted across its polished floors, the Capitol stood like a giant inverted "T" among haunting, century-old, moss-hung oaks. There were poplar and magnolia trees dotting the magnificent grounds, and beds of flowers planted so that whatever the season there were bulbs blossoming. You walked up 48 granite steps through a 50-foot-high entranceway. Carved on either side was a passage from the document of the Louisiana Purchase. Inside, you stepped into the grandiose main lobby called Memorial

Hall. Guides lectured about its volcanic stone floors, bronze fixtures, murals, and high, decorated ceiling. The great hall was the building's hub. Opposite its huge doors, elevators glided up the slender shaft to six acres of plush, air-conditioned State offices. Just behind the bank of elevators was the Governor's office. And, flanking the hall, the marble-walled Senate and House swung out on either side to form the crossbar at the base of the "T."

The Legislative chambers even had electric voting machines whose red and green lights flashed the outcome of every bill—except, curiously, once when the House began action to impeach Long. On that occasion, the machines worked wrong. Burning mad legislators leaped across desks and upon each other. "Crooks . . . I voted no and my light showed yes. . . ." Fists flew, curses resounded, and brass knuckles flashed in Louisiana's staid Renaissance palace that rose in dignity above the Mississippi.

That night, one block from the Capitol, Dr. Weiss picked up his medical bag, kissed his wife good-bye, walked into the moonlight in his white linen suit and Panama hat, and drove off in his car. There was a gun in the glove compartment. A few minutes later, he mounted the Capitol steps and walked through the massive entranceway.

Huey paced the aisles of the House chamber. The night session was closing rapidly. The Ways and Means Committee had acted favorably on 39 of his 42 bills during the afternoon, and now they were rolling nicely through the House. As a U.S. Senator, Long had no business on the floor of the State Legislature. But no one there that night was going to try to stop him. He rambled about, chatting with legislators, rocking back and forth on the dais as he looked down upon the House.

You would have called Huey Long dumpy if he had passed you on the street. He was a compact man, with deep-set, piercing, brown eyes. He had a chubby face, a thick, upturned, bulbous nose, and a ruddy complexion speckled with tiny blotches of pigmentation. He had crisp, curly, ginger-colored hair with a forelock that tumbled wildly, a cleft chin, dewlap jowls, a wide mouth, and a habit of scratching his rear end. A setup for a political cartoonist. But at 42 Long was at the top of his amazing political career. He ruled Louisiana with an iron hand. Some said Huey was just getting up steam, that one day he would take over the country.

A hard-driving farm boy with a yen for the power of public office, Long went through Tulane law school in seven months. He passed the bar exam in 1915. Thirteen years later, he became Louisiana's youngest Governor. He was 34. Long built a crack machine, and Louisiana became his empire. He boasted that he bought legislators "like sacks of potatoes, shuffled 'em like a deck of cards." He claimed there might be smarter men "but they ain't in Loozyana," and dubbed himself "Kingfish" (after the shrewd *Amos 'n' Andy* radio character). "This is the Kingfish speaking," Long would bellow when the telephone rang. His rip-roarin' politics catapulted him into the national spotlight.

At 39, the Kingfish became U.S. Senator. And his

"Share the Wealth" plan for Utopia caught up the longings of depression-poor millions. He was making plans for a White House bid. But that night, September 8, 1935, his dreams came to an end—suddenly, violently, irrevocably.

Long bolted out of the chamber as the House was adjourning. He walked briskly down the hall to Governor O. K. Allen's office. A phalanx of bodyguards followed—among them Murphy Roden (who later became State Public Safety Commissioner).

The eyes of a man in white followed the entourage.

Long barged into the Governor's office. His bodyguards waited in the corridor. John B. Fournet, State Supreme Court Associate Justice, had tried to catch Long as Huey left the House. But the Kingfish had walked too fast for him. Fournet joined the waiting group. Long had some things he wanted to air at a morning caucus. "Get the boys out early," he yelled into the office. "Have them all there." Long wheeled and breezed out as suddenly as he had swept in.

As Huey flashed back into the corridor, witnesses said, Dr. Weiss brushed by the bodyguards. Somebody said it looked as if he were going to shake hands with Long. When Weiss's hand appeared, Long's bodyguards said, there was a gun in it.

Newspapers of every major language in the world reported what happened next. No other event in Louisiana history spurred such a lingering fervor. Some denounced Weiss as an assassin or a madman. Others hailed him as a martyr. His family and friends said he was neither. They swore he was innocent.

Weiss was forgotten in the wash of years. Huey became a modern legend. Generations of Southerners have told and retold the story of his life. His stormy career became the subject of movies, books, radio and television dramas. Strangely, they all pushed into the background the sensational events of the tragedy of September 8th. Nobody in Louisiana today is really sure of exactly what happened in the Statehouse corridor—or why it did. Nobody except those few men who saw it. The witnesses were all Huey's bodyguards or members of the Long machine. They waited eight days to tell their stories to the coroner. Some people insisted that not all the facts were disclosed.

The shooting, never fully investigated, confused by conflicting details, shrouded in secrecy, spawned a host of intriguing mysteries. The mysteries gave rise to legends. The legends persist to this day—more than a half-century later—and, incredibly, the mysteries remain unsolved.

The Kingfish's Sunday

Born Winnfield, Louisiana	August 30, 1893
Married Rose McConnell of Shreveport, Louisiana	1913
Admitted to the Bar	1915
Railroad Commissioner	1918–28
Defeated for Governor	1924
Governor	1928–32
Defeated Impeachment	1929
U.S. Senator	1932–35

"I would describe a demagogue as a politician who don't keep his promises. On that basis, I'm the first man to have power in Loozyana who ain't a demagogue. I kept every promise I ever made to the people of Loozyana. None of these ex's and belly achers that have been fightin' me down there ever kept his promises when he was in office. It was an unheard of thing in Loozyana until Huey P. Long got in."

—Huey Pierce Long

Sunday, September 8, 1935, started as another quiet Sabbath in Baton Rouge. At 5:40 a.m. the sun cast its first rays on the lazy Mississippi winding peacefully through the sleeping Capital. The sky was partly cloudy, the day windless, the barometer falling, the mercury on the rise. It would keep rising and soar to an uncomfortable 95 by mid-afternoon.

At the great Capitol, porters had finished cleaning the Legislative chambers and a committee room upstairs. The House Ways and Means Committee was to meet in that room in a few hours. It was to hear Long explain the reasons for a sheaf of bills that had suddenly summoned the lawmakers into another special session—the fourth of the year and the seventh since the regular session adjourned in July of 1934. It was to be an historic meeting.

From the beginning, there was a sense of urgency. Governor Oscar Kelly (O. K.) Allen, Long's hand-picked crony from his home town of Winnfield, had barely given legislators time to scramble to the Capital. He had notified them early Saturday morning of the opening session Saturday night. Few had complained. The Legislature—some called it the "Longislature" in those days—was solidly pro-Long. And then, there was the matter of $10 a day salary and ten cents a mile travel pay. It was hard to fight that kind of money in the Depression.

Senator Long had journeyed down from Washington with his entourage of bodyguards and taken up residence in his apartment-office on the 24th floor of the Capitol tower. This was important business. Huey wanted to be on the scene to be sure everything went smoothly.

Although few knew it then, one of the chief reasons Huey had called the session was to open his counter-attack on the Roosevelt administration. Washington had cracked down on the Kingfish by turning over patronage to his enemies. It had launched a tax inves-tigation of his Louisiana machine. Now it was threat-ening a Congressional probe of Long's whole dictator-ship in the State. That was the last straw. The Federal Government could go "slap dam' to hell," Long told the press. One State bill would fix prison terms for Federal officials exercising "unconstitutional" powers in the State. Louisiana would "fill the jails so full of them Roosevelt henchmen, you can't see the dust," Huey roared. Another measure would give the State power to control Federal funds in Louisiana. Roose-velt might have money to spend in Louisiana, but he would spend it through Huey or not at all. And as long as he was down for the session, Huey figured there were a few other local matters that could be taken care of—39 of them to be exact.

On Saturday night, portly James A. Noe, president *pro tempore* of the Senate and acting Lieutenant Gov-ernor, called the Senate to order at ten o'clock. It had very little to do that night. All measures were origi-nating in the House. Thirty of 39 State senators had raced to Baton Rouge from all parts of the State. The records show that one of the missing—Senator W. Scott Heywood of the 14th District—wanted to be sure the

Kingfish, his colleagues, and possibly posterity knew he had a valid excuse. "My brother near death which is expected any time," Heywood wired. "Dr. Wade keeping him alive with saline solution. Impossible to leave. Please have this telegram read to the Senate and ask to be put in the record. Best personal regards."

Across spacious Memorial Hall, Speaker Allen J. Ellender (later U.S. Senator) called the House into session. Eighty-five of its 100 members answered the roll call. Father Francis Leon Gassler, who would play a minor role in the drama that was about to unfold, opened the session with a prayer:

"Look down, O Almighty, Eternal Father, upon these tiny children who are here assembled in obedience to the call of authority to devise ways and means for the well-being of our beloved Louisiana. Send forth Thy Spirit so that they may begin their arduous work with Thee and, guided by Thy infinite wisdom, may bring their labors to a successful resolve. For this we pray and for this we plead—Amen."

The House's work was brief, too. The clerk read all the bills—39 of them backed by the Long administration—and, under a suspension of the rules and without objection, the House sent all of the measures to a single committee—the Committee on Ways and Means.

It saved time to refer all bills to one committee, Huey once explained. One committee also saved energy and shoe leather. The Kingfish didn't have to bother hopping around from one room to another. By now, the seventh year of his reign, Long showed up at committee meetings by habit. When he was there, he ran the show with a precision that would have won envy from a circus ringmaster. When Huey nodded, committee members nodded. When Huey frowned, they frowned. When Huey said yes, they said amen.

It was just after nine o'clock the next morning—Sunday morning—when the Ways and Means Committee met in the towering Statehouse. Huey made his entrance clad in immaculate linen, with tie, shirt, shoes and socks to match. Heads turned when Huey entered. As a United States Senator, Long held no official position in the State of Louisiana. But he said he was there to "discuss" the measures—a privilege accorded every Louisiana citizen. Long exchanged greetings with friendly lawmakers, took a seat next to chairman Edmund G. Burke of New Orleans, and signaled for proceedings to start.

Representative Burke handed the first measure—House Bill No. One—to Long for explanation. It seemed a relatively minor item. No one there that morning regarded it with any great interest. It affected only two men. It split an anti-Long voting district in south Louisiana by carving it up and joining its segments to heavy pro-Long areas. Long was making defeat at the polls inevitable for a judge and a district attorney who had opposed him.

"This bill rearranges the 13th and 15th Districts," Long said. "It separates St. Landry and Evangeline Parishes (counties) and puts St. Landry in the judicial district with Acadia, Lafayette and Vermilion. The status of Judge Pavy and District Attorney Garland are not affected. They retain their status until January 1, 1937. . . . When their time comes to run, they go into a new district."

Long put down the bill. He looked out among the faces in the crowded committee room.

"The reason I'm explaining these bills is for the benefit of the audience," he said. "I thought there might be someone here who would like to be heard in opposition to them."

He glanced around, a quizzical smile on his face. There was a dead silence.

Jack Williamson, a 23-year-old Representative from Lakes Charles, broke the stillness.

"Did the people of the District request this change be made?"

The Kingfish turned and looked hard at Williamson for a moment. Then Long answered:

"Yes, the people of Evangeline are for it, and the St. Landry Parish members of the House are for it."

Williamson was the only anti-Long on the 14-man Committee. House Bill No. One passed 13-1.

The Committee moved on to the next measure. House Bill No. Two, Long said, provided for one judge instead of two in East Baton Rouge Parish after November 1936, when the current term expired.

"One judge is enough for East Baton Rouge Parish," said Long. "Judge Favrot was ill for a number of years before he died and the court was presided over by one judge. Besides, this move will save money."

The bill was designed to defeat Judge W. Carruth Jones, a Long opponent, when he sought re-election. The Committee approved it. Chairman Burke came to a bill restoring some of the pay which a third special session had cut from the City Attorney's office in New Orleans. New Orleans was a staunch anti-Long stronghold. A Committee member handed an amendment for the bill to Long. He read it, tore it across the middle, and then into smaller pieces.

"No, we don't want this amendment," he said. "We are providing that the City Attorney in New Orleans should have $6,000 a year and his assistants $4,000. That is enough for the assistants, and I don't think they need $5,000."

The Committee approved the unamended bill.

The procedure was the same on all measures. Burke handed Long a bill—or Long simply picked it up from the pile in front of Burke—and Long rattled off a few sketchy reasons why he considered it necessary. Except for Williamson, the Committee showed no curiosity about them. Lawmakers were all for speed.

Once, Long offered no more explanation than to say, "This is a fine bill." Williamson, his cheeks flushed, was on his feet demanding details.

Huey turned to Assistant Attorney General George Wallace sitting nearby, solemn-faced and bored.

"George will explain any of the fine points," Long said. "I'm told this bill takes out some of the clockwork and gives the hands a chance to move."

The Committee reported the bill favorably.

Burke continued down the list until he reached the key anti-Federal bill. It made it a crime for a Government agency or officer to exercise any Federal power in Louisiana not specifically delegated by the United States Constitution. Now Huey was getting down to business. He was turning to States' rights with a vengeance.

"You know, just the other day a Federal officer in

Natchitoches Parish refused to permit hay to be shipped into another parish of the State," Long explained, easing into the bill informally. "He said that the hay was infested with ticks. Why, they can give almost any kind of excuse and enforce any kind of a ruling they want unless we enact a law like this."

"This simply provides a penalty for violation of Article Ten of the Constitution of the United States," he went on. "In Section One of our bill, we say the same thing that the Constitution of the United States says —that certain rights are reserved to the states and the people. But in Section Two, we go further and say that whoever violates the Constitution of the United States, we make it a misdemeanor punishable by a fine and jail sentence."

Chairman Burke had dropped the bill in the House's hopper, so it carried his name. As an afterthought, Long said, "You know, this bill bearing the name of Edmund Burke will go down in history. When the great lawmaker Burke of England is forgotten, this bill will cause Edmund Burke of Louisiana to be remembered. Hereafter when anyone speaks of Burke the lawmaker, everyone will ask which one you mean."

"What is the purpose of this bill, Senator?" Williamson asked, a feeble voice amidst the general laughter. Williamson knew he had no chance of defeating the measure. But, since the session was open and covered by the press, at least he might embarrass Long by getting him to come out and admit what was really behind this important bill. If he could do this, he would be building up ammunition to fire against Long in the coming election. But Huey was cagey. He could use the cloak of legality with the best of them. And he was glad to oblige.

"What is the purpose of this bill, Senator?" Williamson repeated.

"This is an enabling act to carry out the principles of the Constitution of the United States," Long answered.

"Does it intend to prevent the expenditure of Federal funds in Louisiana?" Williamson asked, trying to draw Long out.

"It intends to prevent violation of the Constitution of the United States," Long answered vaguely.

"What have you in mind by this bill?" Williamson persisted.

"We have in mind the preservation of the Constitution of the United States."

"You are willing to go on with this even though it should mean keeping vast sums of Federal funds out of this State?"

"At any cost," Long fired back, "the Constitution of the United States must be preserved. The Tenth Amendment, reserving to the states all the powers not specifically placed in Congress by the United States Constitution, was written by Thomas Jefferson, and we're still Jeffersonian Democrats in Loozyana."

Applause broke out in the committee room. Some Committee members joined in and clapped. "Hot dog! Pour it on 'em, Huey," someone yelled from the crowd. Long smiled. The rest of the meeting was anti-climactic. On that searing Sunday morning the House Ways and Means Committee passed all 39 administration-backed bills. Three other bills without administration support were rejected. Chairman Burke adjourned the meeting, and spectators and lawmakers crowded around Long.

It could be said that on that day in history—September 8, 1935—Long was the most powerful man in Louisiana, past or present. Twenty years back he had been a nobody. Where had he come from? How had he risen to power so quickly? And, perhaps most important, where was he going from here?

Huey Pierce Long is not easily defined. But those who lump him with the run of the pea-patch Southern demagogues plainly underestimate him. His mind, Raymond Moley once wrote, was an instrument such as is given to few men. He was sure in detail, quick in decision. Chief Justice William Howard Taft said that he was "the most brilliant lawyer who ever practiced before the United States Supreme Court."

Hugh Mulligan of the Associated Press saw him as a man who wore a multi-colored coat: "He was a master political strategist, a bold leader and petty tyrant; a physical coward who surrounded himself with bully boys but still had the courage to take on the President of the United States; a lovable, laughable, rustic clown who gave the people bread and circuses in exchange for political servitude."

It was true. Huey's life was a jumbled kaleidoscope of contradictions.

He mispronounced the simplest words, then used a jaw-buster like "petroglyphic" correctly in the next breath. He said "ain't," then quoted Vergil without faltering.

He ignored messages from leading citizens on occasions. Yet, his secretaries said he never turned down a request for an autograph.

He turned down dozens of social invitations. Then, unannounced and uninvited, he would show up at a highly formal function, startling the hostess with the presence of his bodyguards.

In Washington, frequenters of the Shoreham Club regarded Long as one of the Capital's latest night hawks. Yet at the Congressional Country Club colleagues regarded him as one of the city's earliest risers. He often got to the club just after daybreak for an 18-hole round of golf.

Huey seldom shot under 100. His foursome usually included his male secretary, Earle Christenberry, and two bodyguards. He had few intimate friends. He was ill at ease talking to an intelligent person at close quarters. He never tolerated men of great ability around him and he never delegated power. But he rewarded his loyal followers royally.

He cultivated the image of a country bumpkin. He launched a national campaign to get people to eat potlikker (the juice left over after greens are boiled with proper seasoning), strutted like a peacock before the Louisiana State University band at parades, "coached" the football team from the sidelines, and caused an international incident by receiving, in his pajamas, an outraged German consul. Huey knew that all the world loved a character, and he knew that "characters" usually got the headlines. (Long, in fact, got more press space, radio time, and visitors than any other Senator.)

But all his clowning couldn't hide his less-comic qualities. He was impudent and a braggart. He called officeholders "dime a dozen punks." He abounded in deeds of personal humiliation. He was not beyond hurling the epithet "kinky" or "shinola" in stump speeches to ascribe "nigger blood" to a political opponent. Hoodlums clustered around him. Brutality was a source of his strength. Revenge was never far from his thoughts.

Above all, Huey was a spellbinder. He was at his best on a platform—arms windmilling, voice thundering. "I was born into politics a wedded man with a storm for my bride," he told the United States Senate. He was a brilliant, if rambling, orator. His mist of words caught the fancy of crowds that heard him in legislative halls, on the radio, and on the stump. Many old-timers still remember Huey talking to the plain folks of Louisiana at shady courthouse squares and dusty crossroads. He spoke their language. His humor was earthy and folksy, with a twist of religion thrown in—their humor.

—Paw was bein' baptized late in a sinful life. The preacher led the way while Maw and the chillun watched with the crowd on the creek shore. As Paw was walking out with the water up to his chest, the ace and king of spades floated out of his pants. Then came the queen and the jack. And just as the preacher was going to duck Paw under, out floated the ten of spades. "Don't baptize him, Preacher," Maw yelled. "Preacher, he's a sinner. He's lost forever." "No, he ain't,

Preacher," one of the boys jumped up and shouted. "If Paw can't make it with that hand, he can't make it atall."

There was Huey on the radio—full of stories from Washington, colloquial and homespun as if he were in your own living room. And he had his own way of getting a big audience.

"This is Huey P. Long speaking, ladies an' ge'men. Now before I start my speech, I want each one of you who are listening in to go to the telephone and ring up a half-dozen of your friends. Tell 'em Huey Long is on the air. Tell 'em to tune in and stay tuned in. I'll wait till you get through phonin'. I'm going to tell you things those lyin' newspapers won't tell you. I'm going to tell you the God's truth, so help me. This is Huey Long speakin', ladies and ge'men. Go to your telephone now an' call up all your friends. . . . Well, they're investigatin' me again. They began investigatin' me ever since I was first elected to public office an' what have they found? Paved roads, free bridges, free textbooks for their own chil-ern—an' it never cost 'em a thin dime! Now, they can't understand that. So they're investigatin' me again. . . ."

There was Huey before the press—irascible, tough, unpredictable, always good for a colorful quote when you could get past his deadpan plug-uglies, but shrewd. The papers were against him in his home state. He turned that into an asset. His weapon? Handbills.

"I understand that practically all important news-papers of the State are against you, Senator," a visiting newsman asked once. "Is that true?"

"Yes, it's true, all right, and it's a damn good thing.

We thrive on opposition. Senator Noe, here, will tell you a thing or two about it. Why, up in Monroe and Shreveport, our boys had told us that the papers were a-layin' low and that we'd carry the election only 3-1. Hell, I said, that will never do. It ain't fair for them papers to lay quiet against them bills of ours. Sometimes those sons of bitches make like they're on our side, and we have to get out handbills to convince them to the contrary. Now, as I was sayin', we got out the handbills in Monroe and Shreveport, and after a while the papers started printin' front-page attacks against me and m'bills. And the finish was that we carried the election there 8-1 instead of 3-1."

Finally, there was Huey on the stump. Listen to Long campaigning in St. Martinville in the heart of south Louisiana's Cajun [1] country. Long was running for Governor in 1928, stumping feverishly in the south, where he needed the votes most. Tanned, rawboned, leather-faced Cajun men and women crowded in on the grass. Huey's voice rang out loud and confiding. His arms jumping, his shirt wrinkled and stained with perspiration, he stood beneath fabled Evangeline oak, the setting for Longfellow's famous poem.

"Evangeline is not the only one who waited here in disappointment. Where are the schools that you have waited for your children to have, that have never come?

[1] "Cajun" is the common name for the Acadians, pastoral French who emigrated from Nova Scotia in the 18th century. After the British and French went to war, the Acadians refused to take up arms against their mother country. The British exiled them in 1755, cruelly splitting up families. Many settled in Louisiana, then a French colony. To this day, Old World customs live on among Louisiana's Cajuns—a tradition of *joie de vivre,* good cooking, Catholicism, and a French patois called simply "Cajun."

Where are the roads and the highways that you send your money to build, that are no nearer now than ever before? Where are the institutions to care for the sick and the disabled? Evangeline wept bitter tears in her disappointment, but it lasted through only one life-time. Your tears in this country, around this oak, have lasted for generations."

He stopped and looked into the eyes of the yearning hundreds—the shrimp fishermen and the muskrat hunters and the gallused farmers from the canebrakes. And they looked back in utter silence in Louisiana's bayou land.

"Give me the chance to dry the eyes of those who still weep here."

In the beginning, there was Huey P. Long, Sr., and Caledonia (Miz Cally) Tison Long. Huey's father owned 320 acres of poor soil barely suitable for farming in north-central Louisiana's hard-bitten Winn Parish. Winn Parish was not a slice out of the romantic South. It was anything but. It was a land of hard-working, grim farmers, straight-laced, austere Baptists—"red necks" who toiled under the blistering sun by day and spent their nights in Bible meetings or tending to household chores. "Its harvests were scrawny," Harnett Kane wrote. "What cattle it had were scrawnier; its people were scrawniest." There were few Negroes. It was over-run with hogs and children. It was a bitter land of poor whites who looked with envy on the rich planters with their slaves and their mansions and their graceful liv-ing. Its chief by-product: dissent.

When Louisiana voted to secede to join the Confederacy, Winn Parish protested. Who wanted to die for another man's slaves? Many Winn Parish men joined Union forces or hid out rather than join the Confederate Army. Winn supported William Jennings Bryan. It voted Socialist in 1908 after Eugene Debs visited and spoke.

Into this aura came Huey Pierce Long, Jr., in 1893 —eighth of nine children. This was the legacy his father left:

"There wants to be a revolution, I tell you. I seen this domination of capital, seen it for 70 years. What do these rich folks care for the poor white man? They care nothing—not for his pain, nor his sickness, nor his death. . . .

". . . They'd sooner speak to a nigger than a poor white. They tried to pass a law saying that only them as owned land could vote. And when the war come, the man that owned ten slaves didn't have to fight. . . . Maybe you're surprised to hear talk like that. Well, it was just such talk that my boy was raised under, and that I was raised under."

Huey Sr. owned his cotton fields and his farmhouse. Though made of logs, his cabin home was a roomy, sturdy structure—better than the majority of surrounding homes. On campaigns, Huey was to picture it as a Tobacco Road shack to establish rapport with poor whites. But in his autobiography he candidly said it was a comfortable, well-built, four-room, log house.

Young Huey knew the Bible practically by heart. The family read a chapter a day. Community life centered around the church. Huey was there all day on Sunday. He went to prayer meetings every Wednesday night. He heard the thunder-and-lightning gospel preachers at revival and camp meetings, the sermons about fiery pits and demons. And there was to be an evangelical tone in Huey's speeches that stayed with him even in the Senate.

But Huey detested the grueling farm chores and the humdrum routine of isolated country life. "In the field, the rows were long; the sun was hot; there was little companionship," he was to write. "Rising before the sun, we toiled until dark, after which we did nothing except eat supper, listen to the whippoorwills and go to bed."

Nevertheless, his boyhood was a lively one. At ten, the red-headed hellion ran away from home. As a teenager he worked in a print shop, won debating honors, auctioneered, sold books to farmers, helped (for five dollars) a neighbor campaign for tick inspector and win by 14 votes.

Huey was always a fighter, but not with his fists. He was a physical coward, and the label was to stick with him throughout his political career. Once brother Earl (later three times Governor of Louisiana) came upon him while he was getting beaten up by a bunch of kids. Earl rolled up his sleeves and piled in to help Huey. When Earl looked up a few seconds later, there were Huey's flying heels kicking up a dust storm down the road.

Political foes later told tales of how Huey ran from an 80-year-old former Governor, fled from a one-legged voter, and got a black eye in a washroom after he tried to urinate through another man's legs.

The railroad came to Winn, and Huey Sr. sold land

to it and moved into a better house. He was able to send six of his children to college. But the money ran out when Huey's turn came.

So Huey turned to the road. He became a traveling salesman for Cottolene, a cooking oil. If he couldn't sell a farmer's wife with words—"quit usin' that hog lard," he would say—he would march right into the kitchen and cook supper for the family. His route took him into Louisiana's backwoods, and here he saw at first hand the miserable roads and rural discontent. He spent each night in a different farmhouse, joking, Bible-quoting, damning the rich, building up a backlog of friends he would call on later. The salary was good, but temptations proved too much. Huey was fired for padding his expense account.

But Cottolene gave Huey a wife. At Shreveport, he met Rose McConnell at a baking contest in which she won first prize for the best bride-loaf cake. They were married a short while later. He was 19.

Huey tried his hand at a variety of jobs until Rose persuaded him to study law. Huey's brother Julius had gone to Tulane law school and was now a practicing attorney. The Longs went to New Orleans, and Huey dug into law texts with a passion. He burned the midnight oil in their small two-room apartment, studying up to 18 hours a day. As professors left for home, he often rode the streetcar with them to discuss fine points. Rose helped him all she could. Huey dictated his notes to her. But his weight dropped to 112 pounds. And in eight months their money was gone. Undaunted, Huey appeared before the State Supreme Court and asked it to give him a special exam. The high court did. Huey passed it. And he returned to Winnfield a lawyer. He was 21.

Huey put his half-dollar shingle outside a second-floor, four-dollar-a-month room rented from the bank of Winnfield. It had two kitchen chairs, a pine-topped table, and a kerosene lamp. The corner shoe store let him use its phone.

Old-timers tell a story that in one of his first cases Huey defended a cousin against a charge of stealing a pig. Huey convinced a jury that his kin was the victim of a frame-up. Huey got the hog as his fee.

Oscar K. Allen, who had a farm near the Longs, was another early client. Oscar, a good-hearted, simple man, was being sued for causing a colossal embarrassment. The family of a Winn Parish man who had died in Shreveport asked Allen to have the body sent home. Poor Oscar got the name wrong. The family lugged the coffin over ten miles into the backwoods only to discover at the wake that the body of a Negro was inside. The family hauled the coffin back over those long backwoods miles, and, enraged, told Oscar they were going to sue him. Huey talked them out of it. He won a life-long friend.

In another case, a widow asked Huey to sue a bank for money that she believed the bank owed her. But she didn't have the money for a required legal bond. With typical nerve, Huey marched to the bank and asked one of the directors to lend him money (so he could sue the bank). That director was State Senator John Harper. Harper gave him the loan and some of his personal philosophy, too. One of the chief Parish malcontents, Harper saw most of the country's troubles in its unequal possession of wealth. He decried the fact that 72 percent of the country's wealth was in the hands of only 2 per cent of its people. The point was an eye-opener for Huey. He listened and he remembered.

World War I came. But Huey showed no inclination to fight. Rose had given birth to a child, and Huey drew a deferment. To get more secure draft protection, he sought deferment as a public official—a notary public. "I wasn't mad at nobody," Huey said.

In 1918, four years out of law school, Long ran for the Railroad Commission, a utility-regulating agency (later known as the Public Service Commission). Huey was 25. It was the only State office that had no age limitation.

Long was one of four opponents against the popular incumbent, Commissioner Burk A. Bridges. He stumped the uplands with a fury, selling himself as he sold Cottolene.

Politicians advised him to wear baggy pants and chew tobacco. But Huey had his own ideas.

"I got me lots of white linen suits and wore them fresh. I borrowed enough money to buy the newest and shiniest automobile I could get. I wanted those folks to think I was somebody, and they did."

He bypassed the usual campaign stop-offs—the courthouse points—for the backwoods country towns and farms. He campaigned past sundown, too, bursting in at farmhouses at night. With his boundless energy, he knocked at darkened country homes and hallooed and shouted, "Get 'em all up." What was all that fussin' about? "If the pore country folk is to win against the

Big Uns," Huey answered, "we're gonna have to work day and night."

"They'd always be glad to see somebody that could talk their own language and still had been traveling around," Huey said. "Most times, they wouldn't want to take pay for the night's meal and lodging. But I'd always make 'em take a dollar, which was less'n I'd have to pay in town, and made the man my friend. And I'd get his name and address, too, and sometime later I'd drop him a letter about crops or something."

Huey Pierce Long, the political unknown, won by 625 votes. The victory launched his career.

Standard Oil was Commissioner Huey's made-to-order opponent. Its refineries overspread the river front at Baton Rouge. Its power reached into the Capitol, where it bulldozed legislators. It was an oc-TOE-pus . . . a giant . . . a Colossus . . . , Huey said. Furthermore, he had a personal vendetta to settle. Huey had bought stock in a small oil company and woke up one day to find it worthless after Standard had forced the pipelines to end service to all independents. Huey fought hard and finally succeeded in getting the Commission to declare Standard's pipelines "common carriers" and therefore subject—like a railroad—to the Commission's controls. The courts upheld him.

Huey declared war on all the big corporations. He blocked several railroad mergers. He successfully opposed a telephone rate increase and made refunds retroactive two years. Telephone users got a big refund, and Huey became a minor State hero. He lowered the rate of Shreveport streetcars and of all intrastate railroads. And he didn't overlook Standard Oil.

He helped persuade the Legislature to enact a three-percent severance tax on petroleum from Louisiana wells.

Now he was becoming a personal force in the State. Huey backed John M. Parker, the gentlemen's liberal, for Governor in 1920 with the understanding that Parker would join in Long's all-out war against the Octopus Standard Oil. But after Parker got elected, Huey claimed that the Governor declined to adopt Long's oil program. Enraged and stung, Long broke with Parker and publicly attacked him. A little too vehemently for Parker's taste. Parker sued Long for slander. One of the stories Huey reportedly told about the Governor was this:

—A Chinaman, a Fiji Islander, and the Governor were trying to see who could stay in a room the longest with a polecat. The Chinaman walked into the room. He stayed three minutes and came out sick. Then the Fiji Islander went in and stayed six minutes, and stumbled out green. Finally, the Governor went in and the polecat rushed out puking.

Huey was found guilty. The judge set his fine at one dollar. Long refused to pay. So the judge passed the hat around and collected a dollar to close the case.

In 1924, Huey ran for Governor. He had two opponents in the Democratic primary—Parker's Lieutenant Governor, Hewitt Bouanchaud, a south Louisiana Catholic, and Henry L. Fuqua, a Baton Rouge Protestant and general manager of the State prison.

Long toured the State, spouting his platform from every crossroads—free textbooks, free bridges, good roads, war on Standard Oil and on the big corporations and on "thieves, scalawags, looters, moral lepers, bugs and lice, plundering high-binders and blackguards in full dress."

Long counted heavily on support in the rural north country. He did not have a close-knit organization, and he knew New Orleans and south Louisiana were lost. His problem was not to run too far behind in those two areas.

The Ku Klux Klan, which had become active in some parishes, emerged as the potent force in the campaign. Naturally, Bouanchaud was staunchly anti-Klan. Fuqua was lukewarm. Huey tried to stay uncommitted. In the Cajun south, he talked anti-Klan. In the "red-neck" north, he talked up the Klan. In both places, he passed quickly over to what he claimed was the election's real issue—that his opponents were both "two eggs from the same corporation basket."

On election eve, Huey confidently predicted victory —barring rain. But the rains came. They turned dirt roads of the north into muddy quagmires. They became virtually impassable with a mule and buggy. The first country box reported in. It showed 61 votes cast, 60 for Huey.

"I'm beat," Huey said. "There should have been 100 votes for me and one against me."

Huey was right. He missed the run-off—where Fuqua beat Bouanchaud—by 7,000. (In Louisiana primaries, if no candidate wins a clear majority, the top two face each other in a run-off.) But outside New Orleans, Long narrowly carried the State. The lesson was clear. If Huey maintained his advantage in the north and picked up new votes in south Louisiana and New Orleans, he could win the 1928 election.

Huey devoted the next four years to winning friends and influencing people in vote-shy districts. Came primary time in 1928, he stumped furiously under the slogan (adapted from a speech by William Jennings Bryan), "Every man a king, but no man wears a crown." Election day was sunny. Huey's great unwashed buggied without hindrance to the polls. At 35, Huey was Louisiana's youngest Governor.

So far, it was the old political story of the ambitious young man rising to the top by arousing the people in the hinterlands and blasting big-business interests. The next step seemed obvious. Long would exact his price for peace with the interests he had so long attacked.

But here the familiar pattern ended abruptly. Long's long-range goal was power, not wealth. He wouldn't share his new-found power with anyone.

In 1928, Hoover was President, the stock market was soaring, actresses took baths in champagne, and one-fifth of Louisiana could not read or write. No state had been so badly governed for so many years. Since Reconstruction, Louisiana had been run by an alliance of the New Orleans businessmen and upstate planters. The "old oligarchy" owed allegiance to the railroads, to the utilities and to Standard Oil.

Veteran politicians regarded Huey lightly in the beginning. A buffoon—at best irritating—nothing to worry about. The *New York Times* thought he would carry on the Southern tradition of "light political farce." Huey fooled them all.

To build a political organization, one that owed him complete loyalty, Huey cleaned house with a passion. He fired every State employee he could—down to janitor. Then, he moved on the State boards and commissions. When employees insisted that they were protected, Huey abolished their jobs, cut off State money.

He faced a hostile Legislature. He had only 18 of 100 members of the House supporting him, only nine of 30 Senators. To bottle up his program, his opponents introduced scores of bills and clogged the calendar. Huey matched wits with them. Huey's leaders quickly called up all opposition bills without debate, passed them and cleared the docket for Long's bills. Later, Huey vetoed all opposition measures.

Huey steered his free-textbook bill through to passage. And he included Catholic schools as well as public schools. His opponents thought that they'd snag the bill on that point—using public money for religious education. They fought the bill to the United States Supreme Court. But Huey argued that the books went to the children, not to the schools. Huey won in a case of national significance.

He put a severance tax on oil, gas, timber, sulphur, and other natural resources. The Public Service Commission opposed him. Its appropriation stopped suddenly. It was out of business.

Bond issues were passed for roads. Any legislator who was against him: "the road stopped at his parish." No one seemed to mind if the State paid two dollars per cubic yard for the same gravel that cost private constructors 67½ cents a yard.

When Louisiana's gentlemen-planter Governors were in office, they sat in their office and received reports of legislative activity. Long treated the Legislature as an extension of the Governor's office. He paced up and down the aisles. Sometimes, he would call out "Aye" or "Nay" in response to a machine legislator's name.

A short honeymoon that existed between Huey and some of the big-city presses ended within a year. Huey shouted back, "lyin' newspapers." He never outwardly censored the press, but he did the next best thing. He got his own newspaper, the *Louisiana Progress,* printed in Mississippi to make libel suits more difficult. The paper was an immediate hit. Every State employee was a subscriber. Any firm that hoped to do business with the State bought ads. The *Progress* carried more ads than the *Saturday Evening Post.*

The first Legislative session ended in general triumph for Huey. The anti-Longs clearly saw that they had underestimated Long. He was well on the road to a redistribution of political power, a reshuffling that would be disastrous to the interests of the upper class. They had to counterattack immediately or it would be too late to do anything. The weapon? Impeachment.

The Legislature was in a nasty mood when Long reconvened it in 1929. He had been pushing too many people around. He was biting off more than he could chew, some thought. For one thing, he was trying to pass an occupational tax of five cents a barrel on crude oil to burden his perennial foe, Standard Oil. The tax triggered a raw nerve in the businessman-planter alliance. Standard President D. R. Weller came to Baton

Rouge. Standard threatened to shut down its refineries in Louisiana.

On March 20, 1929, State Representative Lavinius Williams asked the House to enforce its rule preventing lobbying on the floor. Huey left one step ahead of the Sergeant-at-Arms. On March 21, Lieutenant Governor Paul N. Cyr accused Long of approving the leasing of more than $1.5 million of Louisiana land to a Texas company on terms grossly unfair to the State. The same day, Charles Manship, editor of the anti-Long Baton Rouge *State-Times,* announced that Long had tried to intimidate him by threatening to publish that his brother was in the State insane asylum. The New Orleans press published a story about Long prancing around with a half-naked dancer at a French Quarter party. The Shreveport Journal called for an investigation, and the cry echoed in the Legislature's cloakrooms. Long spread the word to adjourn the session, but the momentum was underway. He was too late.

In a tense session they call "Bloody Monday" in Louisiana, a Long legislator made the motion for adjournment. But, as he spoke, Representative Cecil Morgan of Caddo Parish—whom Speaker John Fournet had unsuccessfully tried to gavel into silence— stunned the House:

"I am speaking and I will not yield the floor. I have in my hand an affidavit . . . that the Governor has tried to procure the assassination of a member of this House."

Even while Morgan held the floor, Fournet recognized the motion to adjourn. He called for a vote.

Legislators rushed to their desks. The voting machine flashed a blanket of green—for yes. Fournet slammed his gavel. The House was adjourned.

"I voted no and the machine showed yes," came a chorus of cries. There was bedlam in the House. Legislators argued, shouted, then slugged each other in an all-out battle. Fournet slipped out a side door.

"You damned crook," one voice shouted. "The machine's fixed."

In the rioting, brass knuckles flashed, shirts ripped, fists flew, and heads bumped on desks. Several men wept. Representative Mason Spencer finally got to the rostrum, grabbed the gavel, and got silence. With Fournet and the clerk gone, he called for a voice vote. Seventy-one were against adjournment, nine in favor.

The next day, Fournet apologized. He said that the machine had functioned improperly. A subsequent investigation showed that an anti-Long man was in charge of the voting machine and that Fournet was probably correct. The House impeached Huey on 19 charges.

The Legislature accused him of, among other things, attempted murder, bribery, misappropriation of funds, violent abuse of citizens and officials, intimidation of the press, cavorting with a semi-nude dancer, and conduct unbecoming a Governor. He was charged with everything under which a Louisiana Governor could be charged—except habitual drunkenness. Some thought that should be included, too.

Huey cried like a baby, his face buried in his pillow. "My ground began to slip from under me," he wrote later. "Rats deserting a sinking ship."

But his weeping didn't last long. He was at a grim crossroads. He was battling for his political life. Crying wouldn't help. He sprang into action. Troopers drove from border to border distributing placards that called the proceedings a "Standard Oil plot." Crowds gathered to watch the Kingfish laugh off the charges and recite his favorite poem, "Invictus."

> ". . . In the fell clutch of circumstance
>   I have not winced nor cried aloud:
> Under the bludgeonings of chance
>   My head is bloody but unbowed. . . .

> "It matters not how strait the gate,
>   How charged with punishment the scroll,
> I am the master of my fate:
>   I am the captain of my soul!"

In the swirl of things, brother Earl sank his teeth into an opponent's ear. It took three men to pry him loose.

The solution came at night. Long summoned 15 Senators from their beds. He got them to sign the famous "Round Robin"—for which they were well rewarded. They announced that they held the impeachment charges illegal and would not vote to convict Huey. They constituted one more than one-third of the Senate membership. It required a two-thirds majority vote to pass an impeachment charge. Proceedings halted. Huey was the victor in the toughest battle of his career.

"I used to get things done by saying 'please,' " Huey said. "That didn't work, and now I'm a dynamiter. I dynamite 'em out of my path."

Huey, the dynamiter, blasted ahead full speed from that day forward. Many believe he did more things for Louisiana than any other Governor. He flooded the State with more than half a million free school-books, reduced the number of illiterates by 175,000, raised enrollment from 1,500 to 5,000 at Louisiana State University, doubled the number of charity hospitals, gave Louisiana 2,500 miles of sorely needed paved roads and 6,000 miles of new gravel roads, put bridges over every major river, opened a State University school of medicine in New Orleans, improved mental hospitals, brought homestead exemptions and welfare and old-age payments. And he abolished the poll tax.

The rest of the nation considered Louisiana's government a roaring farce. But to thousands of humble and illiterate in Long's state, he was a popular hero. In many ways, he gave them the social justice that the planter and businessmen politicians had so long denied them.

("Looking back," Pulitzer-Prize-winning newspaper-man Hodding Carter wrote, "I know that part of our failure arose from an unwillingness to approve any Long-sponsored proposal for change, regardless of its merits.")

But Long was a captive of his own insatiable lust for power. And these improvements came with a virtual suspension of democracy. Long loaded the State payroll with his cronies, bludgeoned a supine Legislature into passing his laws, and gradually extended his power until practically every officeholder, court, and municipal government was under his thumb.

During a Legislature committee session, a State Representative, enraged by Long's interference with proceedings, threw a copy of the Constitution at Huey's head.

"Maybe you've heard of this before," the lawmaker shouted.

Long picked it up, looked at the title, and tossed it aside.

"I am the Constitution just now," Huey said.

In 1930, Huey won a United States Senate seat without relinquishing his hold on the State Government. The Lieutenant Governor had become an opponent, so Long didn't take up his Washington post until two years later, after he saw a hand-picked successor elected Governor. Huey told the voters, "With your present Senator, the seat, in effect, has been vacant for years anyhow."

"Long for President" banners went up all over the State after Huey's election to the Senate. The nation laughed. Huey didn't.

Oscar Kelly Allen, the same man who had confused white and Negro corpses back in Winnfield, was Huey's choice for Governor. A less than brilliant man, Oscar's greatest virtue was his swift and uncompromising recognition of who the boss was. When Huey came to town, Oscar moved out of the Governor's office when Huey wanted privacy. "O. K." were apt first and second initials. They called Allen "the vassal." His reflexes were so automatic, he signed bills that Huey approved without hesitation. A story goes that one day a leaf blew in on Oscar's desk. He dipped his pen and signed the leaf.

His Louisiana house in order, Long expanded his influence. He helped elect a Governor in Mississippi and a Senator in Arkansas and played a key role in the 1932 nomination of Franklin D. Roosevelt.

He carried his flamboyance and meanness to Washington. He had no trouble winning the crowds, but his brash ways offended most Senators. When he spoke in the Senate, the galleries were filled, the floor deserted. He was, at first, a supporter of the New Deal. But the administration cut off his patronage when it learned how his Louisiana machine squandered public money and how opposition was suppressed. And Roosevelt's Congressional lieutenants offered no zealous support for Huey's wealth-sharing scheme. Long turned on his heels and became one of FDR's archfoes.

Ostensibly, they parted company over the Share-the-Wealth plan, but the cleavage coincided nicely with Huey's Presidential ambitions. He filibustered to disrupt New Deal programs. He led the Senate rejection of United States membership in the World Court, which Roosevelt had called for.

He compared FDR to a scrootch owl, Hoover to a hoot owl. A hoot owl slammed into the nest, Huey explained, pushed the hen clear off and snatched her as she dropped. "But a scrootch owl slips into the roost and scrootches up to the hen, and talks softly to her. And then, the hen just falls in love with him, and the first thing you know, *there ain't no hen*."

Then, in 1934, Huey launched his own drive for the White House. His glittering "Share-the-Wealth— Every Man a King" plan promised an income of not less than $5,000, an old-age pension of $30 a month, a homestead, a car, and a radio. One poll said he commanded four million votes. Not enough to win. But enough to be a factor in 1936. And a real contender in 1940.

As Huey walked out of that committee hearing in Baton Rouge on the afternoon of September 8, 1935, he had the unmistakable air of a man who knew he was going places. Heads turned. Crowds pushed back to let him through. The Kingfish of the bayou empire passed.

Forgotten on that hot summer day was the first bill on Long's steam-roller list. A minor bill affecting only two men. One of them was Judge Benjamin Pavy, a stubborn old Opelousas judge who had been in office over 20 years. Pavy had opposed Long. But Long had not been able to see Pavy defeated at the polls. So House Bill No. One was to slice up Pavy's vote-heavy territory (St. Landry Parish). It was gerrymandering, pure and simple.

Ironically, Long was never to hear the endless discussion that the bill was to touch off after the moment of truth and the hysteria that were now less than ten hours away.

Forgotten, too, was a prophetic Legislative speech made only a few months before by Mason Spencer, a lonely, anti-Long lawmaker:

"I am not gifted with second sight," Spencer had said, shaking with emotion. "Nor did I see a spot of blood on the moon last night. But I can see blood on the polished floor of this Capitol. For if you ride this thing through, you will travel with the white horse of death."

The Doctor's Sunday (Part One)

Born: Baton Rouge, Louisiana	December 18, 1905
Interned Touro Hospital, New Orleans	1926–28
Graduated Tulane Medical School, New Orleans	1927
Postgraduate Work, Vienna	1928–29
Interned American Hospital, Paris	1929–30
Interned Bellevue Hospital, New York City	1930–32

"In every group of 100 college freshmen, three usually stand head and shoulders above the others. Carl Weiss was one of these."

> —Mrs. Mercedes Garig, teacher of English, Louisiana State University

The day began at the Weiss home in Baton Rouge with the sereneness of a thousand other Sundays. The sun swept across the city, pursuing languid shadows across the grass, streaming through the windows of the little, white cottage on Lakeland Drive. Dr. Weiss, his wife, and their three-month-old son rose from their cocoon of sleep to meet the bright, new morning. September 8, 1935. It would be the most eventful day of their lives.

After breakfast, Dr. Weiss made a brief sick call while Mrs. Weiss bathed and dressed the baby. When he returned, they got into their Buick and drove four blocks to the elder Weisses' eight-room frame house on Fifth Street—one of the first raised homes in the Capital.

The families exchanged greetings, and grandmother Weiss took the baby. Then Carl and his slender, dark-haired wife set out for the ante-bellum Gothic church just around the block, on the corner of Main and Fourth Streets. He had on his white linen suit, black shoes, and Panama hat.

Mockingbirds sang from blossoming crepe myrtle trees. Church bells filled the air. The sun, beaming from a cloudless sky, glinted from the towering steeple of St. Joseph's Catholic Church. It was the Sabbath, the seventh day, the day of rest, and it was summer. The rhythm of the workaday week had lulled into a deep and relaxing sigh of rest. The factories were quiet. The typewriters in the office buildings were silent. The stores were deserted. A woman puttered with flowers in her backyard. A man slept in his hammock, the Sunday comics over his face. A barefoot colored boy fished for whiskered catfish from the banks of the Mississippi.

The Weisses walked by the tall, twin palm trees on the church lawn. As was their habit, they took the short cut through the side door. The sweltering heat followed them inside. Hand fans shimmered through the nave. Air conditioning was as yet unknown. They walked to a pew on the left side front, genuflected, crossed themselves, and waited for Mass to start.

Inside the sacristy, Father Louis Abel Caillouet, a dark-haired, round-faced priest of French ancestry, washed his hands and began the age-old ritual of prayer as he donned each garment for Mass. First the amice of white linen about the neck and shoulders, then the long, dress-like alb, flowing to the shoe tips and tied about the waist with a cincture. The maniple, symbol of sorrow and penance, went over the left arm, and a fringed stole worn for the sacraments slipped around the neck. Over the alb, he put on the robe-like chasuble, white for purity, because it was the birthday of the Virgin Mary.

Father Caillouet, the assistant pastor of St. Joseph's, knew the Weiss family—the father better than his son. He had gotten his glasses from the elder Weiss. The priest was acquainted with the young Weiss as a regular worshiper at Mass and first Fridays, and he had baptized the doctor's baby in June.

The Weisses rose with the congregation as Father Caillouet walked to the foot of the altar. He set the chalice on the altar stone, opened the missal, made the sign of the cross, and began the celebration of the Eucharist.

"In nomine Patris et Filii, et Spiritus Sancti. Amen." ("In the name of the Father and of the Son and of the Holy Spirit. Amen.")

Worshipers crossed themselves.

"Introibo ad altare Dei," the priest continued. ("I will go to the altar of God.")

"Ad Deum qui laetificat juventutem meam," the altar boy answered. ("To God, who makes me young and joyful.")

The Latin phrases swirled through the vast nave and echoed about the rafters as the Mass went on. Dr. Weiss, his knees pressing against the hard kneeling board, closed his eyes for a moment and listened to the familiar sounds from the altar where the miracle of Christ's sacrificial death on the cross was being re-enacted.

"Judica me, Deus, et discerne causam meam de gente non sancta; ab homine iniquo et doloso erue me." ("Give judgment for me, O God, and decide my cause against an unholy people; deliver me from unjust and deceitful men.")

Carl Austin Weiss was born December 18, 1905, in a frame house at 446 North Street in Baton Rouge. His father, Carl Adam Weiss, was a doctor, too—one of the first eye, ear, nose and throat specialists in Louisiana. Colleagues regarded the elder Weiss as a man of stature in the community, a serious, no-nonsense physician who took his professional responsibilities greatly to heart.

"He was the type of man who would take a day off to go fishing and then hate himself for it the next day, because he thought he should have been working," his nurse, Mary Smith Fitzgerald, said. She worked for him for over 20 years.

He was a stern, bald, fanatically punctual man. ("He used to go to 5:15 a.m. Mass," his only daughter said. "At 5:10 a.m., he would be sitting in church waiting for Mass to start. If he wasn't five minutes ahead of time, he considered himself late.")

He wore rimless glasses, suits with vests, and a stickpin in his tie. He never practiced for the dollar, firmly believed in the old Dutch-German attitude: "Do right and stick by it." He rarely admitted he was wrong.

Beneath the tough exterior, he was a kindly man. He usually had a funny story or a peppermint or a toy for the children he treated. His neighbors said he was a man with an abiding interest in his family, his religion, and his practice. He passed these qualities on to his son.

Carl Adam Weiss did not name his first son—Carl Austin—after himself, partly because he never forgot the taunts of playmates who turned his middle name into "Aay-damn, Aay-damn." He had no innate call to medicine, never claimed to. His father, a Bavarian organist and choirmaster who came to New Orleans in 1870, forced him to study medicine, forced him to become a doctor. ("Daddy always said he hated medicine," his daughter said, "and we wondered how on earth he could have made such a success of it, hating it like he did.") He attended Jesuit College in New Orleans and apprenticed as a druggist under one of the old masters. After he became a registered pharmacist, he went on to Tulane, graduating from the medical department in 1900.

The record isn't clear, but it was probably in 1903 that Dr. Weiss moved to Lobdell, a community across the Mississippi River from Baton Rouge. In those days, young physicians often started in country towns to gain experience. Two years later, he married Viola Maine, a quiet-spoken, conservative, Baton Rouge girl of gentle manner and French-Irish extraction. He was 26. She was 24.

He practiced for six years. But he eventually despaired of his ability to cover the whole range of medicine as a general practitioner and decided to specialize. About 1908, although he was then 30 and had two children, Dr. Weiss moved his family to New Orleans and went back to medical school. Some eight years later, he returned to Baton Rouge and opened an eye, ear, nose and throat office in a downtown office building. He gradually built up a big practice. Through two succeeding decades, Dr. Weiss earned a reputation as an original thinker in his branch, a tireless worker, and a dedicated physician. In 1933, the Louisiana Medical Society added the crowning touch. It elected him President.

So it was against this background that young Carl grew up in New Orleans and in Baton Rouge.

Carl was the eldest of three children. He had a sister, Olga Marie, who was two years younger, and a brother, Thomas Edward ("Tom Ed"), twelve years younger.

A teacher remembered Carl as one of the most retiring students she'd ever had. "Quiet dominated his
personality," she said. "It was as if he had discovered
a secret zone of calm in which he moved serenely." A
friend said you sometimes felt you almost had to bar-
gain with Carl for a smile. Others said he had a pleasant sense of humor. He had a scholarly, aesthetic air.
He had blue-gray eyes; an olive complexion; a slight
frame (he weighed 132 and stood 5-10); a shock of dark
hair in front; full lips; even, white teeth; and a long,
straight nose. Thick-lensed glasses sometimes gave him
an owlish look.

Those who knew him said he was "very human . . .
very happy . . . he delighted in the exquisite flavor
of life . . . a thinker and an idealist . . . a gentle,
brilliant man with a good sense of humor . . . a quiet,
undemonstrative man with only a passing interest in
politics . . . a kindly doctor of great ability . . ."

Friends said Carl had a quick temper. Once, when
his little brother fooled around and broke a chisel, Carl
glowered so fiercely that Tom Ed never forgot the incident. ("I didn't know whether he was going to chase
me around the block two or three times . . . but I
understand how he felt.") On another occasion, Carl
heard Monsignor Gassler, St. Joseph's pastor, interrupt
services and growl at a late-comer—telling him to find
a seat. The old German priest didn't like people standing in the back. Carl, disturbed at what he considered
a lack of dignity, marched to the rectory after church
and told the pastor off. Monsignor Gassler was not a
priest you could tell off easily.

A boyhood pal remembers that when the gang

roughhoused, Carl's temper sometimes flashed if he thought an underling was being unduly bullied. He might slap someone hard. He would always recover quickly. He had a friendly disposition and a scrawny build, but he wasn't the kind of person who could be pushed around. His wife, however, does not recall seeing Carl lose his temper. ("People have told me he had a violent temper. I never saw Carl angry in the time I was married to him.")

"Usually, he was a calm and deliberate man, although somewhat high-strung," A. Veazie Pavy, his brother-in-law, said. A nun who assisted Dr. Weiss in operations at Our Lady of the Lake Sanitarium (hospital) also used the word "high-strung" in describing him.

"He took all living too seriously," his mother said. "He works too hard," his father had said. "He ought to rest more."

As a child, Carl was fond of music, fascinated by electricity and mechanics, precocious and inquisitive. At five, visiting a baby cousin, he asked his mother, "What kind of a stork brought that?" Once in downtown "Jesuit" Church in New Orleans, he got to tampering with the lock on the pew—in those days, each pew had a gate and each family had the key to its own pew—and he locked his mother and two aunts in their pew. It was the era of ankle-length, figure-conforming dresses. The ladies were marooned in their pew for hours until someone got the lock to work. At eight, he dismantled an heirloom. His father threw up his arms in despair when he saw the hundreds of tiny parts sprawled on a table. It was an old grandfather's clock that hadn't worked in years. But when Carl put it together, it ran. He was an obedient child. His relatives held him up as an example to his cousins. A standard remark was, "Why can't you be as good as Carl?"

He never cared much for childish amusements. His sister Olga loved playing in the huge toy sections of the downtown department stores when their mother went shopping. But Carl would go on the swing or the see-saw once and then he knew how it worked. And he lost interest.

He was an introvert. His little playmates would shout, "Come on out and play, Carl." But he was happier playing with blocks or building with his erector set or working on a pet project or reading. Carl was forever reading. When he got measles his mother put him in a dark room. He stashed away books underneath his mattress and read in the dim light. He impaired his eyesight. He needed glasses at an early age.

In New Orleans, Carl went to Kruttschnitt kindergarten on Dryades and Foucher Streets and McDonough No. 8 elementary school. But he didn't come into his own until the family moved back to Baton Rouge in 1916, when he was 11.

The Weisses moved into a roomy, one-storey house on Fifth Street that would become the family homestead. There was an electric shop two blocks away, and Carl spent a good deal of time there. His inventive mind soon became the wonder of the neighborhood gang. The boys built a clubhouse behind an old garage. Carl noticed there was an old electric-streetcar line that ran along Main Street, a block away. He learned that you can harness electricity. He captured the streetcar electricity on the galvanized roof of the garage. The clubhouse had lights.

With that venture under his belt, he boldly offered to wire a five-room house rented out by Miss Winnie Costello, a grandaunt. She agreed, but got him to promise that before he pulled a switch he would let her call an electrician to check it over. The electrician said there was nothing left for him to do.

His interest flitted to a variety of subjects. He dabbled in sketching, photography, wood-carving, fishing, tennis, and fencing. His family says he built the first radio in Baton Rouge and was the first to screen a porch. He was a boy scout. He helped pick figs, turned the crank on the ice-cream freezer, ran errands. He learned to drive in his early teens and drove each morning before school to a dairy for milk.

Guns were one of Carl's great interests. Carl's father liked to hunt and kept a number of firearms. Carl was one of the first in the neighborhood to get a rifle. It was a .22-caliber Remington pump gun. Later, he acquired pistols. He learned to take them apart, find out how they worked, and put them together. Because he was nearsighted, Carl was not an exceptional shot. He never cared much about killing animals. He preferred target-shooting.

Carl had a passion for music. His family felt that it was an inherited talent. Carl's grandfather and great-grandfather on his father's side were accomplished musicians. He learned to play piano and saxophone. Later he learned the clarinet to get into the college band. (Saxophonists were a dime a dozen, but the band was desperate for clarinetists.) Carl's approach to music was from a decidedly intellectual standpoint. Instead of playing songs, he loved to go over and over practice exercises. He had exercise books piled a foot high. And his idea of relaxation was to open a practice book and play it from start to finish as you would read a novel. Often, Carl became so absorbed in his music that his mother had to call him to the dinner table three or four times.

Supper was a sacred hour in the Weiss household. Since Dr. Weiss worked long hours and was gone so much, it was the one time the family could be together. Mrs. Weiss used to "wait supper" until her husband got back. Sometimes that wasn't until seven or eight or even nine o'clock at night.

Dr. Weiss was prone to be talkative about politics at mealtime. In later years, Huey Long became a prime topic. Dr. Weiss was opposed to Long. He felt that Long stood for everything that was wrong, dishonest, and conniving. He thought that Long lacked integrity, put a price on every man, and would run roughshod if left to his own means.

Once, by chance, Huey came to see the elder Weiss. The Kingfish had got a speck in his eye, and, "cussing like a sailor," stormed into Dr. Weiss's waiting room demanding immediate attention, Dr. Weiss's nurse said. When he got in, Huey refused an anesthetic. Dr. Weiss went ahead just the same and put cocaine in his eye, and then removed the foreign body. As far as anyone knows, that was the only time they met.

As Dr. Weiss's practice grew, he became friendly with two staunch anti-Longs—both former Louisiana Governors. He counted John M. Parker (Governor from 1920–24) among his patients, and had him home for meals. And he was on close terms with Jared Young Sanders (Governor from 1908–12).

Carl did well in school. He was valedictorian of St. Vincent's Academy, a Catholic school. He graduated at the tender age of 15, and entered Louisiana State University in the fall of 1921. His father discouraged him from a career in medicine. The elder Weiss saw how much of his time was spent away from his family. He was often out of the house before anyone was awake. Sundays, he went to 5:15 Mass so that church would be done with and he would be ready if an emergency happened. He started work at 7:30 a.m., or earlier, when operations were scheduled. Sometimes patients still filled his office at sunset. He felt that there were so many other ways that offered the good life without being at the beck and call of the public. So Carl started college with a career in engineering in mind. He had a B-plus average at LSU during his first two years. But somewhere along the line, Carl felt that engineering was a mistake. The Weiss family got another doctor.

Since LSU had no medical school—Huey Long did not establish it until 1931—Carl transferred to Tulane in New Orleans in his junior year. It was in his undergraduate days that Carl's personality began to mature. He learned to control his shyness, and to a large extent he blossomed from his introverted ways. Once he accomplished this, he made friends easily. "When you got to know Carl, you found he had a wonderful sense of humor," a college chum said. Carl joined Phi Rho Sigma medical fraternity and became popular enough to win the class election for secretary-treasurer. He was bookish but not a bookworm. Music was his great diversion. He played in the band, and later, during his internship, he learned the organ at an old folks' home near New Orleans' Touro Infirmary (hospital). He became good enough to play at song fests that the old folks held at night.

Carl got a bachelor of science degree in 1925 and then continued for two more years in the graduate medical school. (Medical students at Tulane began a heavy schedule of med courses in their junior undergraduate year in those days.) In his final year in graduate school, Touro Infirmary awarded Carl a two-year internship in pathology (the study of tissue changes during a disease). He received an M.D. degree in 1927 at the age of 21. He graduated with an over-all average of 83.

The young doctor stayed on as an interne at Touro for another year, where he worked quietly but with ability and genuine promise. He became a *protégé* of the renowned Dr. Rudolph Matas, president of the International Society of Surgeons. Dr. Matas was on a committee that awarded Carl a highly-prized internship at the famous American Hospital in Paris. The internship began in April 1929. Only two other New Orleans doctors had ever won the award.

On his way to the ship in New York, Carl dropped by Bellevue Hospital. Bellevue had a national reputation as a first-rate training ground for young doctors. Carl's Paris internship was good for only one year. So, looking ahead, he decided to see if he could line up a future internship at Bellevue.

Mrs. Gertrude Reed, a graduate nurse and secretary to Dr. Richard P. Atkins, head of the ear, nose and throat clinic, remembered the bespectacled Southern doctor and the day he walked in.

"He (Dr. Weiss) had a curious scientific—rather than mortal—look about him," she recalled. "He gave the best sales talk I ever heard. He was as sincere as he could be, and so enthused about his work he kept Dr. Atkins spellbound for half an hour. Dr. Atkins was impressed, but he explained a year usually elapsed between such applications and appointments."

Before going to Paris, Dr. Weiss went to Vienna, delving more deeply in postgraduate courses, into the study of the ears, nose and throat. (The eye had by then been made a separate specialty.) Vienna was the medical capital of the world, and some of Europe's foremost physicians gave courses there. Carl had learned German from his grandfather and so had no trouble understanding the lectures.

He was in Vienna during one of the bitterest winters on record. Snow piled waist-high. The Danube froze and cut off Vienna's coal supply. The city rationed water, and there was very little heat at Carl's boardinghouse. Despite the hardships, he found Austria fascinating. He heard Wagner at the great opera house, watched crack European skiers swoosh down the slopes at Semmering, visited wine cellars in the Vienna Woods, saw the lavish, baroque apartments in the Hofburg, and went to Mass at ancient St. Stephen's Cathedral.

When his course ended, Weiss and Dr. John Archinard, a Louisiana interne friend who was then studying at the American Hospital and who corresponded with Carl, took a vacation through Italy. To save money, they traveled third-class on trains, sometimes sitting up through the night on hard, wooden benches, next to peasants. They rode through Hungary, stopping briefly at Budapest, and through Yugoslavia. They saw a Europe on the brink of great shifting forces. Adolf Hitler was rising to power in Germany. Benito Mussolini was making the trains run on time in Italy. In Austria, fascist forces were manipulating social unrest to bring about the dictatorship of Chancellor Englebert Dollfuss. The little chancellor was to become a world figure when his soldiers ruthlessly shot down striking socialist workers. He was assassinated in 1934 by Nazi rebels against his regime. In America, political writers would find comparisons in Huey Long's regime in Louisiana with the European dictatorships.

The two doctors went up and down the Italian coasts to Venice, Florence, Sorrento, Naples, Milan, Genoa and Rome. They saw signs of fascism everywhere. In the movies, films of Mussolini interrupted the feature picture half a dozen times. His face brought the audience to its feet, clapping and shrieking, "Duce! Duce! Duce!" In the streets, the fascisti strutted proudly in polished leather boots and splendid uniforms, their chins jutting like carbon copies of Mussolini. A couple of times, they stomped by Carl and Dr. Archinard, elbowing them off the sidewalk, ready for a fight with the American tourists. The two doctors did not oblige.

"This little Caesar will get his due some day," Carl said. "They're peacocks, not fighters."

In June of 1929 Carl went to Paris to start his work at the American Hospital. The hospital had inherited its name from its patients. After the turn of the century, Americans flocked to Paris. Those settling permanently wanted their own hospital, where an English-speaking staff could treat them according to American methods. So began the American Hospital. It was located in Neuilly-sur-Seine, a picturesque suburb of Paris. It received its first patient in 1910. In 1913, the United States granted it a Federal charter. It became a curious creature—an American corporation existing in France by an act of the U.S. Congress.

Americans, even without funds, had priority. Nevertheless, the list of patients read like an international Who's Who. In one week, King Alexander of Yugoslavia, the Shah of Persia, a pretender to a European throne, a prince, and an ambassador came to the hospital for treatment. Its fame quickly spread.

Carl worked for a year in several clinics under Count Thierry de Martel, the hospital's chief surgeon and one of France's leading physicians.[1] He lived in the internes' quarters near a modern hospital building that had just been dedicated as a memorial to the Allied war dead.

One weekend he made a trip to Belgium, where he visited the famed weapons plant Fabrique Nationale

---

[1] Dr. de Martel, according to a Reuters dispatch, ended his life with poison on the day the Germans took Paris. He was said to have been unwilling to risk being required to serve the Nazi cause.

d'Armes de Guerre in Liége. The plant manufactured the American-designed Browning guns for all European markets. Carl, still intrigued by firearms, added a pistol to his collection. He would take the gun back to the United States, along with other souvenirs. It would make an important reappearance later.

Carl ended his internship in May of 1930, returning to New York, where he paid another visit to Bellevue. Mrs. Reed, the graduate nurse, recalled that day, too.

"After Dr. Weiss had gone to Paris, a vacancy occurred," she said. "Dr. Atkins cabled him to report as soon as possible. The cable was never delivered. We received word that he had left the American Hospital without giving a forwarding address. We had just given up hope of finding him when he walked into the office, smiled, and asked,

" 'How about that appointment?' "

" 'But didn't you get our cable?' "

" 'Cable? No, but I had a hunch and came back three thousand miles sure that you'd have one for me.' "

Carl eagerly accepted the appointment, but first he went home for a reunion. He found his baby brother Tom Ed almost grown, already a freshman in high school. He saw that his father's practice had mushroomed to overflowing proportions. Nothing was ever said, but it was understood that the elder Weiss would dearly love to have his son join him one day.

Friends said Carl returned profoundly influenced by European ways. As far as his conversation went, the influence was confined to cultural, artistic, and professional matters. He seldom talked politics.

"He felt that politics, as he saw it, was an awful lot of wheels spinning," his brother said, "and it really didn't get you very far. He always seemed to have more interesting things to talk about. . . . In fact, I never recall he ever had any strong political philosophy. Just right and wrong. And that was it."

Carl returned to New York and served a brief externship at Bellevue in the summer of 1930, performing the duties of an interne but living outside the hospital. He soon became a regular interne and served two years—until July 1932—working chiefly in the ear, nose and throat division.

He earned a reputation as a thorough and painstaking doctor, if something of a perfectionist.

"He was so insistent upon thoroughness," Dr. J. Hallock Moore, a fellow interne, said, "that he used to personally inspect all tonsillectomies. If the least vestige of a tonsil was not removed, he would raise the roof. It finally got to the point where such a remnant was known as a 'Weiss tag.' "

Dr. Weiss soon was appointed house surgeon.

A few years later, newsmen asked Dr. William H. Dick, another interne, how he remembered Dr. Weiss. He came so highly recommended, Dr. Dick said, few felt that Dr. Weiss would live up to his notices.

"He surpassed them," Dr. Dick said. "Weiss was really a brilliant man."

Strangely, the report of that interview takes off on two widely separate tangents from that point.

This is the account that appeared in the *New York Herald Tribune* the week of September 8, 1935:

" 'I can remember talking with him about politics

down in Louisiana,' Dr. Dick said, 'but he never showed any particular interest in it. His work consumed all his interest then; he had no political aspirations at all.

" 'He felt as a great many people do, that things were being badly managed down there. He certainly was no admirer of Huey Long, but there was nothing to indicate any deep feeling on his part. Weiss was a man of very regular habits, quiet and serious. But he was perfectly normal. He enjoyed going out occasionally, seeing shows and things like that. . . .' "

A second clipping of Dr. Dick's interview was received in the mail by Carl's father in September of 1935. It was accompanied by a short letter postmarked from New York City. The clipping did not include the name of the newspaper or the date it appeared. After a similar beginning, the news story read:

" 'It was curious,' Dr. Dick said. 'Here was Dr. Weiss, handsome, lovable, with as brilliant a mind as I have ever met, and rapidly rising in his field. Sociable as anybody could be in his pleasant Southern way. But mention Huey Long and he became moody, bitter.

" 'He hated Long vehemently. He had the belief fixed in his mind that Louisiana politics were the worst of any state's. He was always a strong-willed and determined man, and on this point he could not be shaken.' "

He went on in the article to say:

" 'Most of his life, though, was wrapped up in his work. He did some of the most constructive work ever performed in Bellevue clinic. Strong-willed, or even hot-headed, as some might call it, he had a certain charm of manner with troublesome patients. I remember that several times patients were turned over to him when nobody else could handle them. He did.' "

Dr. Dick, who said that he became probably the closest New York friend of Dr. Weiss, died in 1952.

Dr. Nelson W. Sissom of East Orange, New Jersey, who spent two years with Dr. Weiss in the Bellevue ear, nose and throat service, was asked in 1962 which of the two versions of Dr. Dick's interviews he believed closer to the truth.

"I would say Dr. Weiss was very much interested in the politics of Louisiana," Dr. Sissom said, "but not to the extent of always talking about them. If the subject was brought up, he would express himself in no uncertain terms. The same applied to Huey Long."

Carl spent weekends exploring the city, going to plays and operas, occasionally with his sister, Olga, who had arrived from a European vacation a few months before and gotten a job in New York. For fun on a dull weekend, they sometimes concocted experimental dishes in Olga's Greenwich Village apartment on East 12th Street.

Carl's relationship with his younger brother was not as close. They were separated by twelve years and by many hundreds of miles. But on his brief visits home, Carl noticed his own old introverted ways beginning to emerge in Tom Ed. On Tom Ed's birthday, Carl tried to call this to his brother's attention in a letter. It was not an easy letter to write. But it made its impression. His brother never forgot it. (In fact, it remains today the sole letter of Carl's which Tom Ed has saved.)

"Dear Butz:" ("Baby Brother" in German)

"Tomorrow will be the 15th of June and your 15th birthday, and this letter is my message of best wishes, of hope for all manner of good things; and by their poverty of expression, judge of their wealth of content. Butz, there is a particular sincerity, an almost egotistical interest in my wishes for your future. Because in you, Butz, are my hopes for all the ambitions I never realized, all the goals I never attained, all the pleasures I rushed past, all things desirable that diffidence, timidity, too sensitive pride can rob one of. We are lately rather strangers to each other, but I follow closely through letters all that you do. More and more, of late, I see evidence of traits that I have, traits I try hard to banish—excusing myself—not actually evil, but unfortunate, and productive of regrets, destructive of pleasures, and more, of highly valuable associations that would ripen through life. These traits will form a barrier, shutting you off from other people, making it ever more difficult to bring yourself to enjoy the interests of your fellows. Knowing all too well the power these tendencies have, I can't expect you to banish them; I try to make you conscious of them, and agnostic to them, so that you may serve yourself of every occasion to combat them. Please pardon this semblance of a sermon; would that I might send in its stead all the pleasure that its application can mean to you. . . ."[2]

In the summer of 1932, Carl came home to go into practice with his father. It began the last chapter of his life—a chapter whose end would be so grotesque that no one then would have believed it possible.

[2] Weiss's letter reveals another side of his personality, according to some observers. "While he was being a loving husband," said David Culbert, professor of history at LSU, "he was also capable of keeping things within his own mind. The letter is the self-analysis of a self contained person who would be capable in his final day of spending a happy day with his family, then stepping out and doing something else." Sharing that view is Charles East, former director of the LSU Press, who has had a lifelong interest in the assassination. East said the letter shows Weiss was "intense, hypercritical—hard on himself, and, therefore, inclined to magnify, to embellish (events). Things that might register 100 on someone else's scale might sail up to 500 or 1,000 on his."

The Doctor's Sunday (Part Two)

Returned to practice in Baton Rouge, La.	1932
Married Louise Yvonne Pavy of Opelousas, La.	1933
Baby born	1935

"Sunday was one of the happiest days in our lives, and Sunday night was the saddest."

—Mrs. Carl Austin Weiss

That summer—the summer of 1932—Carl was the conquering hero back from the wars. A parade of relatives trooped in to welcome him. There was joy in the Weiss home. Old friends came by. Even the Baton Rouge *Morning Advocate* hailed the event. The paper sent a reporter to interview Carl. The newsman wrote, in part:

"Dr. Weiss has always wanted to practice in Baton Rouge, his birthplace, and on his return two weeks ago went into the office with his father, Dr. C. A. Weiss. He jokingly declared that a few gray hairs would aid him immeasurably. However, his large, capable hands, his serious eyes, and friendly smile inspire confidence.

"When asked whether the girls in Baton Rouge and America compared favorably with foreign girls, he answered:

" 'Well, I could hardly be called an expert on that subject. But you see I didn't bring any back with me.' "

Baton Rouge was just a friendly little Southern town in 1932. Growing steadily, but still not too big to obliterate the easy-going pleasantries of small-town sociability. A good town for a young doctor to settle in, raise a family and take over his aging father's thriving practice.

"Le Baton Rouge." The city got its name from early French explorers. One story is that they called it "red stick" because they found a reddened post there—a tall cypress stripped of its bark, dyed by the blood of drying animal skins. The tree marked the boundary line of the Houma and Bayou Goula Indians' hunting grounds. It stood on a bluff—the Mississippi's first highland from the Gulf—on the east bank of the river, some 90 winding miles from New Orleans. A century back, the Capital was just a little upriver cotton port, the farthest-inland deepwater port on the Mississippi. Now, industries, attracted by the all-year temperate climate, cheap labor and shipping accessibility, were moving in by leaps and bounds. One of them, the Esso Standard Oil Company, had established the nation's biggest oil refinery. The plants set the pace for the town's prosperity. Merchants fixed their hours by paydays. When workers got their salaries, banks and stores stayed open until midnight.

Huey's Capitol provided the best view of the city. Carl's mother had never set foot in it—to her it was a giant symbol of a dictator's rise to power—and Carl, as far as his family remembers, may never have been inside either. But every Sunday the Weisses saw scores of rural pilgrims drive by their porch, flocking to look out over Baton Rouge from high atop the Statehouse. To the north lay Our Lady of the Lake Sanitarium, where Carl was to perform scores of tonsillectomies and mastoid and sinus operations in the next few years. Farther north were the ever-burning flares of the city's spreading petro-chemical complex. Westward across the broad Mississippi, Louisiana's great sugar bowl swept out far beyond the horizon. To the south, Louisiana State University's 300-acre campus sprawled across the plains, and farther south were the cypress swamps and remote Cajun lands. To the east, the

Comite and Amite Rivers, dotted with summer cabins (one of them belonging to Carl's father), rolled through quiet woodlands—formerly wild, lush, Indian hunting grounds. The city itself seemed to sleep under the shade of a forest of trees.

In 1935, Baton Rouge had only 30,000 residents. Industry would turn it into a boom town. Its population would multiply five times in the next quarter-century.

Carl, like his father, devoted the great majority of his time to his practice. He thought about it constantly. "He was obsessed with looking so young," a member of his family said. "He used to say, 'They'll think I'm just out of medical school.' He scraped his medical bag against the wall to make it look older. Once, he raised a moustache."

Except for membership in the Kiwanis, Carl was not a joiner. He did go to church regularly. And he regularly attended Mass and Holy Communion on the first Friday of each month. At one time, the young doctor became doubtful of his religion and began to study Catholicism anew. He went at it slowly and carefully. ("Nobody could rush Carl," a relative said. "He was very calm, very deliberate.") When he finished his reassessment, Carl found that his doubts had vanished. In the years to come, he became noted for his piety as much as his professional skill.

Despite the fact that the elder Weiss was pleased to have his son join him, those who knew the senior Weiss feared a clash of personalities. The misgivings proved groundless.

"I remember they used to get into big discussions about cases—or even about medical generalities sometimes," Mrs. Mary Fitzgerald, the office nurse, said. "I can still see Carl standing at the sink washing his hands —he always seemed to be washing his hands. The old doctor sitting bolt upright at his rolled top desk. His back turned, pretending he was at work, arguing. Carl would dry his hands, walking up and down. The conversation would go back and forth. Then, it had gone far enough. Carl would wink at me. He'd toss his towel over that old bald head and say, 'Aw, you win, Skipper.' And walk out."

There were differences of opinion, but the younger Weiss always knew how to handle the "Skipper."

The Weiss office suite was on the seventh floor of the modern Reymond building, which housed a big department store. Carl's father shared a waiting room with another doctor in an adjacent office. Dr. Weiss had two eye chairs—sometimes he treated two patients at once—and two treatment cubicles. He used an adjoining room as a recovery lab and later as an X-ray room. For minor eye operations he had another small room which he shared on weekends with Dr. A. C. Broussard of New Orleans, an orthodontist who had married Dr. Weiss's daughter. Dr. Broussard came to Baton Rouge to see patients every third Saturday.

Carl took care of the ear, nose and throat patients, and his father handled the eye cases. Mrs. Fitzgerald shuttled between the two, and assisted Carl on emergency calls and operations.

"He (Carl) had beautiful hands, long, slender, sensitive fingers," she recalled. "They were so sensitive I could feel them quiver slightly when I slipped on his rubber gloves before an operation. But the second he touched a scalpel, his hands would be still. In the most delicate of operations, his hands were perfectly steady."

Dr. William Cook, a highly respected Baton Rouge physician, summed up the feeling of the doctors of the city toward Carl's professional ability.

"Looking back, I would say he probably bordered on brilliancy. He was probably the best-educated young doctor in ear, nose and throat in Louisiana. He was a dedicated physician and had all the indications of becoming a doctor's doctor—one that a physician turns to when he needs exceptional help. He was the only doctor in Baton Rouge—and I doubt if there were many more anywhere in those days—who could take out a cancer of the larynx and make it look easy."

With all his ability, he was a humble doctor, Mrs. Fitzgerald said. After an operation, when someone would tell him how wonderful he was, it would surprise him.

"Once, on an emergency call to Ethel—a town about twenty miles north of Baton Rouge—we found a child choking to death. It was a diphtheria case. We put the child in the car. The father drove. Carl sat on the back seat trying to keep the boy breathing. He saw it was no use. Carl stopped the car. He took out a pocket knife and opened up the trachea (windpipe). After we got to the hospital, we didn't see Carl for three days. He didn't leave the boy's side. The boy recovered.

"Later, the boy's parents thanked Carl. Carl's answer was, 'I did nothing. God did that. He gave me the power.' "

When he was not busy with patients, Carl was designing devices for surgical work. He invented several mirror devices to help in ear and eye surgery. Other doctors used to have to puncture a bone between the sinus cavity and the nose to catheterize a sinus. Carl brought back from Europe a device that could slip up the nose and wash out the sinus from the natural openings. And he could handle it expertly.

"I learned to do a lot of things as a nurse," Mrs. Fitzgerald said. "I never could do that."

One day in November of 1932, a slender, dark-haired young woman walked into the office. She told the receptionist that her eyes were bothering her. She asked to see the elder Dr. Weiss. She would remember that visit all her life. So would Dr. Weiss.

Louise Yvonne Pavy (Pah-vee'), a new teacher of French at Louisiana State University, had recently returned from study at the Sorbonne. Miss Pavy was the daughter of Judge Benjamin Henry Pavy of Opelousas, the judge who would be the target of a Long gerrymander three years later.

"What have you been doing, young lady?" the old doctor asked as she sat down in his office. He began writing her case history.

"Well, I've been working hard and studying," she said. "I've been in Paris."

"Paris?" the doctor looked up over his glasses. "Did you know my son?"

"No. I knew another doctor in Paris. Dr. Bayoun at the American Hospital."

"Well, you must have known my son. He was at the

American Hospital, too, and he knew Dr. Bayoun there."

"I'm sorry I didn't meet your son."

"Then you must meet him now," Dr. Weiss said. He called Carl in. Carl entered the room, sat down and began talking to the young teacher. They found out that their paths had crossed many times without their meeting.

Yvonne—she used her middle name—had majored in French at Newcomb College (the girls' undergraduate school at Tulane) while Carl was a student there. She had graduated in 1929. She had taught French for the next two years in a little high school in St. Martinville, a picturesque south Louisiana town. In 1931, Yvonne had applied for a fellowship at the Sorbonne. Dr. Rudolph Matas—the same New Orleans surgeon who had helped select Carl for his American Hospital internship some years earlier—had also been a member of the committee that had granted the fellowship to Yvonne. She had arrived in Paris after Carl had returned to America.

Yvonne had lived in Neuilly, only a stone's throw from the American Hospital. She had found Europe as intriguing as Carl had—perhaps more so. Young Frenchmen had escorted her through the old city. American internes had danced with her and had taken her to dinner. She had crossed the Channel to go to June Week at Cambridge. Somewhere in the whirl, the master's degree had got left behind. And that's what had brought her to Baton Rouge and LSU in 1932.

"This is the worst thing I've ever done," the old

doctor said as he returned to his office and saw Carl and Yvonne still talking. "Now get about your business," he said, shooing Carl out.

Three days later, Yvonne returned for her glasses. Going down in the elevator, she ran into Carl.

"My, don't you look like a schoolteacher with the glasses on," he said.

After they said good-bye, Yvonne turned to a girl friend who had accompanied her and said, "I've met the man I'm going to marry."

Yvonne didn't hear from Carl for the next three months. Then, one day, when she returned from Easter vacation, she found a box waiting for her. Inside was an Easter egg. A note read, "Could your bunny beat this?" It was signed, "Carl Weiss." Yvonne rushed to the phone, pausing to shout to her roommate, "That man I told you I was going to marry, he sent me an Easter egg." On the phone, Yvonne thanked Carl. He asked her for a date. That was in April. By early May, they were seeing a lot of each other. On Sundays, Carl and Yvonne began meeting in St. Joseph's Church for Mass and then going to the Weiss home for dinner. Occasionally they drove to the family summer cabin on the Amite River and swam or practiced target shooting or just rocked on the porch swing and lolled in the river breeze. By late May they were going steady. By June, they were staying out into the wee hours. Carl blinked his eyes as his fingers tightened over a scalpel in the operating room the next morning. Yvonne yawned as she pored over the diaries of Alexander Declouet, a Louisiana sugar planter. (She was translating his memoirs for her thesis.) Carl's mother telephoned Yvonne once or twice, reminding her that Carl had to operate early in the morning. The calls were to little avail. Carl popped the question that summer.

In Opelousas there is a luxuriant lawn and a long walkway past two centuries-old oaks laden with Spanish moss leading to the porch of the Pavy home. Carl and Yvonne took that walk on a warm Sunday in June. They had come to meet her family. Inside the spotlessly clean ante-bellum house, Mrs. Pavy squirmed beneath the canopy of her four-poster, hunting for her glasses. She was down with flu, and out through the front window her daughter was coming up the walk with a young doctor who was asking for her hand. Mrs. Pavy had misplaced her glasses. And, *mon Dieu,* without her glasses how could she tell what he looked like?

Judge Pavy waited at the foot of the walk, some of his seven children grouped on the porch behind. Yvonne was glad her father would be the first to greet Carl. Her mother had expressed reservations about the marriage. Both the Pavys and the Veazies—her mother's family—came from old French stock. The Weiss family was of German extraction.

Carl and Yvonne approached the old judge. Benjamin Henry Pavy was a tall, heavy-set man with a gray moustache and a full mane of silver hair. In his blue alpaca coat and white linen trousers, he looked every inch the Southern colonel.

Unlike most Southern colonels, though, Judge Pavy spoke French as fluently as English. He had been born a few miles south of Opelousas in a tiny, French-speaking community called Coulee Croche. The third son of a family of twelve, he had learned to speak French at home, probably before he had learned English. In later years, he made campaign speeches in French to Cajun audiences. He was a self-made man. He had become a lawyer by studying in an attorney's office.

In 1910, at the age of 36, he had won the election for District Judge of the Parishes of St. Landry (where Opelousas is located) and Evangeline. The two parishes then constituted the Thirteenth Judicial District. Voters re-elected him continuously for the next twenty-six years.

Judge Pavy was a jovial, good-natured man, a born raconteur, excitable, convivial, fond of company, especially the company of lawyers. He knew nearly every family in both parishes. He earned a reputation as a painstaking and efficient judge. Appellate courts seldom reversed his rulings. In politics, Pavy was an outspoken, vigorous campaigner. He had strong convictions. The consequence was that he had bitter political opponents. Huey Long became one of the bitterest.

Pavy would not align with Long, because he had no use for the man or his methods. He considered Huey a false prophet, a shallow politician riding to power on the backs of the lower orders, a pied piper duping the masses with illusions of grandeur—behind it all, a dangerous man, a menace, the nearest thing to Hitler in America.

Judge Pavy climaxed a long feud in September of 1932, when he denounced "election thievery" and sentenced five pro-Long election officials to a ten-day sojourn in jail for violating an injunction against "dummy" candidates. Governor Allen pardoned them two hours later.

Long was concerned about Pavy because he couldn't beat him. When you can't beat a man, you can't control him. True, Pavy was judge of only two parishes out of sixty-four. But it was a hole in Huey's armor. Pavy was a man with great appeal all over south central and southwest Louisiana. Long didn't want that hole to uncover an Achilles' heel.

One day Judge Pavy came home from a court session in Ville Platte and told the family that Long had approached him in the courtroom and asked him his price. Someone had apparently advised Huey that he might win Pavy over with a personal appeal. It hadn't worked. The volatile judge had cursed Long and told him to get out of his court.

But that was back in the past. Now he was at home on a beautiful Sunday afternoon, and his daughter and his would-be son-in-law were approaching.

Judge Pavy stepped out and grasped Carl's hand.

"Son, you don't have to say a word. I know all about it, and it's wonderful."

That broke the ice. Carl found no difficulty making friends with the family. Their engagement followed soon afterward. They were married December 27, 1933, in St. Landry Parish Catholic Church in Opelousas.

After a Florida honeymoon, they moved into a second-floor, furnished apartment near the Capitol, and Yvonne continued teaching at LSU. Late in 1934 Yvonne became pregnant. She decided to stay at school as long as she could, partly because it would keep her mind off the baby, and partly because, as a young bride, she was secretly embarrassed to have to break the news to her department head. Carl sensed the latter. One day, he took her to LSU. Instead of driving off to the office, he stayed right there. "I'm going to sit in the car until you tell Mr. Broussard you're pregnant and can't finish the year." That forced the issue. To Yvonne's relief, her boss was exultant.

The stairway to their apartment was steep. Dr. W. L. Edson, Yvonne's doctor, advised Carl that she shouldn't make the climb every day. Carl had spent a great deal of time drawing plans for a house in which he eventually hoped to locate his office. He liked being at home, and he had seen in the East that many doctors had their offices at home. But he was still involved in his father's practice. The new house was very much a part of the future. He needed to move now.

Carl's mother solved the problem. Her family owned a number of houses in Baton Rouge, and she had inherited some. She gave Carl and Yvonne a modest, one-story, three-bedroom, frame bungalow with a screened front porch. It was at 527 Lakeland Drive, a block and a half from the Capitol.

They moved in shortly before the baby was born and started furnishing it carefully, piece by piece. Only one bedroom, the nursery, and part of the living room had been furnished when Yvonne gave birth to a nine-pound thirteen-ounce boy on June 7, 1935. She named him Carl Austin Weiss, Junior.

("When everybody said, 'What are you going to name the baby?' I said, 'I don't know. We never discussed a name.' And Carl said, 'I wouldn't say a word. Let Vonnie decide. Anything Vonnie says will be all right with me.' And so it was Carl Austin Weiss, Junior. By my choice. . . . And he was proud, but didn't say anything.")

While she regained her strength, Carl fixed the house up like a hospital. He hired a trained nurse for the first month (a practical nurse took over later), and he carried the baby into the house.

"You carried him out," he told Yvonne. "I'm going to carry him in."

He was a doting father, his wife said. He took dozens of snapshots, gave the baby his two a.m. bottle, played with him, wheeled his carriage. Yvonne hardly changed a diaper.

Sometime during the week preceding Sunday, September 8, Carl dropped by the Fitzgeralds' home. They sat on the porch, and during the visit Carl showed Mr. Fitzgerald a gun that had jammed. They were unable to get the gun working properly again. Mrs. Fitzgerald said that Carl tossed it into the glove compartment of his car and said nonchalantly, "Never mind. I'll get it fixed."

On Thursday evening preceding Sunday, September 8, Carl came home early.

"Get dressed, Vonnie," Carl said. "We're going to get some more furniture."

They went to Kornmeyer's Furniture Store. They bought a dining room table and chairs, and selected a large china closet from a catalog. The furniture was to be delivered the following week.

Friday night before Sunday, September 8, Carl's

mother dropped by as they started dinner. Carl told her about the new purchases. He also said that he was interested in a gas-heating floor unit to go under the dining room. Like many houses in the deep South, Baton Rouge homes were poorly insulated. Most houses—Carl's included—were heated by simple gas units that protruded from the floor and were spaced throughout the house. The floor unit Carl was looking into was a new central-heating device that he felt would keep them more comfortable through the cold weather. His mother disagreed. She felt that it would be too costly for what she considered to be a doubtful system. Instead, she suggested they continue using the existing heaters for the time being and build a home on her property with a Homestead (savings and loan association) loan. The elder Mrs. Weiss remembers Carl's answer. She wrote it down a few days later and saved it.

"No, Mother. I'm not going into the Homestead. I'll be in this house for ten years at least."

Carl's mother said that night he went to Hummell's Store on St. Charles Street to ask the owner how he felt about the heating plant. Mr. Hummell had had one installed the previous year. He gave Carl a favorable report, and the next morning—a Saturday—Carl went under the house to see how much room there was. His mother said that he telephoned her later that day and told her he was going to get the floor unit and that he had ordered it installed on Monday, September 9, 1935.

At that time in his life, Carl Weiss had four life-insurance policies—two of which had been bought by his father. The elder Weiss had gotten Carl two $5,000 policies—one in 1922 and another in 1930. Carl was paying for one $5,000 endowment policy that he had got in 1933 and a $2,500 endowment that he had started in 1934. The four totaled $17,500. The policies were part of a long-term savings plan for retirement at age 65. One policy had a double-indemnity clause. It was canceled if death was by homicide.

❖ ❖ ❖

"Ne perdas cum impiis, Deus, animam meam, et cum viris sanguinum vitam meam: In quorum manibus iniquitates sunt: dextera eorum repleta est muneribus . . ."

("O God, do not allow me to perish with the wicked: do not destroy my life with sinners whose hands are foul with crime, and heavily weighted with bribes. . . .")

After Mass Carl and Yvonne stopped off at Scheinuk's Florist, on the same block. Carl wanted to pay a bill and have flowers sent to a patient. "Quite a personal touch you're developing," Sam Scheinuk joked. The old florist, a good friend of the family, made up a second little bouquet. "For the baby," Scheinuk said. "He's three months old. I haven't given you a present yet."

Dr. Weiss gave the flowers to his mother when they returned to her house. Then he drove home with Yvonne and the baby to change clothes and get ready for the regular, one o'clock Sunday afternoon dinner at his parents' home. Yvonne doesn't remember exactly when they spoke of the Pavy bill. But they did talk of it that day. And it may well have been during the morning. The bill had been introduced along with a host of other measures late Saturday night, and the Sunday morning *Advocate* carried a complete story on the special session. Sometime that morning, Carl had read the paper.

"You know Long is out to get your father," Carl had said. "Your father is going to be gerrymandered out of office."

Yvonne had watched her father in the rough-and-tumble world of politics all her life. She knew that he was one of the last anti-Long judges on the bench, that he was helping form a slate of candidates to oppose the Long machine in the coming January election. A month ago Marie Pavy, her sister, and Paul D. Pavy, her uncle, had lost their jobs. Marie had been a third grade teacher in Eunice. Paul D. Pavy had been Principal of Opelousas High School. The Long-controlled parish school board dismissed them along with several other teachers who were not allied with the Long administration. And one of Yvonne's close friends had lost her job in another mass school-purge in Baton Rouge. The gerrymander bill did not come as a surprise to Yvonne. She knew that her father was a veteran politician. She was confident that he would take it in stride. There was no extended conversation about the bill, she said. In a little while, it was time to go over for dinner.

The elder Dr. Weiss sat at the head of the table, napkin spread in his lap, his wife to his left. Carl was at the opposite end, his brother to his right, Yvonne to his left. The baby slept in the next room, the door slightly ajar. Martha, the Negro cook, set before them the usual big Sunday dinner of fried chicken, rice, gravy, salad, and all the trimmings.

No one remembers for sure if the Pavy bill was mentioned at that meal. If something was said, the family's best recollection is that the gerrymander was taken as a kind of backhanded compliment. The attitude was—he must be a pretty good judge if they can't vote him out of office.

Carl did not appear preoccupied, his mother said.

"He was chatty as usual at mealtime," she said. "He ate heartily, and after dinner I heard him tell Martha the chicken was delicious."

After dinner, Tom Ed excused himself to go to Donaldsonville with some college chums and hire a band for a rush-week dance. Yvonne went into Olga's bedroom to nurse the baby. She sat in a rocker. Carl stretched out on the bed and they talked quietly together.

The midday temperature soared into the 90's. Someone suggested a drive to their cabin on the Amite River. The cabin was a primitive, three-room, wooden bungalow about an hour's trip from Baton Rouge. You couldn't cook there, but it was isolated and next to the river and fine for relaxing. The family went there for picnics and swims. Sometimes they invited other couples out for summer evenings.

When they got there, Carl set up the swing on the porch for his parents and he and Yvonne changed into their bathing suits.

"She shouldn't be swimming while she's nursing that baby," the elder Dr. Weiss said. But it was a hot day, and Carl gave his approval.

They floated and played in the river. Yvonne stood on Carl's shoulders and jumped into the water. Carl's parents watched from the porch, where they played music from a phonograph for the baby.

"How thin Carl looks," his mother said.

On many outings to the camp, Carl and Yvonne practiced shooting at cans and rocks. Carl was trying to teach her how to fire a gun. ("He always wanted me to do everything he was doing. And so we did target shooting together.") Yvonne said that she does not remember if they went shooting that Sunday. Carl's mother thinks that they did not, although she said that Carl may have brought his gun in his car.

Carl carried Yvonne out, and they changed from their wet suits. The families gathered on the porch, chatting and watching the river glide by. Father and son discussed medicine. The women played with the baby. There was a timelessness about the scene. Clouds drifted along far above. The ripples of the water swept silently by. It was like a vignette from an impressionist's canvas. Who would have dreamed of the horror to come? It was less than six hours away.

Late in the afternoon, the Weisses started back. Mrs. Weiss brought Carl's old bathing suit for Yvonne to patch. Carl and Yvonne had invited another couple to join them at the camp for a picnic supper the following Wednesday evening. Carl dropped his parents off at their house and continued on to his. The elder Weiss recalled that it was about 7:30 p.m.

Carl had a couple of sandwiches and two glasses of milk, Yvonne said. He ate heartily. The baby slept in his buggy close to the kitchen table. Peter, the big German police dog, came over and started licking the infant. Carl pulled the dog away.

"Vonnie, you'd better wash the baby," he said. "I'll put Peter outside."

He put the dog in the backyard, fed him, then helped Yvonne dry the dishes.

A little after eight o'clock, Carl made a telephone call. He called the home of Dr. Webb McGehee, an anesthetist who was to assist him in a tonsillectomy at 7:30 a.m. Monday. He wanted to be sure that Dr. McGehee knew that the operation had been switched from Our Lady of the Lake Sanitarium to Baton Rouge General Hospital. Dr. McGehee said that he knew of the change and would be there.

Dr. Weiss showered, while his wife stretched out on the bed reading the Sunday comics. The baby slept. It had been a long, peaceful Sunday.

A few minutes later, Dr. Weiss stepped into the room. He had discarded his casual camp clothes. He was dressed in the white linen suit, black shoes, and Panama hat that he had worn to Mass.

"Use this," he said, tossing a cake of soap. "You know how the red bugs bite you."

Yvonne often came home from the country covered with insect bites. She glanced up at Carl. He looked handsome in his white suit, she thought. But his hair wasn't combed.

"Carl, go brush your hair before you go out."

He walked back into the bathroom and she turned

again to the paper. She was still reading when he came back in. He kissed her good-bye. She thought he said softly, "I'm making arrangements for an operation to-morrow." She made no comment. She kept on reading. In the back of her mind, she thought that he was going to Our Lady of the Lake Sanitarium, just behind the Capitol. But she didn't ask Carl where he was going. There was no reason. It was part of his routine to make occasional night calls to the hospital. And he had dressed so unhurriedly. Nothing appeared out of the ordinary.

A neighbor, who asked to remain anonymous, called on Yvonne two weeks later and said that she wrote down Yvonne's description of Dr. Weiss's departure and saved it. She said she recorded Yvonne's remarks as follows:

"About nine o'clock, he (Carl) said he had a call to make. There was nothing unusual in his manner. I even recall the last thing he said. He was standing there tying a toy to the top of the buggy for the baby to play with. I said, 'I believe I'll let the baby cry himself to sleep and not rock him.' Carl smiled as if he doubted me and said, 'Well, I'll hurry back as quickly as I can and we'll try it out together.'"

The neighbor said that Mrs. Weiss explained that it had been their practice to rock the baby to sleep after his ten o'clock bottle.

When shown this passage by the author in 1961, Yvonne said that she could not remember if it had happened.

Outside, Dr. Weiss walked in the dim light of a quarter-moon. It was quiet. Crickets chirped. He put his medical bag on the front seat of his Buick, slid in beside it, and started backing out of his narrow driveway. There was a gun in the glove compartment. That, in itself, was not unusual. In those days, it was not uncommon for doctors to carry pistols in Baton Rouge on night calls. They armed themselves against addicts who had attacked physicians from time to time for the narcotics or whiskey they carried in their bags. Dr. Weiss had carried a gun with him ever since he had found a drunk sleeping one off in his car. He kept it wrapped in a flannel sock to keep the dust out. His father said that Carl occasionally put it in his coat pocket when he left the car on night calls.

Mrs. Quincy Ewing, Jr., wife of an Associated Press newsman in Baton Rouge, had finished paying a call at the house of a friend who lived next door to the Weisses. She started the engine and rolled forward a few feet to a point where she blocked the next driveway.

"A man in a car was attempting to back out of the driveway," she recalled. "He saw I was having a little engine trouble and politely indicated he was not in a hurry. He did not speak, but made a gentlemanly gesture to this effect. I got started in a minute and drove home."

Mrs. Ewing said that she did not know Dr. Weiss, so has no way of being sure that it was he. If the man was Dr. Weiss, she added, he seemed calm and relaxed.

Dr. Weiss's path trails off into oblivion as he drove into the night. Theoda Carriere, a private nurse on duty at the Baton Rouge General Hospital, said that she remembered seeing Dr. Weiss there that night.

The hospital was then 15 blocks from Dr. Weiss's home. She said that they met near the rear exit as she got off work. They lived two blocks apart, and Dr. Weiss offered her a ride home, Miss Carriere said. She had transportation, so she declined. However, Miss Carriere placed him at the hospital at about 7:00 p.m., when, according to the Weiss family, Carl would have been still driving home from the Amite camp site.

The only certainty is that sometime shortly after he left home Dr. Weiss's route took him by the Capitol's sunken gardens fronting the Statehouse. Perhaps he was on his way home. Most people out that night were watching the Legislature, and his auto was probably one of the few cars on the road. Evergreens and poplars rustled in the fleeting night shadows among the hundreds of cars parked for blocks and blocks. He turned down Capitol Drive, before the great Statehouse ablaze with lights.

Huey Long was in that building. Nobody can really say for sure when—or if—Dr. Weiss's thoughts turned to Long on that hot, summer night. But, if they did, he may well have been thinking of Huey on that solitary drive.

Some ten days before, a number of Baton Rouge surgeons had talked politics in a hospital amphitheater. The conversation had suddenly become heated. Several doctors had criticized Long. They had called his regime an oppression to the people. One of the surgeons said that he had happened to glance at Dr. Weiss.

"He (Dr. Weiss) had said nothing. But great tears were rolling down his cheeks. He got up and walked out of the room."

Dr. Weiss's mind may have turned to his wife and to her relatives who had lost their jobs. Perhaps he had thought of Judge Pavy. This has never been verified by the author, but a story later made the rounds that Long had been threatening to go on the radio before the January primary and charge that there was "nigger blood" in the Pavy family. That was the supreme Southern insult. The unfounded racial slur would have applied to Dr. Weiss's wife and to his newborn son. (Another version, also unverified by the author's research, was that Long, in his effort to destroy Pavy, had already uttered the remark, and that it had reached Weiss.)

Dr. Weiss parked his car, got out, and started slowly up the Capitol's forty-eight steps, each with the name of a state etched into it.

Later, when it was over, his family was to say that he may have dropped in just to talk to Long. Or perhaps to see Dr. F. Octave Pavy, his wife's uncle and a member of the House (although Yvonne Weiss says that Carl did not know him, and it turned out that Dr. Pavy was not at the Legislature that night). Or, perhaps, attracted by the crowds and the lights, he stopped on impulse to see the special session.

He walked through the great, bronze doors beneath the two eagles protecting the great seal of Louisiana. The light that rushed out framed him in the entranceway. It traced a pattern on his dark features, flowed to his white linen suit, and printed a long silhouette on the Capitol steps. Behind him, a stillness enveloped the night. A riverboat churning up the black Mississippi wailed a lonely cry. Somewhere in the past there was a prophetic line under his portrait in the old college yearbook. It read:

"With knowledge aplenty and friends galore, he is bound to go out and make the world take notice."

Death Casts Its Shadow

"Sure I carry a gun. Sometimes I carry four. Can't tell when somebody's going to shoot the King."
—Huey Pierce Long

Speaker Allen Ellender slammed the gavel at 8:30 p.m. and called the Louisiana House to order. It was to consider the 39 bills approved that morning by the Ways and Means Committee.

There was nothing for the Senate to do until the House took action on the bills, so the Senate was not in session. Ed Desobry, who had come up from the Associated Press bureau in New Orleans to help cover the session, and a few other newsmen assigned to the Senate passed the lull playing poker in the basement pressroom. Before their game was over, they would cover a story that would stop presses all over the world. Elliot Coleman, plainclothes member of the State Bureau of Criminal Identification and Investigation (Huey's secret police), waited for Long in the House. Coleman carried a service revolver under his suit jacket in a holster on his right hip. Within an hour, he would fire that gun. In the Capitol's main lobby (Memorial Hall), State Supreme Court Justice John Fournet, who had recently been elected to the Court, chatted with his father. Fournet had come to see Huey. He wanted to ask a favor for some friends in his district who needed political help. Fournet was to witness a scene that he would never forget. Outside the Capitol, Tom Ed Weiss, Dr. Weiss's brother, circled around in a car with Sigma Pi fraternity brothers and some high-school boys they were rushing. They wanted to go in and "watch the show." But they couldn't find an empty space among the hundreds of jam-packed autos. They didn't want to park way out on the fringe, so they just kept riding. Young Weiss would always regret that he was not in the Capitol that night. A few blocks away, Dr. Arthur Vidrine was finishing dinner at the Heidelberg Hotel. He was in Baton Rouge to try to get an appropriation for his Charity Hospital in New Orleans. Long had lifted Vidrine from obscurity as a young doctor from the country town of Ville Platte and had appointed him head of the huge public hospital. Vidrine would soon be bending cautiously over an operating table holding a life in his hands.

About 8:45 p.m., Huey came down the elevator from his office suite high in the Capitol. With him was his entourage of special bodyguards—Joe Messina, Murphy Roden, and Paul Voitier. Long had spent the afternoon on the 24th floor receiving an endless parade of patronage callers, telling stories from Washington, talking politics. There's no record of what went on, but the best information is that Huey was chiefly concerned with lining up his ticket for the upcoming January primary—tantamount to election in one-party Louisiana.[1] Governor Allen's post was on the block. So was Huey's Senatorship and so were all other Congressional, State and city offices of the Long machine.

Later, there was to be a bitter fight in the ranks of the Long regime as to whom Long named that afternoon to succeed Allen. (Allen couldn't run for re-election, because Louisiana law prohibits the Governor from succeeding himself.) Actually, Huey prob-

[1] In Huey's day, the "parties" were both Democratic factions—Longs and anti-Longs.

ably did not make any final decision. But before the month was out Allen was to announce that Long had told him that he wanted to see Richard Leche, an obscure State appeals judge and Allen's former secretary, as his candidate.

One story goes that Long had called Leche that afternoon to check on his religion. The rural Protestant half of the State had seen that no Catholic had been Governor in the 20th century. "Dick, what's your religion?" Huey had asked. Leche had answered that the kind of immortality that appealed to him was that of the American Indian in his happy hunting grounds. Huey had hung up.

"Hell no, he ain't a Catholic," Huey had said. "He's an Indian. Told me so himself."

(Leche won the election by a landslide. Before his term ended, a Federal grand jury indicted him on mail-fraud charges involving the pocketing of $31,000 in excess profits on trucks and equipment sold to the Louisiana Highway Department. Leche resigned, stood trial, and was sentenced to ten years in prison during the sensational "Louisiana Scandals," in which one man committed suicide and the Federal Government sent scores of State officials to jail for looting Louisiana of an estimated $100,000,000.)

Huey bounded down the Capitol corridor with long, rapid strides. He quickly outdistanced his bodyguards. ("He always walked plump! plump! plump! like he was going somewhere," said a hometown crony. "Businesslike, what I mean.") He brushed past lobbyists, hangers-on, tourists, swung around the corner at the end of the hall, and strode into the House.

Immaculate in linen suit and sporty black-and-white shoes, Huey walked up and down the aisles. He stopped several times to speak to members, shook hands, swapped a joke or two. The customary relaxed ribaldry held sway. Nobody cared much about what was going on. Everyone knew that the bills on the floor would pass overwhelmingly when they got to a vote a few nights later. If a Long legislator got confused and pushed the "no" button, the Kingfish simply dispatched a bodyguard to guide the lawmaker's hand to "yes." There had to be opposition to spark fireworks in the Legislature. There was no opposition.

In fact, there was really no reason for Huey to be in the House that night—everything was running like clockwork; but Huey liked the personal touch.

"He wanted to keep his hand in," the AP's Quincy Ewing said, "wanted to be able to conveniently keep the hell scared out of his legislator-henchmen, face to face, without having to phone them."

A Long rule was never write what you can phone, never phone what you can talk head 'n' head, never talk what you can nod, never nod what you can wink, never wink what you can look.

Huey rambled to the dais, plopped down on a swivel armchair next to Speaker Ellender, and chatted with him,[2] the House Clerk and newsman J. Alan Coogan. Coogan, United Press bureau "manager"—United

---

[2] Senator Ellender, in an interview with the author, said that Huey had talked to him about the upcoming Governor's race. According to Ellender, Huey had already chosen Ellender as his man for the top State post. As it turned out, Ellender was never to get the nomination. Instead, he ran successfully for the U.S. Senate, and accumulated enormous power by holding his seat until he died in 1972.

Press gave Coogan that grandiose title even though he was the only UP newsman in Baton Rouge—was seated nearby at the press table.

"Huey perched on the edge of my desk," Coogan recalled, "and was shooting the breeze about the coming football season and the trip to Nashville, Tenn., when LSU was to play Vandy and Huey was to lead the LSU marching band up Nashville's main street. I had a bulldog (early edition) of a Sunday New York *Daily News,* and the sports section had a big feature from Nashville about how they couldn't wait to see Huey up there. That tickled his vanity immediately, and he was talking to me for at least 45 minues while I got farther and farther behind in my chores."

The report of the Ways and Means Committee was received and read. Representative Isom ("Sit Down") Guillory,[3] the Long House-leader from St. Landry Parish, moved that the rules be suspended to take up the 39 bills that the Committee had rubber-stamped. One legislator objected. The House took a vote, and the Speaker declared the rules suspended. The bills were read a second time and advanced to third and final passage on Monday.

Then the lawmakers turned to a minor but nonetheless indispensable matter—their pay. The House passed a resolution authorizing $15,000 "or so much as may be necessary" to pay themselves for the session. The roll call showed 74 yeas, no nays.

C. E. Frampton, a rawboned, lantern-jawed reporter

---

[3] Guillory, later a State judge, earned the sobriquet "Sit Down" at a House session during which Long, not caring for the drift of Isom's argument in a floor debate, suddenly bellowed, "Sit down, Isom!" Isom sat down.

for the New Orleans *Item-Tribune,* walked over to Huey. Frampton was one member of the press who had no trouble getting access to the Kingfish. He was on the machine payroll as a statistician in the Attorney General's office.

"Do you have any comment on the Florida hurricane?" Frampton asked Huey. A hurricane had ripped through southern Florida earlier in the week, taking the lives of 458 ill-prepared victims. Most of them were jobless veterans of the Depression, working in Federal road-building camps in the Keys. A controversy loomed, because they were not moved out before the storm hit.

"Hell, yes, I've got some comment," Huey said. "Mr. Roosevelt ought to be very happy tonight. Every soldier he gets killed is one less vote against him."

Frampton made a beeline for a phone.

Huey rocked on his heels, looking out at the crowd in the high-domed, marble-walled chamber. Usually, a good number of spectators stood in the back, near the rail that ran behind the last row of desks. But not tonight. Before the House had opened, assistant sergeants at arms had stationed themselves at the entrances to the chamber to stop spectators from going in. House Sergeant at Arms A. J. Thomas had given orders directing to the gallery all persons not having legislative business. On the floor, Brigadier General Louis F. Guerre, head of the State Bureau of Criminal Identification and Investigation, had spaced out his men among the lawmakers.

The reason for the added guard was never made

clear. A scuffle the night before may have precipitated it. Shortly before the House had begun its Saturday-night session, a bodyguard had slapped elderly T. O. Harris of Shreveport. Harris, a former newspaperman who worked as publicity director for the Federal educational program in Louisiana, had encountered Huey near the Clerk's desk. They had exchanged words. A scene had developed. Long later said that Harris had been drunk and had cursed a bodyguard. Harris denied that he had been drunk. He said that he had sworn at Long after Huey had cursed him. "When I cursed Huey back," Harris said, "George McQuiston, one of Long's bodyguards, slapped me in the face. When I asked McQuiston why Long didn't slap me, McQuiston said, 'Come on with me.' He took me to jail and charged me with being drunk, using obscene language and disturbing the peace." Harris had returned to the House chamber that night after posting $15 bond. He had not been bothered thereafter.

It's doubtful, however, that Huey would have filled the Capitol with secret police just to keep an eye on old Harris.

One story that the Long lieutenants later gave out was that Huey had been tipped off about a plot to do him in before the special session adjourned. Another version had it that there was talk of a disgruntled mob storming the Capitol. If either of these stories is true, Long's advisors were apparently somewhat skeptical. Aside from the extra guards and the clearing of the House floor, there were no special precautions. By now, the seventh year of Huey's reign, the bearing of tales of so-called assassination schemes was far from unusual. Such stories were, in fact, commonplace.

"Long was so prodigal in his listing of murder conspiracies in which he was the appointed victim," Thomas O. Harris wrote in *The Kingfish,* "they became almost run of the mill affairs in Louisiana."

Huey had been gripped by a mortal fear of assassination since he had become Governor in 1928. He was the first Governor in Louisiana to hire a bodyguard. He was only a few weeks in office when he phoned the Mayor and reported a suspicious-looking auto driving round and round the mansion. It turned out to be a motorist putting mileage on his new car. A man strolled by the mansion twice daily at the same time. Long called the police. They found that he was going and coming from work.

Huey's fear was not wholly without substance. There was no question but that Long's ruthless politics spawned legions of bitter enemies. They were unorganized and poorly led, but, as the years passed, their grumbling spread through the ranks. Dissatisfaction smoldered in citizens whose taxes the State had arbitrarily raised, anti-Long leaders of rural parishes turned out to pasture, schoolteachers and State workers let go because their politics were "wrong," hitherto-secure representatives of Big Business, submissive legislators who fretted inwardly because they had sold out, idealist New Dealers, and genuinely disturbed bourgeoisie. Louisiana was filled with these people.

And Huey knew it. At first, one guard was enough. As the years passed, his bodyguard grew until it reached the porportions of a military company. Huey was as well protected as the President, as Al Capone in his heyday. No American politician has done more to ensure his personal safety.

Brother Julius Long dubbed the guardsmen "Huey's skull-crackers." There was Joe Messina, a big, beefy ex-house detective. He was Huey's favorite. Once, AP photographer Leon Trice, without asking permission, took a picture of Huey getting off a train in New Orleans. Messina flattened him with a black jack. Simple-minded Joe was completely devoted. He acted as Huey's valet, slept near the Kingfish, rarely let him out of his sight.

Another regular was Murphy Roden, an outwardly quiet, sharpshooting cop from Arcadia, Louisiana. Roden had tried to become a flying cadet at San Antonio, Texas, washed out, and joined the Louisiana State Police. He was familiar with his home territory of north and central Louisiana, and on one of Huey's trips upstate Roden was assigned to drive Long's personal car. Murphy, it was said, could empty a pistol into a four-inch target at 50 feet. Huey took a shine to him, made him his regular driver, then a member of his bodyguard.

When he became Senator, Huey took his top Cossacks to Washington. He breezed in and out of hotel lobbies in the center of a flying wedge. When Huey got on the elevator, it was automatically full. Whenever Long was on the Senate floor, you could look up at the gallery reserved for Senatorial families and special guests and see one or more of Huey's gum-chewing

bodyguards. Before Long left the floor, they were notified by some pre-arranged signal, slipped quietly out,
and picked up Huey at the cloakroom entrance.

Despite the armed guard, Huey couldn't shake his
fear of violent death. It was rumored that he wore a
bullet-proof vest and carried a gun. "Sure I carry a gun.
Sometimes I carry four. Can't tell when somebody's
going to shoot the King." But generally he didn't joke
about it.

A Washington reporter once approached him with
the remark, "I have a couple of shots for you, Senator."
Long retreated a step. A few seconds passed before
Huey realized that the reporter meant *questions*.

A familiar newsman, bent on an interview, walked
into Huey's office through a private door. The door
was usually locked, but this time it wasn't. Long, taken
unaware, leaped to his feet. A guard, his hand reaching
inside his coat, sprang between Long and the intruder.
"Don't do that again," the guard said nervously. "You
don't know what a close shave you had."

The Associated Press bureau in New Orleans had
to phone Long at night every so often to check an
out-of-state rumor that Long had been shot. "I would
pick up the phone and dial Huey's unlisted number,"
Ed Desobry recalled. " 'Sorry to disturb you, Senator,
but we just got another report that someone shot you.'
Usually, Huey would come back with some crack."

"Sorry to disappoint you," Long would say, "but
I'm not even half shot."

Once, Huey's office got a crudely-made bomb in the
mail. It did not go off. As a means of self-protection,
Long proposed a State law requiring the registration

of all firearms. He was constantly ordering State Police raids on suspected gun caches.

There were threats against Long's life in Louisiana. But the evidence is that they were not seriously uttered. They were generally made openly at public mass meetings called to protest a new tyrannical measure. Occasionally, at a caucus of political foes, a frustrated anti-Long would slam his fist on a table and bellow, "Lord, I wish someone would kill the sonofabitch." If these hopeful pronouncements were murder plots, there were hundreds in the State nearly every week.

It was 9:10 p.m. Francis M. Julias, a commercial photographer on assignment for a photo syndicate, took some pictures of Long on the dais. While the flashbulbs popped, Huey spotted James P. O'Connor of New Orleans enjoying a lusty Corona Belvedere cigar. O'Connor, a 29-year-old lawyer and Long-appointed member of the Louisiana Public Service Commission, had spent part of the afternoon with Huey discussing some upcoming rate cases, then stayed on to see the session. The sight of O'Connor puffing away with abandon made Huey suddenly yearn for a cigar. He called O'Connor over and asked the young attorney to get him a few.

The House was winding up its business rapidly. Inside the adjoining Sergeant at Arms office, the telephone rang. It was Frampton, the *Item* reporter, calling from Governor Allen's office. Frampton had telephoned Huey's comments on the hurricane deaths to his paper. But he had overlooked the obvious question —would Huey demand an investigation? City Editor George Coad told Frampton to get back to Huey fast and find out. To save time, Frampton called Long on Allen's private line.

"Certainly, I'm going to ask an investigation," Long roared. "If there was negligence, the Nation is entitled to know who was responsible. Wait, I'll come in there to talk to you." Long hung up abruptly.

Speaker Ellender gave Huey a nod, the signal that he would end the session in a minute or two. Long got up and started through the chamber.

Huey rambled down a side aisle, past the ocean of faces, the fawning expressions, the staring eyes, heels clicking beneath the lavishly decorated ceiling, the ornate chandeliers, the bronze fixtures. He was in the corridor. It was 9:21.

Huey Pierce Long had one minute before catastrophe.

Blood on the Capitol Floor

"It seemed like the whole world exploded."
—Mildred Sanchez

Outside the Capitol a stillness was settling over Baton Rouge. The slow music that was Sunday was coming to an end, gearing down, seeking a new rhythm which was night. A faint breeze from the southeast whispered through the Spanish moss of the great live-oaks. The moon spread a thin layer of silver over the city, over the levee and the great River. At the First Methodist Church, on the corner of North and East Boulevards, the Reverend J. Richard Spann conducted the evening worship service. On the Airline Highway an exhausted motorcade of 150 members of the Young Men's Business Club of New Orleans drove home after a pleasant day's excursion of picnicking and swimming in Baton Rouge. At the "Louisiana" movie house, a Sunday-night audience (paying 25 cents for adults and ten cents for children) saw Gary Cooper in "The Virginian" and a "Betty Boop" cartoon.

A pedestrian walking near a house at 1141 Laurel Street could have heard the excited squeals of teen-age girls. Mildred and Frances Sanchez had begged and gotten permission to go to the special session. They wanted to get Huey's autograph, and Mrs. Sanchez had finally given in when Mr. and Mrs. Frank Odom, their neighbors, had agreed to take them along with their daughter, Patsy.

"The thought of being able to get his (Long's) autograph made wonderful chills run up and down my spine," Mildred recalled. "Wouldn't we be the envy of all the kids on our block!"

At the Capitol, the Odoms went to the gallery and the girls huddled to lay their plans. Mildred suggested that they split up. They could cover more territory that way and have more chances to confront the great Kingfish. The girls agreed. Frances, 13, went to the gallery. Patsy, 14, went by the main floor of the House. And Mildred, 15, circulated through the corridors.

Mildred had been wandering aimlessly and without success for some time when she spotted Dr. Weiss in Memorial Hall. She knew him, since she had visited his office a number of times. Mildred walked over.

"Hello, how are you?" the 29-year-old doctor asked. He patted her on the head, and excused himself. On the spur of the moment, Mildred decided to follow him. A physician was a kind of celebrity to the teen-ager.

"If I follow him, maybe he'll lead me to some equally famous names," she thought. She started after him. She trailed him through Memorial Hall and down a short passageway connecting with the Governor's corridor.

Inside the House, Justice Fournet had the Kingfish under his eye. The 39-year-old judge had tried all night to buttonhole Long. "I got close to him," Fournet said, "but he was talking with friends or milling about in the usual way, and I didn't want to speak in front of people." Fournet took a seat. When Huey bolted from the chamber, Fournet rose to head him off. A crowd blocked his path. The judge's patience went unrewarded. Huey was soon out of sight.

An entourage of plainclothes bodyguards followed the Kingfish. They walked at his side and rear, leaving the front open. Huey bustled through the House lobby into an entranceway opening into the Governor's corridor. Running behind the bank of public elevators, the long, narrow corridor stretched east and west like a belt across the rear of the Capitol. The ten-foot-wide passageway linked the House and Senate chambers to the Governor's office midway down the corridor.

Louis Lesage, a lobbyist for Standard Oil, sat on the window ledge at the end of the ornate hall talking to Roy Heidelberg, owner of the Heidelberg Hotel. Lesage saw Huey wheel into the passageway. Hugo Dore, a pro-Long judge from Ville Platte, approached from the opposite direction. As Lesage recalled the scene, Dore, noted for his quick wit, seized on the surprise meeting to launch into a spur-of-the-moment pantomime of Huey: Dore suddenly stopped and waved his arms in exaggerated fashion, gesturing wildly as if he were the Kingfish thundering from the stump.

Spotting Lesage, Long remarked, "Louie, that's a crazy goddam Frenchman." Long laughed noiselessly, sucking in his breath, and continued down the corridor. His bodyguards were a murmur of voices in the background, a clatter of heels trailing him on the slick marble floor. Down the hall some 50 feet was the Governor's private elevator, in which Long had to ride to get to his 24th-floor suite. But Huey had some business to attend to first. The Kingfish was on his way to the Governor's office, about 80 feet down the passageway. He hurried past the Representatives' room, a coatroom, the Speaker's anteroom, and the elevator, and into a hallway immediately outside the Governor's office.

Here the corridor widened slightly, framed by four recessed marble pillars. The pillars, about a foot or so in diameter, rested at the corners of the hallway, set back from the flow of passersby. A bust of the 17th-century French explorer Robert de La Salle stood midway between the south pillars opposite the Governor's office. It was La Salle who had claimed all the land drained by the Mississippi River for King Louis XIV and named the vast territory "Louisiana" in his honor. La Salle, the first boss of Louisiana, was assassinated by mutinous members of his expedition party in 1687.

Long barged through the big double door leading into the Governor's office suite. The suite opened into a small, oblong reception room with three doors branching off into the Governor's office, anteroom and secretary's room. The bodyguard platoon—Roden, Messina, Voitier, Coleman, and Louis Heard—waited outside. Fournet joined the waiting group. The wait was a brief one. Long breezed out as quickly as he had stormed in. He apparently hadn't found the man he was looking for. Huey wasn't going to wait. Roden skipped out of his way, goose-stepping backward.

"Get the boys out early in the morning and have them all there," Huey said over his shoulder as he flashed back into the hallway. Long had some things on his mind, and he wanted to air them at a caucus.

"Yes, Senator, everybody's been notified to be on hand at nine o'clock," Joe Bates, BCI assistant superintendent, said.

Long walked toward the waiting knot of men standing on a circular design on the floor at the center of the hallway. Witnesses said that a man in a white suit walked into the group from a set-back pillar (nearest the House) and approached Long. Those who would testify at a coroner's inquest eight days later would insist that no words were spoken. Some in Louisiana would never believe this. They would feel there was never a full disclosure of the circumstances that occurred after Weiss advanced.

The rest of the story can only be told by those who surrounded Huey and Dr. Weiss.

"Huey was coming toward me and I noticed his eyes were popping like saucers," Fournet said in an interview. "I saw a man in a linen suit with dark-rimmed glasses—a small fellow with dark hair. And I saw that little black automatic.

"It was a hot night before air conditioning and I perspire freely. I was holding my Panama hat in my right hand and wiping my brow with a handkerchief in my left. By reflex, I reached out and hit the man with my hat, a backhand swipe, and then started pushing him. Simultaneously, Roden grabbed him."

A muffled explosion echoed down the corridor. Blood stained Huey's white shirt about six inches above the belt line. He grabbed the right side of his abdomen. His eyes dilated. His knees sagged, but he did not fall.

The bust of La Salle looked down from its vantage point seven feet above the floor. Mason Spencer's dire prophecy had been fulfilled. Blood flowed in the majestic Capitol.

"When Huey was shot, he spun around, made one outcry—'Ohhhhhhh!'—and ran down the hall," Fournet said. "He ran like a scared deer."

"I dropped my hat," Fournet said. "I was about to grab him (Dr. Weiss) when I twisted a muscle or got a crick in my back. I couldn't move. I stood there frozen."

Weiss and Roden went down on the slippery floor.

"I put my left hand over the gun," Roden said, "and we struggled and fell to the floor and came up again. My eyes were full of smoke and my hands and face were powder burned. At first, I thought it was a free-for-all, and I knew I had the man who had shot the Senator. I jerked loose, pulled my gun."

The other bodyguards sprang forward, pistols drawn.[1] Dr. Weiss surged backward, attempting to regain his balance. He looked up. Death was staring him in the face. In that terrible, endless moment, a lifetime could have swept across his mind. Less than an hour before he had been putting his baby son to bed, telephoning a doctor to confirm an operation in the morning. Only six hours before, he had been swimming with his wife, lolling in the sun with his parents, basking in the exquisite flavor of a summer Sunday. At this very instant his wife was in their kitchen two-tenths of a mile away, listening in the still night to music drifting in from a neighbor's radio, while their baby slept. Weiss was never to know that the child would become a doctor, and interne in the same hospital in which he himself had done his interning.

"I shot ten times," said Roden. He had a .38 caliber Colt super automatic. It fired as fast as he could pull

---

[1] Both United Press and the *New York Times* erroneously reported that Huey's bodyguards cut down Weiss with submachine guns, in addition to pistols.

the trigger. At the same instant, or perhaps even before
Roden could act, Huey's bodyguard platoon opened
up. There was a deafening roar. Steel-jacketed missiles
ricocheted along the corridor, whined through the air,
spattered against the shining walls. Gunsmoke drifted
down the hall in streamers. Men fled. Women screamed
wildly as they ran from the corridor. "It seemed like
the whole world exploded," Mildred Sanchez said. The
arm of a Highway Patrolman engulfed her like a ten-
tacle, snatching the terrified girl against the wall by
one of the pillars. Louis Lesage dived from the window sill, sliding on his stomach into the Representatives' room.

Fred C. Dent and his wife, State Land Register
Lucille May Grace (who kept her maiden name be-
cause she was elected before her marriage), ducked
into a side passageway. State Highway Patrol Chief
Colonel E. P. Roy peeped from behind a door frame,
Dent said.

"What the hell's going on out there?" Roy asked.

"You're the head of the Highway Patrol, Colonel,"
Dent said as he rushed away with his wife. "You get
out there and see."

"Firecrackers," laughed Speaker Ellender in the
House. (It's a Louisiana custom to set off firecrackers
at the close of a Legislative session.) More shots rang
out. Legislators stampeded.

"The first time he was shot, Weiss shivered," Fournet said. "Then, he quit trying to shoot Roden. He
shivered again when the second shot hit."

Weiss started to crumple slowly—like a puppet let
go—sagging face forward. As his knees struck the floor,

his right arm bent as if he were trying to ward off the lethal barrage. His head pillowed on the crook of his arm. A gun skidded across the polished floor. Bullet after bullet pounded into his prone body, shuddering and stiffening under the withering fusillade. The 29-year-old doctor groaned only once, the last sound of his life. And still the guns thundered. They poured lead into his broken, five-foot ten-inch frame from all sides. The body bounced convulsively with each blast until there were no more bullets left.

Blood flowed from 61 wounds. One man said that the whole thing had lasted only six seconds. The action was so fast that nobody knew—or would say—who had fired the first shot.

Roden, in a 1961 interview at Louisiana State Police Headquarters at Baton Rouge, where he was State Public Safety Director, said that Weiss had covered his gun with his hat as he walked toward Long. At first, Roden said, he had thought that it was a toy.

"You didn't see many foreign automatics in those days."

When he grabbed Weiss, Roden continued, he hit the doctor's gun and knocked his arm down.

"If it hadn't been for me, Huey would have been shot through the heart," Roden said. (Fournet held the same opinion about his own effort.)

"The webbing of my right hand caught in the firing mechanism," Roden said. "It was the type of automatic where the whole carriage comes back to eject the cartridge."

Authorities believed that Weiss's gun jammed. Some thought that it stopped shooting because its firing mechanism was faulty. Others felt that Roden's hand had rendered the gun harmless when it stuck in the exposed unloading breech—thus preventing the empty shell that had been fired from coming out.

"The doctor fired a second bullet and it shattered my watch on my left wrist," Roden said. (He was quoted as telling the coroner's jury that he was "of the opinion Weiss fired only *one* shot.") "I had on a pair of new shoes and slipped and fell under him. I got shrapnel in my back from the ricocheting marble chips. They dug it out of my back for six months afterward."

Dr. Joseph Sabatier, an interne, said that he removed burnt powder and particles that appeared to be concrete or tiny pieces of stone from Roden's right hand the next day at Our Lady of the Lake Sanitarium. Roden's left hand had two small abrasions where, Roden said, a bullet had shot his watch off.

Reporter Frampton, waiting for Huey to show up in the Governor's office, had chatted with Governor Allen for a few minutes. Then, thinking that Huey might have forgotten him or been tied up with other business, Frampton got up to find him. He walked from Allen's inner office into the outer reception room toward the main double door.

"Just as my hand clutched the knob, I heard a muffled shot," Frampton said. "Jerking the door open, I saw Senator Long walking away, his hand to his side."

As Frampton recalled the scene 25 years later (in New Orleans' historic Cabildo museum, where he was business manager), he said that he had not been convinced at that moment that Long had really been shot.

"Huey's mind worked so fast," Frampton said, "I thought he may have grabbed his side just to see that man (Weiss) shot."

Frampton later was able to confirm that Huey was wounded. His front-page story the next morning in the now-defunct New Orleans *Item-Tribune* was an exclusive eye-witness account of Weiss's slaying:

"Almost at my feet, I saw Murphy Roden struggling with a white clad man. A shot was fired. I couldn't tell which of the struggling men fired. Roden backed away firing as he stepped backward. The man with whom he had been struggling pitched forward on his face. . . . He gave a strangled cry. Then, a half dozen men, officers in plain clothes, began firing at him. . . . Bullet after bullet thudded into his body."

Frampton said that one of the bodyguards later told him that he spotted Frampton coming out of the Governor's office and thought Frampton was an accomplice. Frampton quoted the bodyguard as saying, "Jesus Christ, I almost killed you. . . . Just as I was about to pull the trigger, I recognized you."

The crash of exploding hand guns drowned out the sound of Speaker Ellender, who was announcing that the House was adjourned until 10 a.m. Monday. The standing-room crowd fled from the gallery. Halls filled with frenzied people pushing each other, jabbering crazily, racing in all directions. Tumult swirled through the Capitol. It was a surrealistic scene, a nightmare.

Reporter Ewing had just left the House press table

to file his copy. Suddenly, the corridor jammed with dozens of panicky spectators, streaking down the passageway.

"They nearly trompled me," Ewing said. "I was like a chip on the ocean, a salmon trying to swim upstream. But I managed to sidestep, elbow or otherwise work my way into the corridor after Long where the shots came from. I reached a point just outside the Governor's office. The crowd had thinned—you never saw a crowd scatter so fast—and with good reason the way those shots were flying in that narrow hall."

When the firing began, Governor Allen locked his office. He hid under his desk. After it was all over, he rushed out, demanding to know what had happened.

"Is Huey hurt?" he asked.

"I don't think so," Frampton replied, although he really didn't know himself.

Then, to no one in particular, Allen said, "Someone give me a pistol. If there's any shooting to be done here, I want to be in on it."

Louis Heard rushed up with a submachine gun that he had snatched from a hidden cache. "Clear the hall," a policeman yelled. "Shoot up and down the hall." BCI agent Coleman said that he grabbed the tommy gun before any shots could be fired.

Through the heavy palls of smoke, Ewing made his way to the body on the floor.

"I saw a slight man in an immaculate white linen suit," Ewing said, "lying on his face at a 45 degree angle against the south wall of the corridor. The white suit was stained by a scarlet circle about a foot in diameter in the middle of his back. The bodyguards were milling around as if demented with Colt .45's in their hands."

Huey had disappeared. Nobody knew where he was. None of the guards would—or could—answer Ewing's questions. And Ewing couldn't even confirm that Long had been shot.

In the basement pressroom, a poker player was stifling a yawn. Suddenly, Wes Gallagher—Louisiana State journalism student and International News Service stringer who would become the General Manager of the Associated Press—burst in.

"Shooting," he screamed, wild-eyed. "Shooting! Upstairs! They're killing everybody!"

("That was the first time in my life I ever saw a man's hair actually stand on end," AP reporter Desobry recalled.)

The poker players bounced into the air at the same instant, upsetting chairs and slamming the table into the wall. Desobry, who had won the pot, took the trouble to scoop it up. The newsmen reached the door in a pack, rammed through, and plunged toward the stairway. It led up to the main floor, where the shooting had taken place. People passed them, running in confusion.

Midway up the stairs, Joe Messina, on his way down, clutched Desobry's arm.

"Where's Huey?" Messina asked frantically. "Where's Huey?"

Desobry mumbled something incoherent on the run. Messina barreled on by. Had Desobry been a few seconds earlier, he would have met the Kingfish on those same stairs.

In the Governor's corridor, the reporters saw plainclothesmen brandishing pistols and machine guns pulled from their hiding places and set up. Desobry picked out the biggest crowd and fought his way into it.

"You could almost hear the feeling of hate and passion all about," Desobry said. "The grim faces looked murderous."

Despite shoving by bodyguards, he managed to push to the front. There was the doctor's body—a sight he would never forget.

"Against the background of that white suit, I could see in bold relief the scores of bullets that had punctured his body," Desobry said. "His back looked like a punchboard with all the numbers out. I went close, leaned down, and looked at him, not to see if he was dead because there could be no doubt of that, but to see if I knew him. He was a stranger."

All this happened in a matter of seconds. Desobry grasped one person after another, trying to pick up the pieces of the story.

"What happened?"

"He shot Huey."

The guards looked menacingly at reporters.

"They did it," one fellow shouted hysterically. "They caused all this! Those damn reporters."

"Shoot 'em all," shrilled another. But the guards' guns were empty. They had poured all their bullets into Weiss.

Another minute passed. Desobry raged about, grabbing anybody to find out if he had seen what had happened. No one would talk. ("That was the dictatorship," Desobry said. "Long was the only one who spoke out in those days.")

At last, he found someone who had seen Long and would admit it. He was a young man.

"He stumbled down those stairs," the man said. "Blood dripped from his mouth. There were two big bullet-holes in his side and stomach."

(Attending physicians said that Long had been shot only once. The "two" holes may have referred to bloodstains on the front and back of Long's suit jacket.)

"What's your name?" Desobry asked.

The man turned as if he himself had been shot, and fled.

Desobry continued probing. He found some more people who said that they had seen Long wounded. Several State officials confirmed it. Desobry ran for the AP teletype in the pressroom.

"Flash," Desobry yelled to operator attendant Joseph A. Conway. "Baton Rouge—Shooting in the Statehouse." The 23-year-old Conway's fingers began punching his first news FLASH.

The bulletin, sent minutes after the shooting, went to New Orleans, where an editor quickly relayed it on the national trunk wire. Randolph Trudeau, a 21-year-old operator attendant, plugged the Baton Rouge circuit directly on the national wire hookup. That eliminated the need for a time-consuming relay from New Orleans. Baton Rouge had the right of way on the vast AP network.

Desobry dashed out, nearly colliding with Ewing. They compared notes. Did they have enough confirmation to flash to the world the news that Huey Long, Louisiana's dictator and stormy petrel of American politics, had been shot? They decided to double check. They corraled people in the area, then huddled again.

"Let's go with it," they agreed.

"Flash," Desobry yelled to the operator.

"Baton Rouge—Huey Long shot!"

That went out all over the United States less than three minutes after the occurrence, Desobry said. It was a clean beat over other services, he said.

Editor and Publisher of September 14, 1935, however, said that there was "wide controversy" over who broke the first flash.

Desobry typed out a short lead to follow the flash:

E O S (Extraordinary Service)

BULLETIN

BATON ROUGE, LA., SEPT. 8 (AP)—SEN. HUEY P. LONG WAS SHOT AND WOUNDED IN THE STATEHOUSE TONIGHT AND AN UNIDENTIFIED MAN WAS SHOT AND KILLED.

About two hours passed before newsmen could get reliable information on the extent of Long's wound.[2]

The AP's opposite number, J. Alan Coogan of United Press, had been delayed by Long's chat and was still at the press table in the House. The UP had recently transferred the 26-year-old Coogan from Jefferson City, Missouri, where he had been Statehouse reporter. He wasn't too happy about the new assignment. The rambunctious Huey was in Washington most of the time, and there wasn't enough action in

[2] Desobry, who stayed in the newspaper business until 1958, when he joined a New Orleans brokerage firm, died of a heart attack in April 1962 at the age of 53. His obituary credited his work on the Long slaying as the distinguishing achievement of his news career.

Louisiana to suit Coogan. Some few days earlier, Coogan had written to the news editor of the UP's southwestern office asking to be sent to a bureau "where something happens once in a while." Suddenly there were shots and the sound of people screaming. Coogan looked up and dashed into the corridor. A little girl threw her arms around him, shrieking. As soon as he could quiet the girl, he made his way to the scene of the shooting. Police barred his path. Coogan got to an elevator and told the operator to take him down to the first-floor pressroom. Messina and Lieutenant Governor Noe, hunting frantically for Huey, rushed in behind him. Hoping to find the Kingfish in his office-apartment, they ordered the operator to take them to the 24th floor. Messina and Noe were crying.

"Is he hit, Jimmy?" Messina asked.

"I'm afraid so, Joe," Noe replied.

Coogan rode the elevator to the 24th floor and then back to the first floor. He saw a crowd packed around a man's body riddled with bullets. By that time, Coogan had enough details to telephone news of the shooting to Earl B. Steele, UP night manager in New Orleans. Steele instantly filed UP's flash:

BATON ROUGE, LA., SEPT. 8 (UP)—SHOOTING IN THE STATEHOUSE, LONG BELIEVED WOUNDED.

Something did happen in Baton Rouge. It was world news.

✧   ✧   ✧

The story was just starting. Who shot Long? And why? How badly was Huey wounded? Who was the

dead man upstairs? Most urgent of all at the moment—
where was the Kingfish?

Even Long's own bodyguards had lost track of him.
They wandered aimlessly, like lost sheep. Messina,
down from the 24th floor, dashed out the main entrance, raced down the terraced steps, and sprinted
futilely through the dark Capitol grounds. Bates ran
into the Governor's office. Some State officials rushed
up the elevator to Long's office-suite.

What happened was this: Huey fled west down the
Governor's corridor in the direction of the Senate. He
turned into a passageway some 40 feet from the shooting scene, entered a four-level staircase leading to the
basement, and went down its 28 steps.

Public Service Commission member James P.
O'Connor had gotten Huey's cigars and finished a cup
of coffee in the nearly deserted basement cafeteria.
O'Connor was starting back to the House when Long
came staggering out of the stairwell. O'Connor was
startled.

"Kingfish, what's the matter?" young O'Connor
said. O'Connor, the son of a New Orleans judge, had
been close to Long ever since Huey had picked him
for a seat on the Commission for Louisiana's First
District. ("I was a young fellow at the time and I was
flattered. Unlike others, I never asked Long about
jobs, money or patronage. I never offered him advice.
He took me to Washington several times. He was like
a father to me.")

"Jimmy, my boy, I'm shot," Huey gasped. He spit
blood over the front of O'Connor's suit jacket.

"The blood came gushing out of his mouth,"
O'Connor said. "At first, I thought he had been shot

in the mouth. Later, in the hospital, I saw a membrane had been cut inside his lower lip."

Huey started reeling. O'Connor grabbed him, helped him toward a rear door. Outside, O'Connor said, he spotted an open four-door Ford sedan. Its owner was nearby.

"The Senator's shot," O'Connor yelled. "Help me get him to the hospital." [3]

The lights from the great Statehouse cast dancing rays upon the Capitol lake, mingling with the twinkling lights from Our Lady of the Lake Sanitarium a quarter-mile away. The three-story, Catholic institution had been founded 12 years earlier by Franciscan Sisters of Calais, France. It was one of Baton Rouge's two hospitals.

The auto raced north on Third Street, along the wooded lakeside lying behind the Capitol. It was quiet. The car's motor merged with the nocturnal songs of crickets and long-horned grasshoppers.

O'Connor sat in the rear with Long sprawling across the back seat, his hands pressed to his wound, his head on O'Connor's shoulder.

"Only once did he say anything," O'Connor said, "And that was to ask, 'I wonder why he shot me?' "

A minute later, O'Connor scrambled out with Long at the hospital. To his utter dismay, he saw the driver suddenly ride off, leaving him alone with Huey. O'Connor half-dragged, half-carried Long up the front walk. There was a rolling stretcher by the entrance.

---

[3] "As the years passed, a dozen other people claimed to have been in that car," O'Connor told the author in 1961. "If there was anyone else in that car except Huey, myself, and that stranger, he was invisible."

He lifted Long onto it and pushed it into the lobby. Sister Michael, a nurse, helped wheel Huey to the elevator and up to a third-floor emergency operating-room. A few minutes later, an interne slit Huey's jacket and shirt as he lay staring at the ceiling with saucer eyes.

"There was a little powder burn and a fleck or two of blood by a small wound and that was all I saw," O'Connor said.

At the electrified Capitol, Huey's bodyguards and uniformed policemen began to restore order. They cleared the main floor of spectators and cordoned off the Governor's corridor. BCI Chief Louis F. Guerre stationed his men at all exits and closed the building. He gave orders not to permit anyone in or out until he was identified. Only State officials or those with business in the Statehouse were allowed in. State Highway Police Chief Roy threw a ring of Highway Patrolmen around Weiss's body. It lay unidentified on the gaudy, multi-colored floor until Dr. Thomas R. Bird, East Baton Rouge Parish Coroner, arrived. There is no record of how long the body remained anonymous. But most observers believed a considerable period of time elapsed. One newspaper and the AP reported that Weiss's identity remained a mystery for more than an hour after the shooting. Bird deputized New Orleans *Item-Tribune* reporter Helen Gilkison to help him search the body. They stepped across the litter of shells to the shattered corpse.

In the dead man's pockets, Dr. Bird said, he found a wallet with six dollars, a fountain pen, a medical-society card, a bone-handled pocket knife, a license issued to practicing physicians, one engraved calling card, and a city tax receipt. His wrist watch was stopped at 9:20. Dr. Bird identified the dead man as Dr. Carl Austin Weiss. He said that he had known Dr. Weiss several years.

The Coroner said that a .32 caliber Belgian Browning automatic bearing serial number 319-436 was picked up next to Weiss's body. The New Orleans *Times-Picayune* reported that Bird said that the gun contained one discharged cartridge and seven loaded cartridges. The *New York Times,* in a dispatch filed by a string (part-time) correspondent, reported that Dr. Bird said that two cartridges had been fired.

Dr. Bird later said that he had found 30 blood-rimmed wounds in the front of the body, 29 in the back, two in the head. One bullet entered the right eye. Another penetrated the tip of the nose. Two bullets were recovered from the body—one a .45, the other a .38. The Coroner said that the body was so badly riddled that he was unable to tell which were the wounds of entry and which the wounds of exit.

Merle Welch, manager of the Rabenhorst Funeral Home, and Jack Unbehagan, one of his assistants, propped the body into a sitting position and police took identification photos. When they lifted Weiss onto a stretcher, so many bullets dropped from his body, someone said that it sounded "like a hailstorm on the floor of the Capitol."

Louisiana went wild with excitement. In Baton Rouge, callers jammed telephone lines. Long-distance calls came in from all parts of the country. Masses of people sprouted at downtown street-corners. Police went on special duty. Hundreds of cars seemed to appear from nowhere and blocked the streets around the Capitol and the hospital.

As Tom Ed Weiss drove along Third Street with his college chums, they noticed a crowd in front of the *State-Times* newspaper office. They stopped and got out. Someone in the crowd said that Long had been shot. Another person said that he had heard that there was a "Dr. Weiss" involved.

"It didn't make sense to me," Tom Ed said, "but my first reaction was—well, possibly, Dad had gotten involved in some scrape. And they took me back home —about four blocks. As I approached, I noticed the front light was on, and Dad was standing on the front steps. I went up the steps and before I could say anything, as I recall, Dad said something like, 'Something's wrong. Your mother is inside. Don't worry her. I'm afraid something has happened to Carl.'

"And I guess I told him that I heard at the *State's* office that Long had been shot and a Dr. Weiss killed. And he said, well, he had heard something over the radio but had turned it off. And he had tried to get Carl by telephone. But the phone was dead. So he said, 'You better go up and see how Yvonne is doing.'"

The music drifted into the window at 527 Lakeland Drive to Yvonne in the kitchen. Suddenly it stopped. "We interrupt this program for a news flash," the announcer said.

"Baton Rouge—Huey Long has been shot in the Capitol, and his assailant killed."

After a while, a crowd started collecting around the house. As Mrs. Weiss recalled the moment, she said she had made no direct connection between the shooting and her husband's absence. But when the crowd began to get larger, she asked herself if something could have happened to Carl. She went to a drawer and found his pistol gone.

A neighbor later asked Yvonne what made her think of looking for Carl's gun.

"I can't explain what happened to me," she said. "I remember Carl always took it (the pistol) on night calls and I tried to persuade myself that there was nothing unusual. . . . I still recall that horrible feeling that came over me and I seemed to sense that something was wrong. Later, I explained it to myself as a warning to me—maybe God preparing me for the shock of what was to follow."

Tom Ed Weiss pushed through the knots of people and rang the doorbell. Yvonne opened the door slowly. Then, recognizing who was there, she pulled it open and cried, "Tom, something's wrong. People are walking all over the front of my house. Where's Carl?"

Tom Ed stood in the doorway groping for words that would cushion the blow. He found none.

"Yvonne," he said, "Carl has been killed."

She screamed, and fell into his arms.

At the elder Weiss's home, Carl's father left to join his son at Yvonne's house. The old doctor hadn't been able to bring himself to break the news to Carl's mother. Perhaps the radio report had been wrong, he thought as he walked into the night. Perhaps there had been a mistake.

In a little while, the doorbell rang at the house on Fifth Street. Carl's mother answered it. Cal Abraham, a newsman for the Baton Rouge *State-Times,* had come for a picture of Carl.

"I'm sorry about the trouble, Mrs. Weiss," Abraham said. What was he talking about? she asked. "I thought you knew," he said. He told her about the shooting. And so Mrs. Weiss learned of her son's death through a reporter.

"Oh, no," she cried. "My son never did that. Not my boy."

She stumbled backward.

"Oh, God, we've been opposed to Long," Abraham quoted her as saying, "but I didn't think he would do a thing like that."

At Our Lady of the Lake, police guards appeared on the hospital grounds and closed the hospital road to all traffic except the cars of doctors and State officials. Pedestrians were not even permitted to walk the road. Residents living in the vicinity of the hospital had to take roundabout routes to get home.

In the operating room, Dr. Arthur Vidrine, who had rushed over from the Legislature, examined Huey's wound and ordered blood tests made for a transfusion. He told Long that an emergency operation would have to be performed to stop internal bleeding.

"Go ahead, if necessary," Long said.

Long's lieutenants started barging into the operating room. Vidrine moved away to talk to them and to arrange for other surgeons to be summoned quickly.

The nun who had helped wheel Long in sat beside him. They were left alone for a moment. The Kingfish, his face pale and sweating, looked up at her.

"How bad is it?"

"Shot cases are always serious," Sister Michael said. "It's best to be ready."

Perspiration beaded across Long's forehead. A drop slid down his nose.

"Then, pray for me, Sister," Huey, a rock-ribbed Baptist, said.

She looked at him without moving for a moment. Then, she folded her hands.

"Yes, but you'll have to pray, too."

The nun prayed aloud. Huey mumbled the words after her. It was the Act of Contrition, the prayer of a dying Catholic.

"Oh, my God, I am heartily sorry for having offended Thee, and I detest all my sins because I dread the loss of heaven and the pains of hell, but most of all because they offend Thee, my God, who art all-good and deserving of all my love. I firmly resolve, with the help of Thy Grace, to confess my sins, to do Penance and to amend my life."

Unto Dust

"Everyone knows how he (Dr. Weiss) died. But written in blood and tears across the incompleted pages of his life is the unanswered question—why?"
—Mercedes Garig, teacher of Carl Weiss
at Louisiana State University

America, struggling slowly out of a depression, was enjoying its Sabbath. War was still six years away. The news was a hodge-podge of humdrum. At Hyde Park, N.Y., President Roosevelt assailed municipal waste in an impromptu talk to a group of neighbors. Dizzy Dean was the day's hero in the world of sports. He hung up his 25th victory as the first-place St. Louis Cardinals split a double-header with the Philadelphia Phillies. At Washington, N.J., an auto struck and injured a striking picket. In Asbury Park, N.J., more than 1,000 persons attended memorial services for the 124 dead of the Morro Castle. The ship had caught fire off the New Jersey coast exactly a year before. In New Haven, Conn., a baptismal ceremony ended in tragedy when Erskine Kidd, 27, Negro, suddenly panicked and lunged away from a preacher and a deacon in Beaver Park lagoon. He drowned as some 50 members of the Second Colored Baptist Church looked on. On Broadway, "Tobacco Road" rolled on through its second year. Judith Anderson and Helen Menken starred in the Pulitzer-Prize-winning play "The Old Maid," and the movie "Top Hat," with Fred Astaire and Ginger Rogers, set a house record at the Radio City Music Hall.

It was on this day that Huey Long was shot and Dr. Carl Austin Weiss killed.

The news burst upon a halcyon nation with the impact of a bomb. Telephones jangled. Telegraphs clattered. Radios blared. In Lynn, Mass., two cutters in a shoe factory fought over the merits of Long. One man suffered a scalp laceration. In Washington, Marvin McIntyre, the President's private secretary, immediately placed a long-distance call to FDR's Hyde Park home. "The President has retired," came a voice from the mansion. "Shall I wake him?" "Not now," McIntyre replied, "but if he wakes later, tell him Huey Long has been shot."

The shooting immediately became the number one story in every newspaper in America. Editors ran it under streamer headlines. It shoved Mussolini's preparations for war against Ethiopia from the lead spot and squeezed it into a one-column head. The break went to morning papers. They reported big extra sales.

By a one-in-a-million coincidence, the Spokane, Washington, *Spokesman-Review* ran a "Ding" (J. N. Darling) cartoon on Long on the front page along with the shooting. The cartoon, headed "The Fates Are Funny That Way," pictured the numerous deaths from highway crashes, earthquakes, lightning, and poisoned foods. The punch line quoted John Q. Public saying to his wife, "But nothing ever seems to happen to Huey Long." The cartoon had been scheduled to run in the Sunday edition but had been held over. The Long shooting came over the wire just before press time, and the cartoon was not pulled for the first edition. It was removed from succeeding editions.

Reams of copy flowed to the foreign press. They asked for more. British and many European and South American newspapers rated the flamboyant, unpredictable Kingfish almost as high as President Roosevelt in news interest. Britain had had no similar event for more than a century. Editors dressed the story with pictures of Long and the Louisiana Capitol. Banner headlines and large-type newspaper placards read:

"HUEY LONG SHOT"
"TURMOIL AFTER SHOOTING"
"FEARS OF COUP D'ÉTAT"
"DICTATOR LIKELY RECOVER"

"Although he never indulged in anti-British utterances," the *Evening Standard* said, "Long does not command any particular sympathy in Great Britain. But Britons feel all parties will unite in the wish he may recover from the assassin's bullet which struck him down."

The *Evening News,* under the caption "Mountebank of Genius," said: "Over here Long was regarded as just another of the oddities of American politics. Over there, however, there are many people who take him seriously. In his own state of Louisiana, he was revered as a little tin god."

The Belfast *Telegraph,* calling Long a "crude, bluff man," said: "The regimes of Hitler and Mussolini are mild in comparison with his dictatorship."

One press-association representative said that the great overseas interest was sparked by the fact that the story fitted the British idea of life in America—gats flashing in a state capitol, and blood and thunder.

Russell B. Long answered the telephone in the Long mansion at 14 Audubon Boulevard in New Orleans' aristocratic University section. Russell (later to follow his father into the U.S. Senate) was then 16—a freshman at LSU. He was the second of Huey's three children. Palmer Reid was 12. Rose was 20. Gilman Mc-

Connell, custodian of the Capitol and Russell's uncle, was on the line. He was a kindly, soft-spoken man. He broke the news gently.

"Russell, there's something bad that happened here," Uncle Gilman said. "I hope it's going to be all right. But it's not good. Your father has been shot. He's in the hospital. I believe it would be well for you and your mother and brother and sister to come up here."

A few minutes later, Lieutenant Governor James Noe, who had rushed to the hospital with Huey's political entourage, called and spoke to Mrs. Long. He told her that Dr. Vidrine had said that Huey's condition was not serious.

The Longs piled into their streamlined DeSoto. Russell took the wheel. They raced along the two-lane Airline Highway to Baton Rouge, some 90 miles away. About 30 miles out of New Orleans, they ran into construction. The road had been torn up. The U.S. Army Engineers were building a spillway to drain the Mississippi River in case of flooding. The Longs went on cautiously. After a while they had to stop. Headlights flashed on a locked gate. The gate was kept open during the day, but engineers padlocked it when the sun went down. They felt that the broken road ahead was too dangerous to drive over at night. Russell and Palmer took out their jack and pried the gate open. They got back into the car and crept through the littered roadway, pushing on to the Capital.

Dr. William H. Cook was half-expecting a call at his Baton Rouge home, but not the one he received. Dr. Cook, born in the little town of Clinton, Louisiana, was a general surgeon who during his later career was to be chief of staff of both Baton Rouge hospitals. Some hours before, he had sent to the hospital a young lady employed by Sears, Roebuck. She had been suffering from acute abdominal pains. The symptoms indicated an appendectomy. The telephone rang. Dr. Cook expected that this call would summon him to an emergency operation.

"Huey Long has been shot," Sister Michael said.

"You're joking," Cook replied, although he knew before he spoke that the nun would not have attempted such a bad joke; but he was taken by surprise and the words flew from his lips.

"Dr. Vidrine asked me to call you to come over."

He went.

Seymour Weiss (no relation to Carl), a former shoe clerk who became major-domo of the plush Roosevelt Hotel in New Orleans and rose to tremendous behind-the-scenes power as unofficial treasurer of the Long machine, answered the phone in his hotel suite. The news stunned Weiss. He had played golf with Huey at Audubon Park only the day before and was expecting to meet Long in New Orleans on Monday. Weiss ordered his car immediately and then called Robert Maestri on the house phone. Maestri, State Conservation Commissioner (and later Mayor of New Orleans) was another wealthy silent power in the Long administration, who also lived at the Roosevelt. Maestri met Weiss in the lobby and off they raced into the night.

"I had just gotten a specially-made Cadillac," Weiss recalled. "I had driven it only 20 miles. Going up to

Baton Rouge, I put my foot on the floorboard and held it there. When we got to the Capital, I found I had burned out the engine."

Lucille May Grace, State Land Register, had been in the Statehouse and had tried to reach Dr. Clarence Lorio, Huey's personal physician in Baton Rouge. Lorio was asleep and wasn't awakened by the telephone. She called his brother, Cecil, a pediatrician. He went to the hospital immediately.

Doctors rushed to the Capital from all parts of the State. From New Orleans came Drs. James D. Rivers, Russell Stone, Louis Levy, Rigney D'Aunoy, Jorda P. Kahle, and others. From Shreveport came Dr. E. L. Sanderson, superintendent of that city's Charity Hospital. Dr. Rufus Jackson was among the Baton Rouge doctors.

The most urgent call of all, perhaps, went to Dr. Urban Maes, outstanding New Orleans surgeon. Maes tried to arrange a flight, but no planes were available. He set out by car, joined by another doctor; but the spillway construction proved too much of an obstacle: Maes ran off the road while weaving through the rough terrain; he landed in a ditch; he was marooned.

The thorny question of political leanings arose for the first time when Dr. Cecil Lorio sought an anesthetist. He called Dr. Henry McKowen, who happened to be an anti-Long. A few days earlier, in fact, McKowen had half-jokingly told Dr. Lorio, "If I ever give Huey an anesthetic, I'll put him to sleep for good." Now he was being asked to do exactly that. McKowen hesitated. He knew that his flippant remark was bound to be repeated, and that if Huey didn't survive perhaps some would question McKowen's motives. He could be jeopardizing his career by this operation. Lorio argued that he knew that McKowen had not been serious when he had made the comment about Huey. A man's life was at stake, Lorio persisted. That was a doctor's first concern.

"All right," McKowen said. "I'll do it if you're with me and watching."

Lorio agreed.

In the emergency room, Vidrine started readying Long for surgery while Lorio made preparations to take Long's blood pressure, so that they would be aware at any given moment how grave Huey's condition was. Huey remained conscious, apparently not in any great degree of pain. Vidrine explained that the bullet wound would have to be cleaned.

"Go ahead and clean it then," Long said, gritting his teeth.

Doctors said that the bullet went completely through Long's body. It left a tiny wound the size of a little-finger tip. The slug apparently flattened out in penetrating Long's torso, Lorio said, because the hole in Huey's back was slightly larger. The bullet entered just below the border of the front right rib cage, about on a vertical line with the nipple, surgeons said. It exited from his back on the same side under the rear ribs. It left a hole near the back midline inside the shoulderblade line.[1]

[1] Dr. Joseph A. Sabatier, Jr., who as a young interne assisted as a scrub nurse in the ensuing surgery, made the following observations about Long's wound in a letter written October 31, 1935: "There were two 'holes' in the body. One on the anterior body wall apparently below the level of the right 12th rib to the right of the mammary line. This

Vidrine started cleaning the wound, talking to Long all the while, trying to keep his mind off his wound. But Huey wouldn't be diverted. He interrupted several times to ask how long he would have to be hospitalized. Whatever Vidrine answered, Long always made the same remark.

"The time doesn't count just so I am assured I will recover."

Then, a minor exchange took place. It lasted only a matter of seconds. Yet, it was to figure importantly in the aftermath of the case.

Jewel O'Neal, a 20-year-old student nurse, was standing behind Vidrine, preparing a hypodermic. She heard Vidrine ask Huey, "How about this place on your lip?" The nurse looked up. She noticed a cut on Long's lower lip and handed Vidrine a towel.

"That's where he hit me," Nurse O'Neal quoted Huey as saying. Long did not elaborate. Nor did Huey mention who "he" was. But Long and Vidrine had previously been discussing the shooting. She made a mental note of the remark and went about her business. The cut curiously would not be mentioned to the press. It would not be made public for eight more days, when a dramatic inquest would finally be held on Dr. Weiss. Miss O'Neal would not be called to testify, but three months later she would sign a notarized statement swearing that she reported the statement accurately.

Hospital technicians found that Lieutenant Gov-

---

was apparently the point of entrance of the bullet. The other 'hole' apparently the point of exit was in the back at approximately the same level."

ernor Noe was of the same blood type as Huey. A pint of blood was taken from Noe, and Huey was moved into a nearby room for a transfusion. Dr. Lorio came in to check Long's pulse and blood pressure. They were alone.

"How did you find out about the shooting?" Huey asked.

"Lucille May Grace called," Lorio said.

Cecil Lorio squeezed the rubber ball that tightened the band on Long's arm. There was a silence. Downstairs an army of onlookers had somehow gotten past police guards. They shuffled up and down outside the hospital, stalking like vultures, their blurred voices drifting upward in the night.

"Am I going to live?"

Long asked the question so matter-of-factly—like asking for a match—that Lorio was taken off guard for the moment. The doctor didn't know the answer. But he said the only thing he could.

"I feel sure everything will come out all right."

Huey started perspiring freely. The droplets on his forehead turned into streams that poured down his face. It was a cold sweat that brought nausea. He munched ice and did not throw up. His face grew pale and drawn. The minutes flew by. He was bleeding internally, and he was in shock.

Each time Lorio took his blood pressure and pulse, Long asked, "What was it?" The blood pressure was falling as the blood escaped from his veins, and the pulse quickened as his heart pumped faster to bring oxygen to the cells. When the pressure and pulse readings come together, it is a strong indication of hemorrhaging. Huey may not have known this. But apparently he knew that it was a bad sign. When the blood pressure dropped to about 90 and the pulse rate climbed above 110, Long said, "Come on. Let's go be operated on."

It was after midnight. The doctors consulted. Cook became first assistant. Lorio took the job of running the surgical tray. (His brother would arrive after the operation started and assist in the surgery.) McKowen was the anesthetist. Vidrine became chief surgeon.

Vidrine was 39 years old, a graduate of Louisiana State and Tulane University school of medicine, and a Rhodes scholar. He owed his meteoric success to Huey. Long had appointed him head of the New Orleans Charity Hospital in 1928, when Vidrine was only 32, then made Vidrine founder and first dean (in 1931) of the State-supported LSU school of medicine. Vidrine held both key posts simultaneously. In speaking of Vidrine, Huey often referred to him as "the world's greatest surgeon." Saving his benefactor's life might not convince the medical world of Long's claim, but it certainly would be repayment in full for the Kingfish's favors.

By now, the hospital floor had filled with Long's lieutenants and hangers-on. Some of the more important politicians pushed their way into the operating-room. Just before Dr. McKowen put the ether cap over Long's face, the Kingfish turned to his men and barked an order:

"I don't want anybody to issue any statements or do any talking until I get out of here. I'll issue all the statements."

The operation started at 12:15 a.m. Monday.

Less than a half-mile away, Dr. Weiss's widow was put to bed under sedation. Carl's mother came over to stay with her. The house soon filled with relatives and friends. The telephone rang with jarring regularity. Background noises crackled during the calls. The line apparently was tapped. After a while, it went dead. Sam Hill Ray, a Jesuit priest, came by to console Carl's mother. He told her that he had seen Carl's body at the Rabenhorst Funeral Home (where it was being prepared for burial) and had given him conditional absolution. Though nobody discussed it then, the question remained—would the Church sanction a religious burial? The canon law of the Catholic Church forbids a Catholic funeral for those who die in mortal sin.

The police were strangely conspicuous by their absence. No authorities came to the Weiss home to question them, or even to advise them that Carl had been killed.

Young Tom Ed left, hoping to get into the Capitol to find out what had happened. He ran into some cousins who lived down the street, and they drove him. They found all the Capitol doors locked. As they drove around to the building's rear, they saw a hearse driving off. It did not dawn on Tom Ed until much later that it carried his brother's body. It was around 11:30 p.m., and Tom Ed remembered that Carl's car was gone. They went to the front of the Capitol, and just to the left of the terraced steps they found Carl's Buick. It was the only car remaining, and it was unlocked. Tom Ed opened the door. He found his brother's medical bag on the front floor on the passenger side. Carl's usual practice was to bind his surgical instruments in canvas rolls and tuck them neatly inside his bag.

"It appeared as though somebody had gone through his bag, because the instruments were arranged in a disorderly fashion," Tom Ed said. "They were half sticking out of the bag. As I recall it, the dashboard compartment looked as though it had been rummaged through. And there was a white cotton sock, cotton flannel, lying on the floor. I recognized it as being the sock he usually kept his gun in, because it had a little grease on it."

When Tom Ed returned, he found his father standing alone by a bedroom dresser. Carl's glasses were in front of him. The elder Weiss had gone to the funeral home to identify the body. He had found his son clad only in his shorts. One eye was shot out. Morticians had started the embalming process. Wax raised his smashed nose. Surgical thread stitched his shattered chest and abdomen. He looked like a tattered rag doll sewn up. His father asked that his casket be closed.

Tom Ed watched his father from a darkened hallway. The tough old doctor held a handkerchief. He was sobbing, and a flood of tears poured into his vest.

"The question in the minds and on the tongues of all of us was what happened," Tom Ed said. "We just didn't know."

Since ancient times, surgeons have looked upon the abdominal cavity as one of the most vulnerable parts of the body. Stabbing and gunshot wounds in this soft, yielding region have always been considered serious.

Over 100,000 soldiers died as the result of penetrating abdominal wounds in World War I. The abdomen is filled with nearly 30 feet of slithering intestines, the stomach, the liver, the kidneys, and other organs. A bullet can't pass through the area without perforating something. If there is evidence of considerable bleeding, a transfusion is beneficial to bolster the patient's strength under surgery. If time and the victim's condition allow, pre-operative tests are made to try to find out if organs have been damaged. Bloody urine is almost invariably conclusive proof of serious injury to the urethra, the bladder, one or both ureters, or possibly a kidney. Under the knife, a surgeon follows the track of the bullet, systematically examining every organ and tortuous loop of bowel to see if it has been torn. The probe must be exhaustive, or a damaged artery or organ can be missed. If this happens, the bleeding can continue internally—like a forgotten water faucet running on. Peritonitis (the same acute inflammation that occurs when the appendix ruptures) and shock account for a considerable number of fatalities. But hemorrhaging is said to claim most deaths.

In 1935, abdominal wounds presented more problems than they do today. A quarter-century ago doctors did not have antibiotics such as penicillin or sulfa drugs as aids. They were able to use blood for resuscitation and in treatment of shock, but they were without the improved surgical techniques and knowledge that came into existence from the massive volume of abdominal-wound cases that military surgeons handled in the Spanish Civil War, World War II, and the Korean conflict. The mortality rate from penetrating abdominal wounds in 1935 was estimated at 65 per cent. From 1959 to 1961, the busy Charity Hospital in New Orleans reported only some 20 percent of its abdominal wound cases resulted in death.

The ether cap went over Long's face, and in a few moments his breathing became protracted and irregular. The doctors grouped around him like great, shrouded ghosts in their white surgical gowns and masks. Long's political lieutenants stayed right there in the operating room, watching their boss's fate, perhaps believing that their presence would ensure that there would be no "funny business" (though it's difficult to see how they could know).

Vidrine, of course, was a Long appointee, and loyal. Lorio was also pro-Long, mainly due to his brother's close ties to Huey. Cook was middle-of-the-road. He was a personal friend of Seymour Weiss and acquainted with Huey and his brother Earl. McKowen, an anti-Long, would be one of Dr. Weiss's pallbearers in a few hours.

"I thought it looked like a pretty good job," Seymour Weiss said later.

"The room was full of people who didn't belong there," Fred Dent said. "Most of them wore surgical gowns. But some had only regular street clothes. I myself was pressed against the center of the operating table opposite Vidrine. Cook was at one end and Lorio at the other. I saw a green pea that Long ate for supper roll out of Huey's insides. I often wondered how a bunch of politicians could have been allowed in a room like that when a man's life was at stake."

"It was a vaudeville show," Lorio said. "Everybody that seemed to have a political ambition was lined up in that operating room."

As the surgery proceeded, Long's henchmen called out, "How's he doing, Doc? Did you find the bullet?"

Vidrine was under great pressure, Dr. Lorio said. It was a "very trying situation," Dr. Cook said.

Details of the operation were not made public. In fact, there seems to have been an effort made through the years to see that they remained secret. Newspaper accounts were confined to a single written medical bulletin issued by Vidrine shortly after surgery, occasional oral statements to the press by various doctors, and conflicting leaks from Long's associates and nurses. They were for the most part incomplete, barely informative, and unreliable.

The only authentic report seems to have been a little-known article published in 1948 by Dr. Frank L. Loria of New Orleans. Dr. Loria, a former instructor at the Tulane University school of medicine and specialist in abdominal surgery, included the Long case in a 29-page monograph entitled "Historical Aspects of Penetrating Wounds of the Abdomen," published in the authoritative *Surgery, Gynecology and Obstetrics,* the official scientific journal of the American College of Surgeons. Even as a doctor, Loria had met with difficulty in research. Vidrine, said Loria, had been "unable" to give him access to the hospital record, and apparently had discussed the case with no great enthusiasm, in fact almost reluctantly. Nevertheless, Loria had succeeded in interviewing Vidrine,

Cook, and Cecil Lorio, and had sent a questionnaire to the hospital, which, he said, had been "adequately" filled out.

Loria wrote:

> "Under ether anesthesia, the abdomen was opened by an upper right rectus muscle-splitting incision. Very little blood was found in the peritoneal cavity. The liver, gall bladder, and stomach were free of injury. A small hematoma, about the size of a silver dollar, was found in the mesentery of the small intestine. The only intraperitoneal damage found was a 'small' perforation of the hepatic flexure, which accounted for a slight amount of soiling of the peritoneum. Both the wounds of entrance and exit in the colon were sutured and further spillage was stopped. The abdomen was closed in layers as usual." [2]

Translating the technical medical terminology into laymen's language, this reads as follows:

Under ether anesthesia, the abdomen was opened to the upper right of the navel with an up-and-down incision. Vidrine cut into the rectus muscle stretching over the abdomen from the ribs to the pelvic bone. Very little blood was found inside the lining of the abdominal cavity. The liver, gall bladder, and stomach were free of injury. A small clot of blood, about the size of a silver dollar, was found in the tissue of the small intestine. The only damage found inside the abdominal lining was a "small" puncture of the colon at a point under the liver where the looping colon curves sideways to travel across the body. That puncture accounted for a slight escape of waste matter into the abdominal cavity. Both the colon's wounds, of exit

[2] By permission of *Surgery, Gynecology and Obstetrics*.

and of entrance, were sewed up and further spillage stopped. The abdomen was closed in layers as usual.

As Huey was rolled out, Governor Allen asked Vidrine, "What do you think his chances are?"

"Governor," Vidrine said, "it all depends on fate."

After Long was moved to room 325, a dust-covered auto chugged in from Winnfield carrying Huey's 83-year-old father. With him was Long's youngest brother, Earl (who would hold Louisiana's Governorship three times). Earl was later hastily reconciled at the hospital with two other brothers—Julius, a Shreveport lawyer, and George, a dentist in Tulsa, Oklahoma. The Long brothers had been at odds for years.

The mass vigil began. In the corridor outside his room, Huey's political leaders milled around, talking in hushed tones. In a suite below, relatives and some family members stood by. Huey's wife and three children arrived too late to see him and went immediately to the Heidelberg Hotel. In the lobby, a lucky newsman who had slipped into the hospital waited. Ringing the building was a brigade of Highway Patrolmen. Outside, the curious congregated. People throughout the State and the Nation kept tuned to their radios, listening for news bulletins.

Early Monday Dr. Vidrine dictated five sentences to Earle Christenberry, Long's personal secretary. Christenberry wrote them on a sheet of hospital stationery and issued the first medical bulletin:

"Senator Long was wounded by one bullet entering the upper right side, emerging from the back. The colon was punctured in two places. The first blood transfusion has been given the Senator with good results. The condition of Senator Long is thoroughly satisfactory. It will be 72 to 90 hours before further developments can be expected."

Louisiana and the Nation waited.

❖   ❖   ❖

"I am convinced beyond any doubt that my son did not go into the Capitol to kill Long."

The elder Dr. Weiss met the press Monday on the porch of his home. He framed his thoughts slowly, sorrowfully, shaking his head sometimes. At other times, he held his body stiffly erect.

"My son was too happy to think of doing what he is accused of trying," the 57-year-old physician said, "too brilliant, too good, too superbly happy with his wife and child, too much in love with them to want to end his life after such a murder. He would have known that it was suicide he was walking into, cold, deliberate self-destruction under the guns of bodyguards."

Carl's mother, too, was at a loss to account for the shooting.

"We had no word, no intimation, nothing," she said, her eyes swollen and red. "All that we know is that he took living seriously. Right with him was right above everything else.

"We were just a happy family group," she went on. "We have always been so proud of him. His future was brilliant. He had the whole world in front of him."

"When he did a thing like that," the Associated Press quoted the elder Mrs. Weiss as saying, "he must have known he would be instantly killed. They didn't have to kill him at all. He weighed about 140 pounds and one man could have handled him without shooting him at all."

"Would the Pavy gerrymander have been a motive for the shooting?" a newsman asked Carl's father.

"Absolutely not," Dr. Weiss said. "He had no reason to take that seriously because the judge did not take it seriously."

Dr. F. Octave Pavy, the judge's brother, sat next to Dr. Weiss, rocking slowly.

"The judge was joking about it yesterday," Pavy agreed. "The judge didn't take it to heart. No one else had any reason to think about it twice."

("Mother was delighted," Yvonne Weiss recalled years later, "because Papa didn't make much money as a judge. He had wonderful connections and my brother was practicing law. My mother was elated. The ambition of her life was to get him out of that judge-ship. Get him off the bench. So there was no great grief. Nobody was complaining. Judge Pavy himself, Papa himself, never felt an injustice was being done to him personally. It was just the fact that it wasn't legally right. He didn't feel that he was personally suffering from it.")

In Opelousas, Judge Pavy was confined to his home the day after the shooting. A doctor spent the night with him. At first, his family thought that he had had a heart attack. Later, it was reported that he was suffering from a nervous condition. The old judge was said to be near a breakdown. He was unable to attend Carl's funeral. Judge Pavy eventually recovered, but the gnawing belief that he may—however innocently—have triggered or contributed even indirectly to the tragedy lingered and disturbed him until his dying day.

("It was a terrific shock to my father," Yvonne Weiss said. "He grieved from it all his life, because he blamed himself, thinking if he hadn't been involved in politics so strongly, maybe Carl. . . . But he never discussed it with Carl. He never could understand how Carl got involved in it, because they (the Pavys) never thought of him (Carl) in any connection with anything like that.")

"Whatever happened there between him (Carl Weiss) and the Senator and those who killed him," the elder Dr. Weiss said, "I do not think I shall ever know. That is something we'll never know. And what happened there, what brought him there, will always be between him and his Maker."

Around the corner from the Weiss home, each pair of hands of the four electric clocks on St. Joseph's steeple were coming together. In a few moments its sweet-sounding bell—which a priest had salvaged years ago from a sunken Mississippi River steam packet—would toll midday. Monsignor Leon Gassler and a number of his subordinate priests sat in the sacristy. They were conferring about the Weiss funeral. Strictly speaking, if Carl shot Huey, he died in mortal sin and must be refused a Church burial. But did Weiss really shoot Huey? Monsignor Gassler couldn't believe it. Where a question arose, he knew he should inform the Archbishop in New Orleans. However, the Archbishop, Joseph Francis Rummel, was brand-new and foreign to the area. Rummel had been born in Germany and had come from another diocese in a midwestern state. Gassler had known Carl the better part of the young doctor's life. He made the decision himself.

"Strictly, in case of doubt, the Archbishop should have been consulted," Father Sam Hill Ray, a member of that solemn conference, said. "However, it was not clearly proven that Carl Weiss shot Huey. We had no proof that he was an assassin, as stated in the press. Therefore, Monsignor Gassler gave him the benefit of the doubt, especially for the sake of the family.

"It was Sunday night when the tragedy occurred. Carl had been to Holy Communion right there in St. Joseph's Church, as Monsignor Gassler knew. That was in his favor. Moreover, the Archbishop had only recently come to Louisiana and had had no time to be informed of Louisiana politics. It would be difficult to explain all this to him. Therefore, by a human interpretation—so characteristic of the beloved Monsignor—we decided the best thing to do was bury Carl in the Church and inform the Archbishop later." [3]

"In paradisum deducant te Angeli: in tuo adventu suscipiant te Martyres, et perducant te in civitatem sanctam Jerusalem."

[3] Archbishop Rummel, an outspoken pontiff who startled many in his Deep South archdiocese two decades later by declaring segregation "morally wrong and sinful" and then integrating Catholic schools in 1962, eventually spoke out on the propriety of the Church funeral. *The Register,* a Catholic publication, on October 20, 1935, said that the Archbishop described Weiss as a practicing Catholic to the very last day of his life,

("May the angels lead thee into paradise: may the martyrs receive thee at thy coming, and lead thee into the holy city of Jerusalem.")

Several hundred persons, including many notables, attended the funeral services for Weiss. It was a dreary day. A thunderstorm sent a heavy rain lashing down from a lead-hued sky. Following the wishes of the family—who wanted to remember Carl as they had seen him at the Sunday outing—the casket remained closed. Morticians had worked six hours preparing the body for burial just the same. Members of the family arrived at Rabenhorst Funeral Home just before services were to start at 4 p.m. Shielding their faces from photographers, they fled into the chapel and knelt in prayer before the plain, gray casket. A blanket of flowers covered the coffin. Tall tapers burned. Nuns from St. Joseph's Orphanage sat near the body. Over 150 floral displays filled every room of the mortuary. One offering bore a card from "Some Hendersonville, North Carolina, Democrats." Two of the wreaths came from Kiwanis and the Young Men's Business Club, to which Carl belonged. Almost all members were there.

Monsignor Gassler entered the funeral parlor with three acolytes, sprinkled holy water on the casket, and intoned the litany for the dead. Mourners filled the small parlor to capacity. Outside, people congregated

---

a man who never discussed politics. Archbishop Rummel, in the interview, expressed no opinion on the shooting. "It happened so suddenly," Rummel said, "there was no certainty." Rummel added: To have Weiss involved was so extraordinary in view of his life habits, that, if he did the shooting, only one thing could account for it—a temporary mental aberration. Hence, the Church's position favoring Catholic burial whether Weiss did, or did not, shoot Huey.

under every shade tree, awning, and shed roof that offered shelter from the rain. Traffic jammed the streets. "It seemed unreal," Carl's brother said.

After brief services, six colleagues of Dr. Weiss—Drs. Henry McKowen, Ashton Robins, J. L. Beven, W. L. Edson, Tom Spec Jones, and M. W. Matthews—bore the casket to a hearse. A slow cortege made its way through the rain to St. Joseph's Church. There, only a day before, Carl and his wife of less than two years had heard Mass.

The high-vaulted church was nearly filled. Among those present were former Governor Parker, Congressman J. Y. Sanders, Jr., and District Attorney John Fred Odom. Odom had by then failed in two attempts to get Long's bodyguards to appear at an inquest. He would meet with two more failures before their dramatic appearance in a week. Mourners included patients; nurses; business, civic and social leaders; and practically every doctor in Baton Rouge.

Carl's widow, dressed in white, with a black straw hat and a fan partly covering her face, entered with her young brother-in-law, Tom Ed. With her were her mother, Mrs. Benjamin Pavy of Opelousas, and Carl's father, walking with a firm, military-like bearing. The dead man's mother was accompanied by a brother. Carl's sister, Mrs. A. C. Broussard of New Orleans, was with her husband.

Pallbearers carried the casket into the church while photographers popped away. One of Dr. Weiss's cousins attacked a cameraman and attempted to smash his plates.

Preceded by acolytes, robed and vested priests

walked slowly up the aisle and placed a cross before
the bier. Many clergymen of the area sat near the
casket. Six deacons kneeled at their lecterns—three on
each side of the altar. Blinking points of candlelight
flickered over the faces of the mournful. A choir sang
resurrection psalms and Monsignor Gassler recited the
Office of the Dead. Once, Yvonne Weiss sagged, but
she quickly regained composure. The service took less
than half an hour.

Once again, the slow cortege crept through the
streets shimmering with glistening pools of rain. A
line of cars extending several blocks followed to Roselawn Cemetery. Curtains were drawn in the car occupied by the Weiss family.

Practically all who attended the service continued
to the sodden turf of the cemetery. Some stood ankle-
deep in water, bareheaded, under a driving rain, while
a priest pronounced last rites. The rain drummed a
staccato accompaniment on hundreds of umbrellas and
the taut canvas of the canopy under which the family
huddled by the open grave. Two members were not
present—Judge Pavy, and Weiss's three-month-old son,
who was left in the care of a nurse.

The casket sank slowly from sight. Tom Ed Weiss
braced the young widow. A plain family headstone
would rise over his grave. A marker, in the shade of a
moss-festooned oak, would bear the solitary inscrip-
tion: "Carl Austin Weiss, M.D., Dec. 18, 1905–Sept.
8, 1935."

Thousands stood with the rain beating down until
the last spade of earth was in place and the family

started to leave. Newsmen reached Carl's mother as she walked toward a car.

"Thank God, my son didn't kill him," she said, quivering, her face streaked with tears. "I'm grateful to God for that. My boy is dead, but I wouldn't want to have that on his soul."

"Fac, quaesumus, Domine, hanc cum servo tuo defuncto misericordiam, ut factorum suorum in poenis non recipiat vicem, qui tuam in votis tenuit voluntatem; ut sicut hic eum vera fides junxit fidelium turmis, ita illic eum tua miseratio societ angelicis choris. Per Christum Dominum nostrum. Amen."

("Grant to Thy servant departed, O Lord, we beseech Thee, this favor, that he who prayed that Thy will might be done may not receive punishment for his deeds; and that even as here on earth the true faith joined him to the ranks of the faithful, so in heaven by Thy Mercy may he have fellowship with the choirs of angels. Through Christ our Lord. Amen.")

Between Life and Death

"Oh, God. Don't let me die. I've a few more things to accomplish."

—Huey Pierce Long

The question—"Who shot Huey?"—had *apparently* been answered. It was true that Weiss's motive was something of a riddle. It seemed difficult for the young doctor's friends to believe that a political maneuver or even a racial slur—if it ever had been made—could have prompted such extreme action on the part of the non-politically minded, mild-mannered specialist. Nevertheless, Dr. Weiss had been at the scene of the crime, and his gun had been fired. It seemed an open-and-shut case.

Attention shifted to Huey. The Kingfish was battling for life. The Nation clamored for news.

The *New York Times* reported that Dr. Vidrine had said that the bullet had miraculously not hit any vital organ. Unless complications arose, Vidrine had added, Long had "a good chance" to recover.

At 6 a.m., secretary Christenberry left his chief's side and said: "He has improved more in the last 15 minutes than during all of the night."

At 8:30 a.m., it was reported that physicians had said that Huey was gaining strength.

Receiving those tidbits as they filtered down was the AP's Quincy Ewing. He was for a while the only newsman not on Long's payroll to crack the palace guard. Ewing had spotted Lieutenant Governor Noe rush into a police car at the rear of the Capitol. Ewing, playing a hunch, had pushed his way in; it was loaded with State officials. A cop started to toss him out. "Let 'm stay," Noe interceded. In the hospital, Ewing became a pool liaison man between doctors and the press. Newsmen from all over the country had flocked to Louisiana. "There was nothing I could do but sit in the main lounge, keep my ears open, and talk to such sources as I could," Ewing said. "At first, it wasn't bad. Immediately after the shooting, Long's followers feared he was dead or dying. Then, somehow, after Huey was examined and it was discovered the bullet had gone completely through him, they got the idea he wasn't hurt much."

Gerald L. K. Smith, a preacher who had abandoned a prosperous church in Shreveport to become Huey's "Share the Wealth" organizer, paced up and down.

"This is great," Smith said, grinning and slapping Ewing on the back. "He's not going to die. He'll get well and what a fine piece of propaganda it'll make. The corporations have been trying to kill him, we've said. Now we can say—'You see.' "

Sometime Monday morning, Opal Beasley, correspondent for the now-defunct Universal Service, persuaded a physician to take her to the corridor outside Long's sickroom. On a gallery beyond the inner sanctum, she saw Governor Allen, Seymour Weiss, Fournet, and close friends of Huey. Members of the Long family occupied a room nearby and walked nervously about a covered front porch running outside the window.

"Senator Long is progressing nicely," the physician, who asked that his name be withheld, said. "He has a good chance to recover."

Huey drifted in and out of consciousness, talking rationally at times, mumbling and making little sense at others. He spoke about his upcoming biography, *My First Days In the White House*. It would be a best seller, he said. It would have "200 words to a page." Brother Earl Long and Seymour Weiss heard him stir. They hurried over.

"Hello, Earl. Hello, Seymour," Huey muttered.

When Governor Allen tiptoed over, the Kingfish blustered:

"Move over, Oscar, and give me some air."

Sometimes, Huey did not appear to see things clearly. When nurses brought in an oxygen tent, he fought it off, convinced it was a device to take his picture.

Though the official line held firm to its opening note of optimism, it, in fact, had already become apparent to some of the doctors that Long was not responding to treatment.

"The post-operative course of the case continued steadily on the downgrade," Dr. Loria wrote. "Evidence of shock and internal hemorrhage appeared to become progressively worse."

In time, the true situation began to leak out. C. P. Liter of the Baton Rouge *Morning Advocate* contacted nurses, who told him that Huey was passing blood in his urine. Liter, whose newspaper was an AP member, relayed this to Ewing by telephone. They continued to swap information, and, as the morning wore on, Ewing said, they began to feel that the Kingfish was slipping instead of getting better.

The first break in the official line came at noon Monday. Secretary Christenberry told the press that Huey was losing blood. Another transfusion was necessary. At 1 p.m. a second pint of blood passed into Long's veins. The donor declined to have his name made public.

At 3 p.m. nurses brought more oxygen and adrenalin to Long's room.

At 6 p.m. Noe said that the Senator was "doing fine."

At 7 p.m. attendants coming from the bedside reported a serious decline.

Sometime Monday evening Dr. E. L. Sanderson, Huey's appointee as head of Shreveport's Charity Hospital, told the Shreveport *Times* by telephone:

"Senator Long won't respond to treatment. His condition is extremely critical. We don't know yet which way his case is going. The next 12 hours should tell the story; he is very low."

At 8:30 p.m. Dr. Vidrine said Huey "is holding his own."

And so it went. Back and forth like a seesaw. The vigil dragged through the long night.

Downstairs, another tense drama was being played out. Ewing was joined in the lobby by James Marlow of the New Orleans *Times-Picayune* (later a wire-service news-analyst), James Bushong of the New Orleans *Item,* I. I. Femrite of United Press, and others. There were phones in a small room nearby. Some 40 plainclothes police prowled through the hospital. All were armed—some with submachine guns. Outside, another dozen stood shoulder-to-shoulder across the top steps. Colonel Roy had issued orders to shoot any photographer caught taking pictures around the hospital. Bodyguards warned reporters not to try to go upstairs to Long's room.

"We didn't try the stairs," Marlow said. "We knew better. Over the years, the Senator's bodyguards had smashed newsmen's faces and heads."

Gloom was everywhere. And everywhere people spoke in hushed tones. Lieutenant Governor Noe, wan from loss of blood and disheveled from lack of sleep, shuffled down the stairs and out into the night for a breath of fresh air. Reporters flocked over for questions. He shook his head. Earle Christenberry sat with his face in his hands. A couple of bodyguards who had been up for 24 hours stretched on a couch. Paul Voitier slumped in a lounge chair fast asleep, snoring. Robert Brothers, dapper and with cane, rushed in. Brothers, Long's aide, had come from Washington. He disappeared upstairs. Ten minutes later, he came down. He was sobbing.

All sorts of rumors flew around. One was that Long was much better after the second blood transfusion. Another was that there was no change. A third said that doctors had learned of an additional injury not previously reported. Huey was failing.

"Liter and I jointly became convinced Long was dying instead of getting better," Ewing said. "I put out a flash flatly saying he was dying. The flash met with howls of denials from Long's followers. We stuck with it."

The vigil went on. Every few minutes, the voice of the switchboard operator echoed through the still corridor. "There's no change," she told countless inquirers. Some calls came from as far as London. Governor Allen, head bowed, entered the hospital with Noe and Abe Shushan, director of the Orleans Levee Board. Allen's wife was sick. He had spent the night dashing from the hospital to the mansion and back. He trudged wearily to Huey's room.

Outside, rain started falling. Lights from the great Capitol gleamed dully. The darkness, vast and brooding, blanketed the city.

Doctors made a third transfusion. Blood came from Dr. Willard Ellender of Houma, Speaker Ellender's brother. Long's pulse slowed, then climbed from 91 to 118. A fourth transfusion was carried out. A fifth followed later.

At 10:30 p.m., the head nurse told Long's friends calling the hospital, "There is little hope." Attendants hauled another tank of oxygen into Long's room.

At 11:30 p.m., Seymour Weiss told a New Orleans newspaper, "We do not expect Senator Long to live through the night. The Senator is sinking rapidly. He has been given all the blood transfusions he can take. He is partly conscious but cannot talk."

What the press did not know then was that shortly after the operation Dr. Russell Stone of New Orleans had carried out a catheterization test (introduction of a long, tubular instrument into the urinary tract). The contents of the urinary tract held the answer to the question that had puzzled doctors: Why was Huey failing to rally? Long's urine contained much blood. The blood pointed to a kidney wound. Only a second emergency operation could stop the bleeding. But Long, fighting to recover from the shock of one operation,

Left: Carl Austin Weiss, in New Orleans about a month before the shooting. *Courtesy State Library of Louisiana*

Below: Huey P. Long addressing the Democratic National Convention in 1932

Pallbearers carry Huey Long's coffin before his great statehouse as mourners look on. Newspapers said it was the largest crowd ever assembled in the state. Pallbearers include: Gov. O. K. Allen (left front); Seymour Weiss (right front, light suit with handkerchief in breast pocket); Justice John B. Fournet (behind Weiss); Robert Maestri (head visible), later Mayor of New Orleans. Merle Welsh, the funeral director, is at left two persons down from Allen. *International News Photo*

Opposite page, bottom: The 900-pound rusted steel vault bearing Carl Austin Weiss's remains was unearthed in 1991 and was examined by a team of forensic scientists. Professor James E. Starrs is at right (wearing white hat). Others are: (far left) Lucien Haag, firearms expert (with name badge); Dr. Irving Sopher, medical examiner (white-haired man bending over vault); and Douglas Ubelaker, physical anthropologist (with glasses behind Starrs). *Courtesy Baton Rouge* Morning Advocate *(Mike Hults)*

On a gray, rainy day, Dr. Carl Austin Weiss's coffin is carried into St. Joseph's Roman Catholic Church. Every pew was filled with mourners, including a former governor and a former congressman. The man on the left is Dr. Henry McKowen, the man on the far right is Dr. Tom Spec Jones--both Baton Rouge physicians who were colleagues of Dr. Weiss. Another local physician, whose face can be seen over Jones's shoulder is Dr. M. W. Matthews. In front center is Merle Welsh, the funeral director, and the man at rear is Welsh's assistant, Jack Unbehagen. *AP Photo*

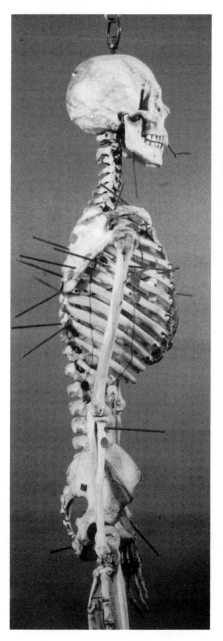

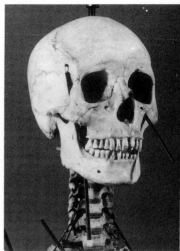

Above: This laboratory skull shows the entry site of the bullet that struck Weiss below his left eye. *Left:* Black plastic straws glued to this laboratory skeleton (not that of Dr. Weiss) show the entry sites and trajectory angles of bullets fired by Huey Long's bodyguards. Only those missiles that hit bone are recorded. *Both courtesy Smithsonian Institution*

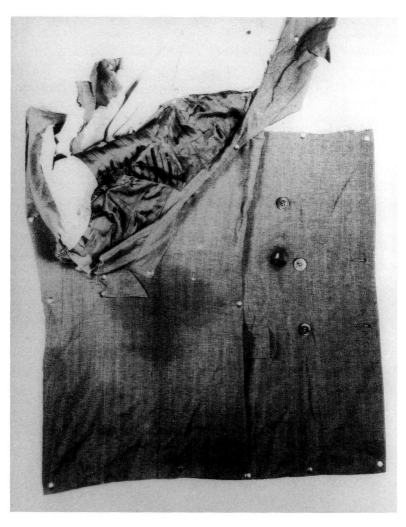

Right: Police photograph of the jacket allegedly worn by Huey Long on the night he was fatally shot. The bullet hole can be seen to the left of the second button; it is ringed with a black stain believed to be powder burns. *Courtesy Louisiana State Police*

Huey Long lies buried beneath this monument and 12-foot high bronze statue that stands before the capitol in Baton Rouge. *Collection of David H. Zinman*

Murphy Roden (right), one of Long's bodyguards, being sworn in as Louisiana commissioner of public safety by Jack P. F. Gremillion, then the state attorney general.

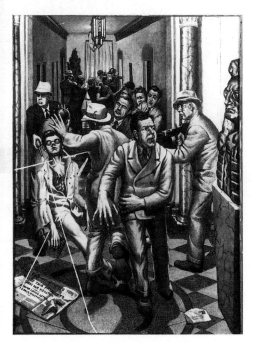

John McCrady's painting of Huey Long's assassination originally appeared in the June 26, 1939 issue of *Life* magazine. The late artist took some liberties. He gave one of the bodyguards a submachine gun instead of a hand gun and inserted himself in the scene. He is the shocked witness behind Long. *Courtesy of Mr. and Mrs. Keith Marshall*

Above, left: Senator Russell Long leaving the senate chamber in 1981; *above, right:* Dr. Carl Austin Weiss, Jr., at his office in Garden City, Long Island, in 1991 © *David H. Zinman*

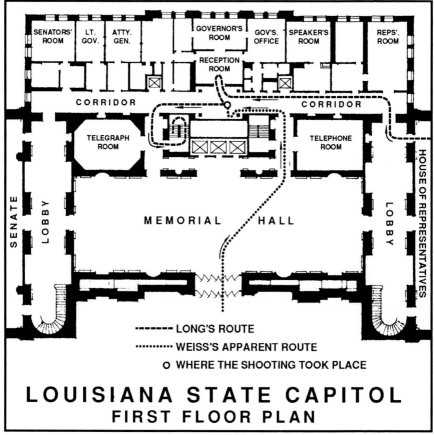

-------- LONG'S ROUTE

··········· WEISS'S APPARENT ROUTE

O WHERE THE SHOOTING TOOK PLACE

LOUISIANA STATE CAPITOL
FIRST FLOOR PLAN

was too weak. He might die on the operating table. More surgery would be fatal, Stone said. He advised against it.

Tuesday came.

At about 1:30 a.m. Dr. P. Jorda Kahle, New Orleans urologist, plunged a long needle into Huey's back in the region of the right kidney. Kahle drew pure blood. There was a massive internal hemorrhage behind the abdominal wall.

In a little while, the first faint sounds of a death rattle could be heard. Saliva appeared at Huey's mouth as he thrashed around inside his oxygen tent. The Kingfish was dying.

There is a story that some of Long's lieutenants pleaded frantically with Huey for the key to his lockbox, which contained important private papers and campaign contributions. Long refused. He said that he wasn't going to die. But, gradually getting weaker, sinking by degrees, and getting a hint from one doctor that he would not live, the Kingfish yielded. When his family opened the box some weeks after his death, it was reportedly found empty.

The clock showed 3 a.m. Mrs. Long and Huey's three children hurried through the hospital lobby. They talked with doctors briefly outside Long's room, then entered.

"We saw him just before he died," Russell Long recalled. "He was in sort of a coma and I'm not sure he recognized my mother or me. My mother reminded me of a very small girl the way she smiled and waved at him when she left the room."

A nurse agreed to blink the lights to signal the end

to friends and kin on a nearby porch. There was nothing to do now but wait. Death came with agonizing slowness. Two private nurses and a black-garbed nun moved noiselessly in his room. Huey lay on his back staring fixedly at the ceiling. He struggled for breath, wheezing, then coughing, his chest rising and falling with labored undulations. The pulsations grew fainter, then stopped. At 4:06 a.m., the lights in the sickroom blinked. Huey did not see them. Death came 30 hours and 44 minutes after he was shot.

"He must have had a stroke before he died," Commissioner O'Connor said. "His whole face was to one side. His jaw had gotten out of whack."

United Press claimed a three-minute beat on the Kingfish's death. It got it thanks to the enterprise of I. I. Femrite, UP bureau manager in New Orleans at the time. Femrite had raced to Baton Rouge and had gotten a friend of Huey's to slip him past the bodyguards. Femrite had reached the corridor outside Long's room about 3 a.m. and had talked to doctors and nurses as they left the room. An hour later, a doctor had come out and said, "Huey's dead." Femrite had a world beat.

Controlling his excitement, he forced himself to walk slowly down the stairs past other newsmen in the lobby to a basement telephone. He dictated the flash to Coogan in the Capitol pressroom, which by now was swarming with out-of-town reporters. Coogan quietly tossed the flash to his teletype operator, camouflaging its importance with the offhand remark, "Here's some more malarky for you." The operator, playing the game, kept a deadpan expression as he punched the flash. Nobody in the pressroom paid any attention.

The bulletin reached the big Eastern papers around dawn. The New York *Daily News* bannered the story. The bulletin prompted editors to roll out early-morning extras in Washington and in hundreds of cities throughout the country. A stunned Nation woke up on Tuesday, September 10, 1935, to find that Huey Long, Kingfish of the Bayous, dictator of a political empire unique in American history, was dead.

Things started to happen fast. A bodyguard came down and whispered to a woman reporter. Marlow of the New Orleans *Times-Picayune* tried to hear.

"Get back," the bodyguard barked. Marlow got back.

Then, a strange twist of affairs took place.

"I heard him say Long had just died," Marlow said. "I ran for the stairs. It was a reflex action. I couldn't phone that Long was dead with nothing to go on but a whisper. I had to go up to his room to verify it. . . . Suddenly, all the bodyguards were running for the stairs. Then, the fight set in. I thought, 'Here's where I get it.' But I was near the stairs. I couldn't turn back. The bodyguards were all around. They had me squeezed in. I thought, 'What a way to get it.'

"And just as suddenly the guards melted away and let me through. I went upstairs, walking, no longer running, the bodyguards walking slowly behind me, not interfering.

"What happened to them at that moment when they had me surrounded and then let me through? I can't be sure. They used to keep in shape beating up newspapermen. Maybe they realized the boss was dead and they didn't have anything more to do.

"Maybe something else. Maybe they suddenly realized the one man who had always stood between them and punishment for their violence was gone and they were defenseless. I don't know. For that one moment, the fight was out of the Long machine.

". . . That moment when I reached the stairs with the bodyguards was the end of an era. . . ."

Governor Allen met the press. He was sobbing and nearly prostrate from the gruelling wait. Newsmen crowded around. With great effort, he pulled himself together. His frame shook from head to foot.

"This marks the death of Huey P. Long," Allen said in a voice so husky it was barely audible, "the passing of the greatest hero for the common right of all the people in America. His name will exist and be remembered in the annals of the State of Louisiana and all America."

Seymour Weiss stood by, biting his lips. He said that Long had been unconscious since before midnight. "He fought like a tiger to live," said Weiss.

"What was the last thing Huey said?" a reporter asked.

"I can't remember," Weiss said.

"Yes, yes," Allen broke in. "The last thing he said when he was still conscious was, 'I wonder what will happen to my poor university boys.'"

Weiss said that Long had expressed no other wish than that he hoped he would live.

Others close to Long were of the opinion that Huey had lain in a coma. If he had talked at all, he had muttered incoherently, talked gibberish. O'Connor, who had been in Huey's room, said that he did not believe that Long had ever become conscious after surgery.

"Long never opened his mouth again," O'Connor said. "I'm convinced he never regained consciousness."

Nevertheless, Dr. Sanderson, the family physician in Shreveport, gave a detailed account of Huey's last remarks. The AP released it as an exclusive. Sanderson wrote, in part:

"When his wife entered the room a few hours before death, he (Long) said:

" 'Here is my sweetheart.'

"As she stooped over to kiss him, it was about this time that he said:

" 'Oh, God. Don't let me die. I've a few more things to accomplish.'

"I really believe his last words were those pertaining to LSU. . . .

"When he passed away, it was like the snuffing out of a candle. There was no struggle whatsoever."

No autopsy was made—despite the fact that a New Orleans pathologist was on the scene when Huey died. Dr. Loria, in his monograph, said: "Mrs. Long objected to an autopsy, and, consequently, none was performed."

Death resulted from uncontrolled internal bleeding, attending physicians said. Surgeons studying the facts, as Dr. Loria was able to glean them, believed that doctors had failed to discover an injury to the right kidney. Nothing was mentioned about a kidney injury in Vidrine's medical bulletin. In the excitement, a preoperative urine examination—which could have disclosed kidney damage—apparently had not been made. (If one had been performed, Dr. Cecil Lorio said, he did not know of it.) Some physicians wondered

why surgeons had not continued to probe into the
back regions (where the major damage was) after finding such a small amount of blood in Long's abdomen.
Apparently, the rear abdominal wall, lying between
the intestines and the kidneys, had acted as a screen.
The blood had welled up unseen behind it. It had
flowed unchecked until Long bled to death.

"(Cecil) Lorio was later of the opinion that the renal
vessels (leading into the kidneys) had probably been
torn by the bullet in its course through the body,"
Loria wrote. "Certainly, without the energetic post-
operative treatment, especially the frequent transfusions of blood, death would have very likely super-
vened much sooner.

"Although no autopsy was performed, the condition
of the intra-peritoneal viscera (within the abdominal
cavity) and other structures, and the course of the
bullet—which was rather unmistakable because of the
entrance and exit points—pointed rather suspiciously
to an injury of the right kidney, and possibly of the
right renal vessels as the source of the hemorrhage.

"The fact that Senator Long died in slightly more
than 30 hours, in spite of an unusually large number
of blood transfusions, would seem to indicate that the
injury to the vessel, or vessels, which undoubtedly continued to permit the escape of blood as fast as it was
administered, was quite large."

Rain still fell outside the hospital, blending on the
grass with the dewy mist of dawn. A hot wind ruffled
the smooth surface of the Capitol lake. Upstairs, Huey
Long lay alone in death.

"After Long died," O'Connor said, "the hangers-on

all vanished. You never saw a place empty so fast. They all cleared out."

❖   ❖   ❖

On Monday night, before Huey died, the Weiss family closed their house up on Fifth Street and left Baton Rouge. Carl's wife and baby returned with the Pavy family to Opelousas. The Weisses drove to New Orleans.

The elder Dr. Weiss knew that the situation was tense. He had heard that there was a possibility of mob action. Word had even reached him that there was talk of a lynch gang. Friends had assured him that no one was going to lay a hand on him or his family. But the Capital was like an armed camp. Anything could happen. Dr. Weiss felt that, for the safety of all concerned, it would be best to leave. They stayed in seclusion for four days at the Reed Hotel on St. Charles Avenue in New Orleans. When they returned Thursday after Long's burial, the Weisses found hundreds of letters and telegrams on the porch. They came from all over the country. Scores of letters were from people they did not know. Some were notes of condolence. Others were from cranks and people who condemned the shooting. And then the family learned something that surprised them. Many persons looked on Carl as a martyr.

> September 14, 1935
> Berkeley, California

Dear Mrs. Weiss:

Dr. Weiss gave his life in order that the liberty of Louisiana might be preserved and its soil freed from the blight of ignorance and tyranny. Your husband died a martyr and a hero. When history is written, your husband's brow will wear the wreath of honor.

An Exiled Louisianian

September 10, 1935
Mexico City

Dear Dr. Weiss:

I hope you will not think it an intrusion if I, who am so much of a stranger to you, write this to express, no matter how poorly, my profound sympathy . . . That your son did a deed of such self-sacrifice, such courage and self-abrogation does not soften the sharpness of your pain just now, I know, but it will in the future. Such things are rare. I feel very deeply for you and his mother.

Sincerely,
Katherine M. Hill

EMPORIA, KANSAS
(Via Western Union)
SEPTEMBER 10, 1935

. . . THE HEROISM AND SELF-SACRIFICE WHICH PROMPTED YOUR HUSBAND'S ACT HAVE EXCITED THE ADMIRATION OF A GROUP OF AMERICANS WHO MET ACCIDENTALLY ON THIS TRAIN AND CAME FROM ALL WALKS OF LIFE. WE BELIEVE THIS EXPRESSION TO YOU EXPRESSES THE OPINION OF MILLIONS OF OUR FELLOW CITIZENS. OUR HEARTFELT COMPASSION AND SYMPATHY TO YOU AND YOURS.

SEVEN FRIENDS

Frank Hartley Anderson, a Birmingham, Alabama, artist and architect, began a movement to erect a monument to Dr. Weiss in Washington. "Dr. Weiss died a martyr," Anderson said, "and as such deserves an honored place in the history of this country."

The martyr theme even appeared in the editorial columns of a number of newspapers. One of them was the *Pittsburgh Press:*

> "Among the fortunately few political assassins who have stained the Republic's history with blood, the killer of Senator Long was unique in that he was seemingly sane and selfless, a type familiar to the Old World tyrannies but new to this country. . . .
>
> "Former American assassins were different. John Wilkes Booth, who shot Lincoln, was a fanatic. Charles Jules Guiteau, who shot Garfield, was an embittered office seeker. Leon Czolgosz, who shot McKinley, was an anarchist. So was Giuseppe Zangara, who sought Franklin Roosevelt's life in Miami and killed Mayor Anton Cermak of Chicago. The attackers of Theodore Roosevelt and Mayor Gaynor were both unbalanced.
>
> "Dr. Weiss was unlike all these. He cannot be dismissed as just another crack-brain. Czarist Russia, that trod so long and so cruelly upon the people, gave birth to many such assassins. Pray heaven that future conditions in our country may be such that Dr. Weiss will be our last [*selfless Old World-like assassin*] as well as our first."

The Weiss family flatly rejected the martyr theory. They lent no support to Anderson's monument campaign. It petered out. In 1963 when this book was first published, the family position remained unchanged— as it does today.

"We never assumed that he was a martyr," Dr. Thomas Weiss, Carl's brother, said.

If the response to Dr. Weiss's death was large, it was enormous for the Kingfish. From all over the country came comments and messages of condolence to his widow.

PRESIDENT ROOSEVELT's first statement on Long's wounding was: "I deeply regret the attempt made upon the life of Senator Long of Louisiana. The spirit of violence is un-American and has no place in a consideration of public affairs, least of all at a time when a calm and dispassionate approach to the problems of the day is so essential."

After Huey's death, FDR sent this wire to Mrs. Long: "Mrs. Roosevelt and I want you and yours to know that you have our very deep sympathy in your loss."

WILLIAM GREEN, President of the American Federation of Labor: "Labor shares with all classes of people the common sorrow which they experience over his tragic death. He was regarded as the champion of the rights of the common people, and as a proven advocate of economic and social phases which he believed would promote social justice."

NORMAN THOMAS, Socialist candidate for President: "The death of Huey Long removes the ablest and most colorful forerunner of American fascism."

CLARENCE DARROW, lawyer: "I admired Huey Long in many ways. I knew him and liked him. As a man, he stood for what was right in political life."

FATHER COUGHLIN: "The death of Senator Huey Long is the most regrettable thing in modern history."

JACK DEMPSEY: "Our nation has lost a fighter who battled to the last ditch for what he thought was right. The world will miss him, and I grieve at the passing of a true friend."

SENATOR W. E. BORAH, Republican, Idaho: "Upon one thing all lovers of order and law must agree, that is, in condemning the manner which was chosen to destroy him."

Among the thousands of letters, phone calls and telegrams that poured in were those from Secretary of War George Derm; Interior Secretary Harold Ickes; Postmaster General James Farley; Senators Barkley of Kentucky, George and Talmadge of Georgia, Norris of Nebraska, Connally of Texas, O'Mahoney of Wyoming, Harrison of Mississippi, Nye of North Dakota, McCarran of Nevada, Black of Alabama, Barbour of New Jersey; Governors Lehman of New York, Connor of Mississippi, Graves of Alabama, LaFollette of Wisconsin; newspaper-chain publisher Frank Gannett; and the singing Boswell Sisters.

Practically every newspaper in the United States and many overseas commented editorially on Long's demise. As the Kingfish did not enjoy a good press in life, neither did he in death.

KANSAS CITY STAR: "A spectacular figure has been taken from the national scene. But his untimely removal cannot be mourned as a national loss."

PHILADELPHIA RECORD: "The murder of Baton Rouge. . . . is a warning that the path of a dictator on this continent is overhung by peril."

AMERICAN PROGRESS, (Long's newspaper): "Huey Long is dead. Today in Louisiana from the red clay hills of Winn to the bayous of Cameron, from the piney woods of the Florida parishes to the muddy waters of the Sabine river, a whole state mourns the passing of a great man."

MILWAUKEE SENTINEL: "The deed of a single individual, embittered by the autocratic rule of the Kingfish, creates no cause for astonishment. No man can carry matters with so high a hand, no man can deliberately invite animosities and reprisals as Long has done without danger of raising some enemy who will adopt the tactics of the assassin."

CLEVELAND PLAIN DEALER: "The Kingdom of Long . . . has left its mark on Louisiana. One's hope is that by wholly peaceful and lawful means the memory of the Long regime may be wiped out and Louisiana brought back to the Union."

BIRMINGHAM AGE-HERALD: "The true spirit of Longism is perhaps best shown by the treatment accorded his attacker. Perhaps Dr. Weiss could not have been seized and disarmed after he fired. Perhaps it was necessary to shoot him. But only a spirit of revenge and blood-lust prompted the action of Long's bodyguards in firing many shots into the body of Dr. Weiss after it lay on the floor. If the attack upon the Senator is a stain upon our civilization, then the mutilation of the body of Dr. Weiss is an atrocity worthy only of barbarians and savages."

In Italy, the press saw no connection between Long's Louisiana dictatorship and that of Mussolini. In Paris, newspapers said that Huey's death removed Roosevelt's most formidable election rival. In Germany, the Berlin *Tageblatt* said that the United States would now be fertile soil for extremist propaganda, which may get a shot in the arm through Long's assassination. In Austria, the Vienna *Tageblatt* attributed the shooting to FDR's New Deal, which, it said, "has aroused such passions." In England, the Manchester *Guardian* said: "The tragedy of Huey Long is that he might have been a great Democrat."

Huey's body was removed to the Rabenhorst Funeral Home, the same mortuary that had prepared the body of Dr. Weiss for the grave a day before. There, on the second floor, Dr. Bird, the Coroner, convened an informal coroner's jury. On the way to the undertaker's, Bird collected three men from various parts of town— G. C. Brian, Jake Goslinski, and Tom Davis. He took them into Rabenhorst's, past a cordon of police. Two mortuary workers—Unbehagan and W. M. Knobloch —completed the five-man jury. No witnesses were heard. Bird explained the facts of the case as he knew them. The jury reached a quick verdict: "Death was the result of pistol wound of abdomen (homicidal)." Each man got two dollars, the standard juror's fee in those days.

Many anticipated that Long would be laid to rest in the family burial plot in the red clay hills of his home town of Winnfield. But the State Legislature, with the consent of Mrs. Long, passed a concurrent resolution providing for Long's remains to lie in a tomb on the Capitol grounds. Lawmakers then passed all 39 of Huey's measures approved in committee, including the Pavy gerrymander bill.

Mortuary assistant Unbehagan, after being turned back by overprotective Highway Police, finally got into the mortuary to help Merle Welch, the harried funeral-home manager, ready Long's body for burial.

Unbehagan said that he had noticed discoloration on Long's face. "There was a dark spot over the chin," he recalled, "I had to cover it with color. I may have put some wax over it."

Seymour Weiss and Governor Allen took charge of the important burial arrangements. They picked for the Kingfish a massive, $5,000, double-walled, bronze casket—actually one coffin inside another—hermetically sealed. For Huey's funeral attire they chose, of all things, a tuxedo—a strange garb for the ex-country boy and friend of the poor. For Long's tomb, State Senators Harvey Peltier and Coleman Lindsey representing the Senate, and State Representatives Lorris Wimberly, Smith Hoffpauir and Frank J. Stitch, representing the House, picked a central spot in the sunken gardens fronting the terraced steps of the Capitol. Workmen labored all night under the glare of electric floodlights to prepare the grave. They sank a concrete crypt seven feet into the earth in the center of a shrubbery-studded circle. Into it they lowered a seamless copper box inside which the bronze casket was to be permanently sealed. Later, a concrete-and-steel slab covered the grave, and a bronze statue was erected.

"They poured so much concrete on him," one red neck among the thousands that swarmed to the funeral said, "Huey couldn't get out of his grave on Judgment Day."

At 1:35 p.m. Wednesday a hearse bore Long's body to the Capitol. A huge throng looked on as police carefully carried the heavy casket through the great bronze door of Memorial Hall. They placed the bier on black-draped standards. Huey lay under a bas relief of himself presented by the Confederate Veterans in "grateful appreciation" of his help and assistance. The spot was not far from the scene of the shooting.

Attendants opened the upper section of the coffin, revealing Long in dinner jacket, stiff-bosomed shirt, and black bow tie. A wandering lock of crispy-curly red hair fell over his forehead.

The bereaved widow and Long's family were admitted first and remained alone with Huey. Over a thousand floral pieces surrounded the casket. Roses, asters, chrysanthemums, lilies, dahlias, marigolds, orchids—flowers of every description. They blanketed the marble floor, pressed against the stone walls, overflowed to the chambers of the Senate and House and even to the mezzanine. The Capitol was thick with their sweet odor. It was estimated that flowers took up an acre of space, cost more than $25,000.

From the mezzanine, Governor Allen and Seymour Weiss peered at the body silently. They stood motionless for a long time. Finally, without removing his eyes from the casket, Allen said, "Seymour, he was a fine-looking man." Weiss nodded, and the two walked away.

When the family left the bier, the vast assemblage surged into the building to take a last glimpse of Huey. Opinions varied on his appearance. Some came away saying that he had his characteristic ruddy glow. Others said that he appeared to be "so heavily painted, he looked like a vaudeville performer." (Undertaker assistant Unbehagan said that Seymour Weiss, feeling that Long was "too pale," had kept insisting that more color be added.)

Long lay in state one full day—from 2 p.m. Wednesday, September 11, to 3 p.m. Thursday, September 12. Eight militiamen stood at rigid attention behind the casket. With them as guard of honor were two Louisiana State University students and four members of the LSU band in purple and gold uniforms Long had designed.

Lines stretched for blocks. Hour by hour, the vast multitude filed by, bareheaded. "Move along, please," said a guard, "there's thousands more behind you." There was a mingled crowd. Negro and white, rich and poor, men and women, and everywhere Huey's loyal Unwashed that poured out of the hills and bayous. Red necks from north Louisiana and Cajuns from the south. They showed up in dusty overalls, ill-fitting Sunday clothes, rubbing shoulders with city folk in tailored suits. They came from places with such unfamiliar names as Dry Prong, Bayou Boeuf, Cow Island, Echo, Tickfaw, Waterproof, Grand Encore, Turkey Creek, Plain Dealing, Pointe a la Hache, Yscloskey, and Zwolle. They passed in a never-ending stream. Whatever them lyin' newspapers said, the country people knew that Huey was their best friend. Handkerchiefs fluttered everywhere. Smothered sobs echoed in the solemn rotunda. The great line moved on and on. It was estimated that more than 22,000 persons viewed the body.

Seymour Weiss called all the news photographers in

and asked them to swear not to take Long's picture in the casket. Oscar Valedon, a New Orleans *States* photographer, crossed his fingers. "What did Weiss ever do for me?" Valedon thought. He set his camera, hid it under his coat, and went up to the mezzanine. Looking down on Huey, he leaned over, whipped out his camera, clicked it, and dashed out the building. Valedon moved quickly. He knew what Huey's bodyguards might do to him if they caught him. His picture showed Huey lying in his coffin in his fancy clothes. It was a classic. A wire service picked it up. The picture got wide play in editions all over the country. As late as 1960, it was still used to illustrate magazine articles about the Kingfish.

On Thursday, the day of Huey's funeral, roads into Baton Rouge were black with cars in every direction. Beyond the Mississippi, at Port Allen, the lines of autos waiting to ferry across to the Capital extended bumper to bumper for more than four miles. Six trains left New Orleans' Union Station carrying some 7,000 persons. Schools throughout the State were closed for the day. The criminal courts and the sheriffs' and clerks' offices were padlocked. By noon, so many people had gathered outside the Capitol that police had to rope off a barrier to keep open a lane for the funeral procession.

A scorching summer sun blazed in the sky. The mercury soared into the 90's. Men and women took off their shoes, occasionally deserting their places up front to seek shade under trees. Some people stretched out on lawns of nearby homes, knocking on the doors to beg for water. Soda pop, hot dog and ice cream vendors arrived. They were overwhelmed.

Parents lifted umbrellas to shield children from the blistering rays. Babies napped on the grass. A child fainted after standing in the sun for hours. Her Negro nurse laid the child down on the concrete and began screaming. Highway police quieted her and took the child to the shade, where they revived her.

A sunshower started. "Happy is the dead that the rain rains on," an old woman cried. The sprinkle ended and the sun came out again, turning the pools of rainwater to steam.

People congregated in every conceivable point of vantage. Spectators perched in century-old oaks and climbed to the tops of statues. State officials peered from Capitol offices. In the distance you could see silhouettes dotting the roofs of buildings. A great noise swirled up from the massive throng.

"It was the biggest crowd I ever saw," Senator Russell Long said. Newspapers reported that over 100,000 came to see Huey buried. The figure was probably exaggerated, but it certainly was one of the largest—if not the largest—crowds assembled in Louisiana to that time.

At about 3 p.m. the doors to Memorial Hall closed. Police cleared the rotunda. Attendants started shifting floral pieces to the grave to make an avenue of flowers along the line where the coffin would be borne. There were so many flowers that Colonel Roy deputized 60 men to help remove them. Working as fast as they could, the men rushed through the corridors for more than an hour before all the flowers were out of the building. The throng trampled many of the floral pieces later, as they crashed through police lines. Some snatched wreaths away for souvenirs—not only after the funeral but even while the flowers were being placed in the sunken garden.

At 4:25 p.m. a hush fell over the throng. The funeral procession appeared at the top of the Capitol steps. The Reverend Gerald L. K. Smith, who in later years would champion the cause of anti-Semitism, led the way. He had been selected to deliver the eulogy. Seymour Weiss said that he had made the choice—one he quickly regretted. ("Choosing Smith for that speech was a great mistake," Weiss said. "It made him. He (Smith) capitalized on it, glorified himself, had thousands of copies printed and distributed.") Smith, a tall, handsome man, stood, prayerbook in hand, his eyes sweeping over the sea of humanity. He started the long, slow walk to the grave. The roped-in crowd surged for a closer look. Police held it back.

The casket began its deliberate descent accompanied by the muffled beat of a drum, the mournful music of a band. Six pallbearers—Governor Allen, Lieutenant Governor Noe, Ellender, Weiss, Fournet, and Maestri —bore the coffin, glittering in the bright sun, down the long flight of steps. Highway police helped distribute the weight of the great bier. Mrs. Long and her children followed. Huey's old father was absent. He was so prostrate with grief that he couldn't leave his hotel room.

The procession moved through the sunken garden. Women held vanity cases as periscopes to see over heads. Over the hushed crowd came the music of a dirge transcribed from Long's own song, "Every Man a King." It blended with distant chimes of a carillon. Airplanes crossed overhead. Flags flew at half-staff. The whir of newsreel cameras sounded faintly.

"This place marks not the resting place of Huey Long. It marks only the burial place for his body," Smith said. "His spirit shall never rest as long as hungry bodies cry for food, as long as human frames stand naked, as long as homeless wretches haunt this land of plenty."

No one moved. All eyes fixed on Smith, standing at a microphone at the grave, every inch a match for Huey as a spellbinder. ("It was a political speech to himself," Senator Russell Long said. "He anointed himself as Long's successor. He made a tremendous impression.")

"The ideals which he planted in our hearts have created a gnawing hunger of a new order," Smith said. "This hunger pain, this parching thirst for better things, can only be healed and satisfied by the completion of that victory toward which he led us.

"In answer to a query in his home one Sunday which I made, he replied, 'I know, Brother Smith, that the arms of God are about me every moment.'

"I believe that God consented to this fate in order that by this dramatic exit, he might retire from this battleground of political torture to find the quiet of eternity, while at the same time, his torch was left to light our way."

The microphone failed to carry Smith's voice to loudspeakers at the fringes of the multitude. The crowd, surging across the gardens, ground electrical wires into the earth and caused a short circuit. But

Smith's silver-toned voice thundered out like cannon volleys.

"He was a builder, a trail blazer, a ruthless foe of decay, a burner of red tape, a violent enemy of retrogression. Progress was the sweetheart of his soul. He divorced the past, he wedded the present, he wooed the future.

". . . Drama was his natural art. A humorist of superior quality; an actor whose stage was his work, whose scenery, the people about him. When he passed, all eyes were fastened on him, watching tensely to see something that had never been done before—listening intently for something that had never been said before; and he never disappointed. . . .

"To you, the officials of state . . . count memorable the day you first heard the mention of his name. The time will come when to say that you even touched his hand will be the most potent interest in your life.

"This blood which dropped upon this soil shall seal our hearts together. Take up the torch, complete the task. . . .

"I was with him when he died. I said, 'Amen,' as he breathed his last. His final prayer was this, 'Oh, God, don't let me die. I have a few more things to do.' This work which he left undone we *must* complete. As one with no political ambition, and who seeks no gratuities at the hand of the State, I challenge you, my comrades, to complete the task.

"Complete the task.

"Oh, God, why did we have to lose him? . . . He was the Stradivarius whose notes rose in competition with jealous drums, envious tom-toms. His was the un-finished symphony."

Seymour Weiss broke a few orchids from the blanket of flowers covering the casket. He handed one to Mrs. Long, one to her daughter Rose, and one to each of Long's brothers.

A lowering device sent the casket into its copper vault with a metallic clang of finality. Many thought that that moment would close the book on the story of Huey and Dr. Weiss. They were wrong. It was just starting.[1]

---

[1] There still remains controversy about Long's last words, which, in fact, are so self-serving, it seems likely his cronies made them up to bolster his image as a martyr. Mark T. Carleton, associate professor of history at Louisiana State University, had an alternate version. He said a retired nurse, who was in the hospital room taking Long's pulse, says his final utterance was simply, "Shit." Carleton said that was probably the most logical of the various accounts (see pages 174–175). "Here he was, 42 years old. He's dying and he knows it. He was not going to be president or rightful ruler of the universe. He is not even going to be on this earth after a few more seconds. He is angry and extremely frustrated. He is running out of breath. And so he ended his life with a four-letter word. But, of course, the legend wouldn't tolerate that."

The Inquest

". . . I killed him because he killed Senator Long. . . ."
—Joe Messina, bodyguard

District Attorney John Fred Odom of East Baton Rouge Parish, the official charged with any court action that might stem from the double slaying, was a heavy-set, bespectacled man with narrow shoulders, a paunch, and a double chin. Odom, 53, was raised on a farm in rural St. Helena Parish in southeast Louisiana. A popular, well-liked prosecutor, he was a good mixer, prone to cussing, fond of swapping stories, persuasive in a courtroom. Two generations of voters had re-elected him without interruption since 1916—going on 30 years. (Although he did not know it then, Odom, one of the State's anti-Long leaders, was serving his last term. The Long machine candidate, charging that Odom was part and parcel of an anti-Long faction that had plotted Huey's death, would defeat him in the January primary.)

Odom and Dr. Bird, the Coroner, scheduled an inquest for Monday, September 9, the morning after the shooting. Huey's last words before going under surgery forbade any statements from anyone but him. When the five-man coroner's jury—Merle Welsh, G. C. Brian, Jake Goslinski, W. M. Knobloch, and Tom Davis—convened at 10 a.m., Huey lay unconscious. But he was alive, and while he lived he was still the Kingfish. No Long officials or bodyguards showed up.

Two men did testify—newsman Frampton and John D'Armond, New Orleans hotel employee and former member of the State BCI. But neither had seen the first shot or witnessed the events just prior to it. D'Armond testified that he had been inside the Governor's office and hadn't come out until the shooting was all over. Frampton had also been inside the Governor's office. He had had his hand on the corridor door knob but hadn't opened it until after the first shot. Repeating under oath the gist of his first-person news story, Frampton testified that, as he had opened the door, he had seen Long walking from the corridor, holding his side. Frampton said that he had seen Weiss and Roden struggling. He testified that three or four seconds had elapsed between the first shot—which he had heard but had not seen—and the others. (This would be a point of disagreement. Other witnesses would later testify that there were two shots fired close together, a lull, and then a great volley.)

"Did anyone but Roden put his hands on Dr. Weiss?" Odom asked.

"I don't think so," Frampton said.

(This point, too, would lead to conflicting testimony.)

Dr. Bird made a brief statement reporting the number of wounds he had counted in Weiss's body. Then he adjourned the inquest until 4 p.m. in the hope that the bodyguards would show up. They did not. The inquest was recessed a second time, until Tuesday at 2 p.m. Tuesday came. Once more, no witnesses appeared. The hearing was recessed a third time, until Thursday, September 12. This was the day Huey was buried. Again, no one turned up.

It soon became apparent that the leaderless Long

machine looked on the inquest as political dynamite. It was open to the public. Whatever developed could be used in the impending election campaign. Nobody knew what Odom, a political foe, had up his sleeve.

Actually, Odom was in the dark. Primarily, he wanted to hold the inquest to air the reason that the doctor had been instantly slain and his body riddled with 61 bullet holes. Those opposed to Long called Weiss's death a lynching. Friends of the slain specialist said that Long's bodyguards could have taken Weiss into custody. They had had Weiss down. Their number could have easily held him prisoner. Instead, Weiss's adherents said, Huey's Cossacks had appointed themselves judge, jury and executioner—sealing Weiss's lips forever. If they had merely been trying to protect their boss, they had been much too late.

Because none of the bodyguards had showed up to testify, stories began circulating that Long, careless of those who got in his way, may even have provoked what happened with a word, a gesture, or a shove. The Weiss family pledged full support to Odom's investigation.

It was reported that State Attorney General Gaston L. Porterie intended to supersede Odom in the inquest probe. Whispers of "whitewash" started spreading through the Capital. Why wouldn't the bodyguards come forward under oath? The plan to supersede was soon abandoned. Those high in the Long forces counseled against it. State officials met with the bodyguards in Porterie's office in the Capitol. Odom got word that witnesses would show up. The inquest was re-scheduled for the fourth time.

At 10 a.m. on Monday, September 16, eight days after the shooting, some 400 sweltering spectators jammed every available inch of the roasting-hot East Baton Rouge Parish courtroom. Nobody cared much about the summer heat that day. The bodyguards were going to tell their story.[2] Everybody in Louisiana wanted to hear it.

"The inquest had all the aspects of a Roman holiday," Dr. William H. Cook said. He had been called as one of Huey's attending physicians.

Attorney General Porterie and Associate Justice Fournet were among the early arrivals. Brigadier General Guerre, BCI chief, led the platoon of bodyguards. Weiss's father was advised to go to a certain area and stay there. He was told not to do anything more than go in and out. Former Governor Parker accompanied him.

The air was charged with electricity. Officials of the Long machine and Huey's bodyguards sat up front on one side of the courtroom. An anti-Long group sat opposite them. Many on both sides had guns under their coats. Few tried to conceal them.

Odom and Bird were together at a long table. Porterie took a seat beside Odom. He told reporters that he came as an "observer."

Fireworks erupted almost immediately. Gerald L. K. Smith, called as the second witness, marched to the witness box. Still standing, and without waiting to be sworn, he announced that he wished to make a state-

[2] Neither the bodyguards nor any member of the Long faction who saw the entire shooting had made a public statement. The comments of Roden and Fournet on the shooting came from interviews with the author in 1960 and 1961.

ment. Before Odom could reply, Smith roared in the vibrant voice he used on the platform:[3]

"I want to say I respect your court, and I respect you, Dr. Bird, but I also want to say that this district attorney has been named as a murder plot conspirator and I refuse to respect him and to be questioned by him."

Odom's eyes bulged. His mouth hung open. A shocked silence fell over the court.

"When a man asks the questions who has not shared in the conspiracies, I will answer them," Smith bellowed. He stretched his arms and flailed the air. "He (Odom) plotted to kill the man I loved. I worshiped my hero."

With eyes blazing, Smith stepped down from the rostrum and walked within a foot of Odom. Long adherents applauded wildly. As Smith stalked out of the chamber, several men slapped his back and shook his hand. Long's bodyguards rose, but Odom's investigators were there in number and they got to their feet also.

Odom, shaken, rose slowly. With lips trembling, he addressed the court in a tone as subdued as Smith's was challenging.

"I care nothing for his opinion of me or of my acts," Odom said. "But if he or anybody else says I engaged in any plot to kill Senator Huey Long, he is a willful, malicious and vicious liar."

Another part of the crowd let out a lusty cheer— about equal in volume to the preceding outburst.

---

[3] Inquest quotations are from the September 17, 1935, account in The New Orleans *Times-Picayune*, which filled all or parts of 11 columns, and from the Associated Press wire story, which ran nearly 5,000 words.

There was a silence. Then Odom laughed. It proved infectious and snapped the tension. Odom called the next witness. The courtroom settled down to the business at hand.

The testimony of Justice Fournet, the first witness, had laid the groundwork for all the eye-witness accounts.

After the oath had been administered, Odom had inquired, "Were you present at the Capitol last Sunday night about 9:20 o'clock?"

"Yes, sir," Fournet had replied.

"Did you witness the shooting in which Carl Austin Weiss and Senator Long lost their lives?" Fournet had been asked.

"I did."

"Will you please state in your own words what you saw," the District Attorney had said.

"Well, I was in the House of Representatives," Fournet had responded. "I wanted to see Huey and talk to him. When Huey started out of the House of Representatives, I left behind him. As usual, he walked very fast. As I entered the corridor leading to the Governor's office, there were several people there, and I asked them where Huey had gone. They told me he had gone to the Governor's office. I walked leisurely toward the office and met Joe Messina. As we approached the Governor's office, Huey walked out in our direction. He reached the big circle in the middle of the corridor and was facing in the direction of the House of Representatives (east). Huey made some statement about getting everybody on hand early the next day, and somebody told him that had been attended to.

"At that time, a small man in a white, or almost white suit, flashed among us, and flashed a gun and shot almost immediately. I immediately put my hand on the man's arm, my left hand, trying to deflect the bullet. There was quite a bit of confusion. One of the boys grabbed him (Weiss). I shoved him (Weiss) and whoever was holding him, and he (Weiss) fell to the floor. They both went down. The doctor did not go all the way to the floor. He was in a crouching position, trying to fire the gun again. He tried to jerk the gun loose from the man I have since learned was Roden. I made another effort to grab him. The doctor was bending over when I was about to grab him when they shot him. I stepped back. . . ."

Q. — At the time you saw Roden grab Dr. Weiss was the doctor trying to fire again?

A. — Yes. It looked like he was trying to shoot Roden.

Q. — To what portion of Senator Long's body was Dr. Weiss's weapon pressed?

A. — It's hard to say. It was from the front and upward from him. I did not see the doctor draw the pistol. He made one step forward and he shot as I put my hand on him. I shoved the doctor and the man who grabbed him. The doctor was in a crouching position trying to shoot Roden who was holding on to the gun.

Q. — Who fired the first shot after Senator Long was shot?

A. — I cannot say who fired the first shot after Dr. Weiss shot Senator Long. The shooting came from in back of me.

Q. — Did Roden fire the first shot after Senator Long was shot?

A. — I cannot say. It happened so fast. I cannot think the man on the floor (Roden) fired the first shot after Senator Long was shot. Roden was on the floor attempting to rise.

Q. — How many shots were fired?

A. — I was a machine gunner during the war, and machine guns shoot about 60 shots a minute. The shooting sounded as fast as a machine gun. There were two, three, or four men shooting at the same time. It sounded like the guns were all automatic pistols. I did not see any machine guns. Dr. Weiss went down very slowly. When the first bullet struck him, he quivered, and then shots poured in from both sides. The first two shots were so close together I thought the doctor fired both shots. Senator Long was of the same opinion. Senator Long told me that I kept the doctor from hitting him with the second shot. After the second shot, there was no cessation in the shooting. It was one continuous movement. If Dr. Weiss was shot forty or fifty times, he was shot as fast as they could shoot with three or four automatic pistols. I heard some people later express the opinion that machine guns were used, the shots were so close together.

Q. — Was Dr. Weiss shot after he was on the floor?

A. — The shooting was continuous. Some may have hit him after he was on the floor.

Odom had been finished with the witness. Attorney General Porterie had had a question.

Q. — Was there any conversation between Senator Long and Dr. Weiss?

A. — None. Dr. Weiss came amongst us, took one step, and fired. There was no outcry except when Huey was shot. He made an outcry and grabbed his side.

After Fournet had left the stand, Smith made his dramatic statement and stormed out. Then Odom called Dr. Cook. It was not clear why Odom wanted him to testify, since Cook had not seen the shooting. It became obvious as soon as he started testifying.

Cook said that he had attended Long at the hospital and had noticed that Huey had an abrasion of the mouth.

"Dr. Henry McKowen, who was called to administer the anesthesia, called attention to an abrasion on Senator Long's lower lip," Cook said. "It was an abrasion or brush burn. When it was wiped with anesthetic, it oozed a little."

Q. — Did it appear to be a fresh abrasion?

A. — Yes.

This was the first public disclosure of an injury to Long's face.[4] Attorney General Porterie was on his feet immediately. Addressing Dr. Cook, Porterie asked:

"A man having been shot as Senator Long was, and

[4] Dr. Joseph A. Sabatier, Jr., who had acted as a scrub nurse in the operation but had not been summoned to the inquest, also reported seeing blood on Long's lips. In a letter written on October 31, 1935, he wrote: "When Sen. Long was brought into the operating room, there were quite a few spots of blood on the edges of his lips. I overheard at this time that he had quite severe fever blisters on his lips and had bruised them in all of the commotion at the capitol."

making his way down four winding flights of stairs could have struck against an angle of marble or iron?"

"Any contusion or trauma could have caused it," Dr. Cook said.

"A knock against a hard surface could have caused it?"

"Yes."

The moment was allowed to pass without further probing of the injury that would puzzle investigators of the shooting for years to come.

Dr. J. Webb McGehee took the stand. His presence surprised Porterie. McGehee had not seen the shooting. Nor had he attended Long.

"Speaking in an advisory capacity," Porterie said before questioning started, "Do you think this testimony by a physician who was not in attendance is relevant?"

"I'm going to show something else," Odom replied icily. He turned to the witness.

Q. — Doctor, did you have an appointment with Dr. Weiss to administer an anesthetic Monday a week ago?

A. — I had an engagement to administer the anesthetic for an operation to be performed by Dr. Weiss last Monday. And I last spoke to him personally Friday (September 6) a week ago. I spoke to him on the telephone at 8:15 p.m. Sunday (September 8) a week ago. He asked me if I knew the operation for the following day had been changed from Our Lady of the Lake to the General Hospital. I told him I knew that.

The point Odom was getting on the record, of course, was that an hour before the shooting Weiss checked arrangements for an operation the next morning—a peculiar act for a man with murder on his mind.

District Attorney C. Sidney Frederick of Washington, Louisiana, took the stand. He said that, during the shooting, he had stood in an adjoining corridor, peeking around the wall. He said that the first two shots were fired quickly. There was a brief lapse between the second and third shots.

Q. — Did you see the shooting?

A. — No. I can't say I saw any particular person fire any particular shot.

.　.　.

Q. — Did you see the body before the firing ceased?

A. — Yes. I was one of the first to reach it.

Q. — Where was it?

A. — It was lying in the corridor by the side of a large, marble pillar.

Q. — When you first saw the body, was it down?

A. — I couldn't say positively.

Q. — After the body was on the floor, did you see anybody fire?

A. — I will answer it like this. There were shots fired after the body was on the floor.

J. T. Cockerham of Denham Springs testified that he had heard the shooting as he stood in Memorial Hall around the corridor from the slaying. Cockerham said that there was a little time between the second and third shots.

Cooper Jean of Baker, the next witness, said that he had stood at the entrance to the Capitol and heard the shots. He noted that there has been a lapse of time between the second and third shots.

Earl Straughn, who had been around a bend from the fatal scene, took the stand.

Q. — Where were you in the State Capitol?

A. — About five steps from where you go into the end of the hall.

Q. — In the House lobby?

A. — Yes.

Q. — Did you go out into the hall?

A. — I was headed that way and stopped.

Q. — You did see the shooting?

A. — No. I later walked down the hall and saw a man in a white suit lying on the floor. I got within fifteen feet of the man on the floor, and then they made us go out of the corridor.

Q. — Did anybody have guns?

A. — Yes.

Q. — Who had guns?

A. — I couldn't say. I don't know them personally or by sight.

Q. — What sort of guns?

A. — Policemen pistols—six-shooters, not automatics.

Q. — How many men had guns?

A. — Four or five.

Q. — Could you give any idea how many shots were fired?

A. — A couple, and then 25 or 30. That is my estimate.

State Representative C. A. Riddle of Avoyelles Parish, a Long machine politician, was the next witness. He was asked if he had been in the Capitol when the shooting had occurred. Riddle said that he had been.

Q. — Did you see the shooting?

A. — I think I did. When the House adjourned, I came out the right side door and turned into the corridor leading to the Governor's office. Senator Long came out of what I thought was the door to the office of the secretary to the Governor, and toward me. He stopped about six feet from a column in the corridor where the circle is. I thought that was a good time to invite him to speak at a barbecue we were planning to hold in Marksville. When I was five or six feet away from him, a gun popped. There was a young fellow with a pistol pointed at Senator Long. I saw several inches of the barrel, which was very bright. Someone grabbed him, and then it sounded like firecrackers . . .

Q. — Did the man who fired the shot come between you and Senator Long?

A. — No. He came more diagonally. He came forward, and at the time the gun popped off it looked like he was holding it with both hands.

Q. — Did you hear any conversation or any remarks between this man and Senator Long?

A. — None whatsoever.

Q. — Did you recognize who did the general firing?

A. — No, I didn't look at them. I thought it was bandits and racketeers.

Q. — Did you see this man put his hands on Senator Long?

A. — No. He just came forward with a gun.

Q. — Did you see Senator Long put his hands on him?

A. — No.

Q. — Did you see Justice Fournet put his hands on the man?

A. — I did not recognize Justice Fournet. I heard Justice Fournet testify today, but I don't remember seeing him. My mind was on Senator Long. I loved him very much.

Bodyguard Joe Messina took the stand, and was quickly overcome with emotion. He had to exert great effort to talk coherently. Odom began questioning.

Q. — You understand your constitutional rights?

A. — I do.

Q. — Were you present in the Statehouse at the time of the shooting?

A. — At this time, I want to make a statement. In the first place, Senator Long was a very close friend of mine, and, in the next place, there was a plot or conspiracy before. My friend, Sidney Songy, came to me and begged me to take him to Senator Long because he wanted to confess to a crime they wanted him to do that he couldn't do. (Tears welled in Messina's eyes. His words came in choking, spasmodic bursts.) They wanted him to kill Long, but he could not bring himself to pull it off. We got lots of stuff we seized—pistols, bullets, hand grenades, and things like that. (Messina's voice broke completely. He wept. His sentences became incoherent. Only the last words were audible.) . . . the cowardly way that man killed the Senator. (Gathering himself together) Now go ahead and ask your questions.

Q. — Go on and tell us what you know about the shooting.

A. — When Weiss shot, I saw Senator Long jump back and I knew that he had been killed. I ran up, pulled my gun, and emptied it at the man who shot Senator Long.

Q. — Was Dr. Weiss being held by Roden?

A. — I ran up and shot the man who had shot Senator Long.

Q. — Did you recognize the man scuffling with Weiss on the floor as Roden?

A. — Yes.

Q. — Why did you shoot Dr. Weiss?

A. — To keep him from shooting Roden, myself or anyone else.

Q. — Was his pistol pointed at you or Roden?

A. — I don't know.

Q. — Did you shoot him because he was about to shoot you or because he shot Senator Long?

A. — One reason was, I killed him because he killed Senator Long and another reason he would have shot anyone in there.

Q. — What did you do after the shooting?

A. — I put my pistol in my pocket and went downstairs hunting for Senator Long.

. . .

Q. — What bodyguards were there?

A. — George McQuiston, Murphy Roden, and myself. Those are all I recall.

Q. — Did you see Dr. Weiss approach Senator Long?

A. — I saw Weiss a moment after the shot was fired.

Q. — Were you behind Senator Long?

A. — I ran up. I recognized Roden and began firing on Weiss.

Q. — Did you fire on Weiss before he broke loose?

A. — No. I fired at the man with the pistol.

Q. — You are employed by the State Bureau of Criminal Identification and Investigation?

A. — Yes.

Q. — How long have you been thus employed?

A. — Since last February.

Q. — You were detailed to attend Senator Long?

A. — Yes.

Q. — Under orders of General Guerre?

A. — Yes.

Q. — What were those orders?

A. — To stop any violence.

Q. — To Senator Long?

A. — To Senator Long or anyone else.

Messina stepped down.

George McQuiston was called. He walked to the stand but did not sit down.

"I am advised by Attorney General Porterie that you do not wish to make any statements," Odom said.

"I don't care to make any statement whatever," Mc-Quiston said. He was excused without comment.

Mrs. O. P. Kennedy, who had been in the Capitol, said that she knew nothing of the shooting. She was excused.

Gordon Latham corroborated earlier testimony that there were two shots close together, a short lull, and then a volley.

Dr. Carl Adam Weiss was called. He requested that no pictures be made of him on the stand, and Dr. Bird told photographers not to take any. Sitting forward in the witness chair, Dr. Weiss described his son's last day in a low but firm voice.

Q. — Did you see your son on Sunday, the day of the shooting which resulted in the deaths of Dr. Weiss and Senator Long?

A. — Yes, I was with him practically all day. I was with him until 7:30 that night. My son and his wife came with their baby to our house early in the morning. They left the baby with me and my wife while they went to St. Joseph's Church for Mass. After Mass, Mrs. Weiss returned to my home while my son stopped at Scheinuk's Florist to inquire about a patient who had consulted him the day before. Mr. Scheinuk gave my son a bouquet of flowers, saying he had not sent flowers when the baby was born three months before. My son came home saying, 'Look what Mr. Scheinuk sent the baby.' My son and his wife went to their home and returned to take dinner at my house. He came to my house for dinner at 1 p.m. My son ate heartily and joked during the dinner. After dinner, we went to my camp at the Amite River. My wife and I kept the baby while my son and his wife went in swimming. We returned to my house from the camp at 7:30 (p.m.) and my son and his wife and baby went to their house from my house.

Dr. Weiss said that at about 9:50 p.m. Carl's wife telephoned and asked if Carl was at his house. She said that he had gone to make a call.

Q. — Did your son usually carry a pistol out at night?
A. — Occasionally he did.
Q. — Do you know the reason?

A. — Recently, there were intruders in our garage.

Dr. Weiss said that his son was 29 years old and of slight build. He weighed 132 pounds. "When he was in swimming at the camp Sunday, I remarked to my wife that 'the boy is skin and bones.' My wife said, 'Yes, we have got to make him take a rest. He's been working so hard lately.' "

Bodyguard Murphy Roden volunteered to testify, after being advised by Odom that he did not have to appear because he was a participant.

"I have no objection to testifying," said Roden. He identified himself as a resident of Arcadia in Bienville Parish, and an employee of the State Bureau of Criminal Identification and Investigation. He said that he had been assigned to guard Senator Long since January 15.

Q. — Were you discharging your duties last Sunday night?

A. — Yes.

Q. — Who assigned you to guard Senator Long?

A. — General Guerre. My assignment had been to stay with Senator Long and see that no one harmed him. I had been with him since January 15.

Q. — In Washington, too?

A. — Yes. I had a commission from the Metropolitan Police Department in Washington.

Q. — And you were paid by the State of Louisiana?

A. — Yes.

Q. — Please state in your own words what you saw the day of the shooting that resulted in the deaths of Dr. Weiss and Senator Long.

A. — I was in the House of Representatives when it adjourned. Senator Long stopped to talk to Mason Spencer and then walked out of the House to the Governor's office. I followed him and stopped at the door. He was inside only a second when he walked out. I backed out. He walked to the circle in the center of the corridor. He had called to someone to have everybody there Monday morning. At this moment, somebody brushed by me, pulled a gun, thrust it at the Senator's stomach, and fired. I grabbed him (Dr. Weiss) and we fell to the floor. I jerked loose, got up, pulled my gun, and began firing.

Q. — You testified that both of you were on the floor. Is that correct?

A. — Yes. That floor is slippery and you can't stand on it.

Q. — Did he (Weiss) say anything?

A. — Not a word.

Q. — Did Senator Long say anything?

A. — No. He just let out a yell of some kind when he was shot.

Q. — Did Dr. Weiss act as if he had been shot before you broke loose from him?

A. — No. If he was, I couldn't tell it. Understand, I had smoke in my eyes and couldn't see much.

Q. — Did the man still have a gun when you broke loose from him and started shooting?

A. — Yes. I couldn't get it away from him.

Q. — How many times did you shoot?

A. — Ten times with a .38 Colt automatic.

Q. — Just why did you shoot Dr. Weiss?

A. — To keep from being shot.

Q. — What was your purpose in trying to get the gun?

A. — To stop the fire. I was a member of the National Guard, and the first duty of a soldier is to put the enemy's weapon out of commission.

Q. — How old are you?

A. — Thirty.

Q. — How much do you weigh?

A. — About 150 pounds.

Q. — How tall are you?

A. — Five feet seven and a half inches.

Q. — Were any shots fired after you ceased firing?

A. — I couldn't say. It was all over in a second. The others were behind me.

Q. — How many shots did Dr. Weiss fire?

A. — I am of the opinion that only *one* shot was fired.

(This last statement was curious in view of the fact that Roden later said that a bullet from Dr. Weiss's gun had shot off his watch.)

Louis LeSage, the next witness, said that he had been in the hall but hadn't seen the shooting.

BCI agent Elliot Coleman of Tensas Parish in northeast Louisiana said that Brigadier General Guerre had assigned him to the Capitol "to keep down any disturbance or lawlessness." Coleman, who had become a deputy at 17 and had been elected Sheriff of Tensas Parish in 1936 and for 24 consecutive years, said that he had trailed Long as Huey had left the House.

"The Senator went in the secretary's office, stayed a minute and then came out," Coleman said. "As the

Senator came out, a party stepped in front of him, pulled a gun, and shot him. I struck at the man who shot Senator Long but missed him, and hit someone else. Roden grabbed him and they fell against a marble column. I struck Weiss again as they fell. (This was the first time it was revealed that Weiss was struck— or for that matter, even touched—by anyone but Roden and Fournet.) I then fired two shots.

Q. — Was Judge Fournet with Senator Long?

A. — He testified here. I judge that he was.

Q. — Did anyone else attempt to disarm him (Weiss)?

A. — I couldn't say.

Q. — Did you grapple with him?

A. — No. I hit at him once and missed, and then I struck him again.

Q. — Was he grappling with Roden when you shot? Had they been grappling?

A. — Oh, yes.

.   .   .

Q. — Can you say who fired the second shot?

A. — No, I couldn't. I thought it was his (Weiss's) gun.

Joe Bates, BCI assistant superintendent, who gave the Cossacks their orders, said just before the House had adjourned, Long had told him to notify Huey's friends to be at a caucus the next morning.

"I did it and came on out (of the House) and started toward the Governor's office," Bates said. "I got as far as Mr. Ellender's office (House Speaker) when I heard Mr. Long say to Mr. Fournet something about a meeting. I told him that everybody had been notified. About that time, a man in white walked up to Senator Long. I thought he was going to shake hands. He shot him (Long). Senator Long said, 'I'm shot,' and ran out in a crouched position, holding his hand to his stomach."

Bates said that he had lost sight of Long momentarily, then ran up and down the corridor trying to find him. Later, Bates said that he had gone to the hospital.

"Joe Messina came out of Senator Long's room and asked me who shot the Senator. I said I didn't know," Bates went on. "He said Senator Long wanted to know. I left the hospital and got in a traffic jam."

Q. — Did you fire any shots?

A. — No. My gun was never drawn from my pocket.

Q. — What bodyguards were there?

A. — Roden, Messina, Voitier. That's all I can recall.

Q. — How many shots did Weiss fire?

A. — I thought there was one. That's my opinion.

Q. — You don't know who shot Weiss?

A. — No.

Louis Heard, a policeman, said that he had not seen the shooting.

"When Long walked out of the House," said Heard, "I walked out after him. He went into the Governor's office, and turned back toward the House. I thought he was going back toward the House, and I turned and started back there. I heard a shot and turned around again."

Q. — You didn't shoot?

A. — No. But I had my pistol out.

Q. — Who was with Senator Long?

A. — Roden and Messina were the only ones I saw.

Q. — You were assigned to attend Senator Long by General Guerre?

A. — Yes.

Q. — What were General Guerre's orders?

A. — Just to keep down any disturbance.

Paul Voitier said that he had been to Washington as Long's bodyguard and had been ordered to stay with Huey the night of the shooting.

Q. — Did you see the shooting?

A. — Yes. I was about two feet from Senator Long and about one foot from Dr. Weiss.

Q. — Tell the jury what happened immediately before the shooting.

A. — Senator Long walked out of the secretary's office before the shooting and said to somebody, I think it was Joe Bates, that he would like to have all of his men there the next morning. There was one or two seconds, and then a man walked up with a gun in his right hand and his left hand over the gun. There was a shot and Senator Long said, 'I'm shot.' Judge Fournet knocked Weiss's hand down. Coleman struck Weiss after Weiss had shot the Senator. He punched again and missed, and I think he struck Senator Long, where his lip was bleeding.

(Coleman, however, later said that he had *not* struck Long. In a letter written to the author on June 29, 1961, Coleman said: "I struck Weiss on the jaw, not in the face, and he staggered back against the marble column. He still held onto the pistol, apparently in an effort to shoot Roden. There was one shot fired and Weiss dropped to the floor. *No one hit Long in the face* (the author's italics) that I know of. I certainly did not.")

(Another discrepancy between Coleman's and Voitier's versions was the sequence of punches. Coleman's testimony was that he had missed Weiss on the first try but connected on the second punch. Voitier said just the opposite. He testified that Coleman had hit Weiss with the first blow, but had missed the second swing. So the two bodyguards not only disagreed on the recipients of Coleman's punches but also on their sequence.)

Odom, continuing his questioning, asked Voitier if he had shot Weiss in the front or in the back.

A. — In the front. I fired between Fournet and Roden. I fired four times, backed away, and then fired again.

Q. — Why did you shoot him?

A. — I shot him mostly because he shot Senator Long and because he was trying to shoot me and anybody else.

✧   ✧   ✧

Twenty-three persons testified at the inquest. The jury returned the obvious verdict: "Dr. Carl A. Weiss came to his death as the result of pistol wounds of the head, chest and abdomen (homicidal)."

Except for the difference in the number of wounds, the wording of the Weiss verdict was identical with that in the Long case. Some newsmen criticized the juries for failing to fix blame in either death. (The juries actually could have gone further if they'd had a mind to, but the law did not require it. "It is customary in

Louisiana for coroner's juries to establish only the cause of death," Odom said, "but in many cases, they have attempted to fix the blame. It is the duty of the coroner to determine the cause, but the custom and procedure governing inquests permit the exercise of much latitude.")

All eyewitnesses gave basically the same story. In substance, they agreed with the version that they had heard Judge Fournet present at the outset: Weiss was the aggressor, approached Long without a word and shot, then was himself gunned down by the bodyguards. The preponderance of testimony was that two shots came close together, then a pause, then a fusillade. None of the witnesses sustained the suspicion that an altercation may have preceded the shooting. The eyewitnesses were all bodyguards or Long partisans.

There remained a number of conflicts and unexplained details.

1. How many bullets had Weiss fired? Dr. Bird had stated that two cartridges had been fired, one of which remained in the gun when it apparently jammed. Roden and Bates both testified—in practically the same language—that they were of the opinion that Weiss had shot only once.

2. BCI McQuiston's refusal to testify—Weiss adherents found it difficult to understand why a State law-enforcement officer, who was among a group defending a Senator from attack, remained mute before an official body investigating the death of the assailant.

3. BCI Coleman's actions—Fournet, Roden and Messina—all on top of the shooting—testified prior to Coleman. None of the three mentioned Coleman's

striking Weiss. It was Coleman himself who volunteered the information toward the close of the hearing. Bodyguard Voitier, who followed Coleman to the stand some minutes later, supported the story, although differing on the sequence of blows, then speculated that Coleman's wild punch had caught Huey on the mouth. Coleman offered no such suggestion in his own testimony and flatly denied striking Long when questioned in 1961.

4. The motive? It was still a mystery to the Weiss family and close friends. They could not accept the theory that Weiss, who took no outward interest in politics, was a martyr, or else shot Long because of a political grievance or an alleged racial slur directed against his father-in-law (of less than two years).

5. Most puzzling of all was Long's bruised mouth. Long's lip had not been cut when he had walked out of the Governor's office at about 9:22 p.m. It was first noticed when Commissioner O'Connor met Long at the bottom of the Capitol stairwell right after the shooting, at approximately 9:23 p.m. Ergo, Huey's mouth was injured sometime between 9:22 and 9:23, somewhere between the Governor's office and the bottom of the stairwell. How? Coleman, though he testified that he had struck Weiss, said that he had not hit Long. If Coleman had not struck Huey, who had? Attorney General Porterie brought up the possibility that the wounded Huey could have cut his lip by running into a ledge while fleeing downstairs. Weiss adherents said that this theory sounded as improbable as a man emerging from a barroom ruckus explaining his black eye by saying that he had walked into a door. "No satisfactory

explanation of Long's bruised mouth could be furnished," one newsman wrote after the inquest. Many agreed.

As Odom, the elder Weiss, and the bodyguards left the courtroom to go their separate ways after that long, tense day, the final phase of the affair was already building momentum. It would be the longest and, in many ways, the most intriguing episode. Although they did not know it then, each would play a key role in the last chapter of the Kingfish's slaying.

Aftermath (Part One)

Voice. I would draw in a lottery to go out and kill Long. It would take one man, one gun and one bullet.
> —Transcript of DeSoto Hotel Conference, New Orleans, July 22, 1935.

A bitter power-struggle boiled within the Long machine. Huey left half a dozen political leaders. None overshadowed the other. Their only common tie was allegiance to the Kingfish. Could the leaderless Long forces survive the impending January election? Political pundits said, "No." The King was dead. There was no crown prince.

"Politically, Louisiana was in a whirlpool today," Ralph Wheatley, AP bureau chief in New Orleans, wrote. "It has no direction. . . . His (Long's) death gave great courage to his political opponents."

"Louisiana was assured of a complete change in politics," the United Press said. ". . . The whole strange system of political rule that Long devised for Louisiana and presided over was doomed. . . . A bloodless upheaval is certain."

Both AP and UP proved to be dead wrong. The Long machine later patched up its squabbles and rallied behind Richard Leche, little-known State appeals judge and former secretary to Governor Allen. But, at the moment, nobody dreamed that that would happen. A power struggle was on. The Long ship of state was rudderless, falling apart, running scared. Huey's men needed something, anything, to turn the tide.

Huey's death, itself, provided the answer.

George Norris, UP political writer, spelled out the strategy:

"The charge of murder will be laid in the lap of the opposition," Norris wrote. "His (Long's) blood will be on their hands. There will be no mincing of words. In next year's (January's) momentous election, for which a senator, governor and other officials are to be elected, the assassination of Huey Long will be the issue."

Nothing is as politically potent as the issue of martyrdom.

The ball started rolling even before the concrete had hardened over Huey's grave. Earle Christenberry, Long's secretary, called a press conference in the Governor's office on Wednesday night, September 11—less than 16 hours after Huey died. "Nervously"—that's the adjective the *New York Times* used—Christenberry told a tale that appeared on front pages of morning editions the next day.

He claimed that Dr. Weiss had been at a meeting in a New Orleans hotel of anti-Longs that had plotted Huey's death. The conspirators had drawn straws. Dr. Weiss had picked the short one, then had carried out the terrible role that fate had chosen for him.

Huey's death, charged Christenberry, lay in the laps of the anti-Longs.

Few stories appearing as follow-ups to the Long slaying achieved as much publicity as this one. Governor Allen himself even took up the torch in print by publishing a three-part, "as told to" article espousing the "murder plot" theory. It ran in a pulp detective magazine.

Beyond the borders of Louisiana the stories puzzled millions unfamiliar with Louisiana politics. Within the State the charges came as no surprise even to the most illiterate. And therein lies an intriguing tale.

Three utterly fantastic events in the last year of

Huey's life had set the stage for Christenberry's statements. The three together were almost without paral-
lel in American history. Louisianians refer to them as
(1) The Battle of the Airport, (2) The Songy Affair,
and (3) Huey's "One Man, One Gun, One Bullet"
speech.

Long forces claimed that these episodes clearly fore-
shadowed the Kingfish's slaying. Whether this is true
or not, they go to the core of the death-plot accusation;
and no story of Huey and Dr. Weiss could be understood or called complete without them.

✧   ✧   ✧

It started with a tiff between Long and Standard
Oil—a political power feud that seemed far removed
from violent death. In December 1934, Huey called a
special session to renew his personal war against
Standard, the Oc-TOE-pus. Long's Legislature imposed
a five-cent-a-barrel tax on crude oil. Standard struck
back by announcing that 1,000 men would have to be
fired at the Baton Rouge plant.

The actions triggered a series of rapid-fire events
that neither Huey nor Standard was prepared for.

Embittered workers, facing dismissal in the midst of
depression, held a mass rally protesting the tax. Out
of that protest emerged the Square Deal Association, a
workingmen's group pledged "to rid the state of ob-
noxious dictatorial laws." The Dealers quickly took on
a martial air. They drilled, wore blue shirts. There was
vague talk of violence.

Things quieted down. Then, a month later, in January of 1935, a rumor spread that Huey's men had kid-

naped one of the Square Dealers—a man named Sidney
Songy. Word went around town like wild-fire. Huey, it
was whispered, was trying to get Songy to reveal the
names of the Dealer leaders. Then the Kingfish would
seize them and try them on charges of conspiring
against Long. Shouldering shotguns, some 300 opponents of Long gathered at the Baton Rouge courthouse and ran the State employees out. The group held
the building several hours. But they had no leader-
ship. Nobody knew what to do next. A few speeches
were made. A minister prayed. The men finally broke
up after being told that the kidnaped Dealer had been
released.

Huey's feud with Standard had spawned a forceful
group within his own state. The Kingfish was ready to
take force into account. His method was simplicity itself. He called out the militia, his personal army. Governor Allen declared martial law that night. National
Guardsmen appeared in the city's downtown area,
tacking up signs forbidding the carrying of arms and
their sale.

The next morning some 100 armed citizens showed
up at the Baton Rouge airport. Huey's army—Guardsmen and Highway Patrol—rushed out to disperse
them. Louisianians named the comic-opera fiasco that
followed "The Battle of the Airport." The civilians
stood their ground, barricading themselves behind
their cars. The horde of militia advanced slowly, their
rifles leveled, ordering the citizens to surrender. About
half of them did. Others ran for their cars or to the
woods. The Guard opened up with tear gas. A shot-

gun went off, apparently accidentally, wounding one civilian. The uprising was quelled.

But Long was far from through. That afternoon he called a hearing to probe charges that the Dealers had planned to assassinate him. His star witness was none other than Sidney Songy. The man the Dealers thought had been kidnaped was actually a Long plant in their own organization.

An extremely *ex parte* hearing was held before District Judge J. D. (Red) Womack, a Long appointee, in a Capitol room guarded by BCI agents.

Songy testified that he had attended meetings where plans of a scheme to kill Huey had been discussed. Under questioning by Long, Songy "confessed" that he had been the lookout man. His part had been to learn when Huey was to leave Baton Rouge for New Orleans, then to notify the plotters so that an ambush could be arranged.

"The plan was to block your car at Dead Man's Curve 18 miles out of Baton Rouge and then 50 to 75 men were to be there to assassinate you in your car," Songy testified.

Songy said that, while the planning had been going on, he had made daily reports to bodyguard Messina, who had relayed them to his boss.

Long roared that he intended to prove that four sheriffs, one district attorney, probably one judge, and a large corporation—Standard Oil—had all participated in the plot. The probe achieved nationwide publicity. But, amazingly, after airing the charges, Huey suddenly dropped the whole thing. Holding the law in the palm of his hand, Long brought no criminal proceedings against any of the alleged plotters.

In Washington, Representative J. Y. Sanders, Jr., Democrat, Louisiana, said that Huey really didn't want to bring the alleged instigators of the plot to trial. Long only wanted the political effect of charging "assassination."

Sanders said that the alleged plot conveniently served to advertise Huey to the country. It let the nation know what a power Long was in Louisiana and how "the interests" wanted him out of the way.

"Some 2,000 years ago, Nero used to uncover plots against his person as the excuse to rid himself of Romans who were too popular with the people or who had money and jobs that he wanted," Sanders told the House. "Human nature changes little."

It was later learned that Songy was a former prohibition informer who had lost his value to Government officials because his information could no longer be trusted. Assistant U.S. Attorney Fair Hardin said that Songy had blackmailed bootleggers in St. Landry Parish for two years. Songy, said Hardin, had posed as a Federal officer and clubbed bribes out of bootleggers by threatening to expose them. At the same time, he had given Federal authorities tips—thus retaining his standing with both groups. Songy's dubious background never reached the public across the country, nor did his subsequent career, which was equally interesting. Soon after testifying about the assassination plot, Songy got a State job in the office of the Superintendent of Public Accounts. He didn't hold it long. Within two years, the Federal Government indicted him for bootlegging and for impersonating a Federal officer. He was convicted and sentenced twice. While he was in jail, former associates who shared a cell with him beat him to within an inch of his life. They accused him of being a "stool pigeon."

If Long's opponents thought that the Songy hearing would close the book on assassination episodes, they were mistaken. The most sensational of all charges exploded just a few months later on the floor of the U.S. Senate. On August 9, 1935, Huey rose and unleashed a blistering, if rambling, tirade against the Roosevelt administration. In the midst of it, he disclosed that a pro-Roosevelt faction had met in the DeSoto Hotel in New Orleans to plot his murder. Before skeptical and somewhat inattentive colleagues, Long claimed that members of Congress from Louisiana—coming up for re-election against the Long ticket—were among the plotters. A dictaphone had been planted in the meeting room, and Herbert Christenberry, an attorney and brother of Long's personal secretary, and B. W. Cason, secretary of the Louisiana Senate (later convicted on two counts of perjury on another matter during the "Louisiana Scandals"), had overheard the scheme and certified a transcript of the record.

"Here is what happened among the Congressmen representing Roosevelt 'The Little' himself, representing Franklin Delano Roosevelt, the first, the last, the littlest," said Huey, waving the transcript.

"Conference. July 22, 1925. Room 506. DeSoto Hotel. Beginning at 10:10 a.m. . . .

"I want Senators to get this. . . . I have got two very fine citizens of Louisiana whose words will be accepted by 999 men out of a thousand, and I think a thousand out of a thousand, who were present and listened to this dictagraph.

> " 'Voice. I would draw in a lottery to go out and kill Long. It would take one man, one gun and one bullet.
> " 'Voice. Single handed?
> " 'Voice. Yes; that's the only way to do it. I once told his brother-in-law I would do it if he interfered with my law practice—

"They were never able to identify who this was—

> " 'Voice. Long is potentially beaten right now. Sixty percent of the people want him in the Gulf of Mexico weighted with chains. The trouble is getting the various elements together. . . .
> " 'Voice. I haven't the slightest doubt that Roosevelt would pardon anyone who killed Long.'

(Laughter.)

"And this gets even funnier. I want Senators to hear the succeeding line. This gets even funnier. I read the language after midnight when I was alone in my room, and got a little bit more shaky, but it is funny in daylight. I will read that line again:

> " 'Voice. I haven't the slightest doubt but that Roosevelt would pardon anyone who killed Long.
> " 'Voice. But how could it be done?
> " 'Voice. The best way would be to just hang around Washington and kill him right in the Senate.' "

(Laughter.)

"This is a great meeting of the higher element that is sent from Washington, D.C., with assurance that they had a right to indict anybody they wanted to, to hire anybody they wanted to, to fire anybody they wanted to, with all the money they needed. It is a great meeting they held for the President of the United States down in New Orleans.

"I will read that last line:

" 'Voice. The best way would be to just hang around Washington and kill him right in the Senate.'

"Now here is where I get a lease on life. Here is something to show Senators where something comes in and gives me a break:

" 'Voice. I once thought that would be necessary, but I don't think it is now.'

"So it seems like temporarily I got a respite on the matter."

Now, the night after Huey's death, Earle Christenberry attempted to link Dr. Weiss to the "murder" conference—even though Weiss's name did not appear in the transcript Huey read. Christenberry explained the omission this way:

There were a number of unfamiliar names in the report, Christenberry said, one of which was a "Dr. Wise." Huey decided not to use the names of people he did not know.

"Earle, in a matter as grave as this, we can't do anybody an injustice," Christenberry quoted Long as saying. "So whenever there is any doubt about the identity of a person, scratch out the name and I'll leave it out in my speech."

Thus, the unfamiliar name "Dr. Wise" was eliminated before Huey's Senate speech, Christenberry said.

"It is my firm conviction," Christenberry told reporters, "that Dr. Wise and Dr. Carl Austin Weiss, Jr. (sic) were one and the same man. . . . It is my opinion that at a later date, in another secret meeting, Dr. Weiss drew the short straw. . . . He was the one chosen to kill Huey Long."

Dr. Weiss's family and close friends categorically denied Christenberry's charge. They said that more than a dozen persons could attest to the fact that Dr. Weiss was with his family or treating patients through every hour of July 21 and 22—dates of the anti-Long DeSoto caucus.

Relatives said that Dr. Weiss, his wife and baby spent Sunday, July 21, at Judge Pavy's home in Opelousas —more than 150 miles from New Orleans. Judge Pavy said that they had arrived at about 11 a.m. and stayed until about 4 p.m. Kenneth Boagnia, an Opelousas attorney, and Helen Garland, daughter of the St. Landry Paris District Attorney, said that they had visited the Pavys that day, and confirmed Dr. Weiss's presence during those hours.

Statements of patients and records in Dr. Weiss's office showed that he had spent a full day treating persons on Monday, July 22. One of his patients was Charlotte Davis, Long's niece.

W. C. Perrault, Opelousas attorney and prominent anti-Long, said that he had attended the New Orleans conference on July 22 and "Dr. Weiss positively was not there."

In rebuttal, the Long forces produced a notarized statement by D. F. Robicheaux, a DeSoto bellboy, to the effect that he had seen a man "who very much resembled a picture of Dr. Weiss" at the political gathering. Robicheaux was unable to state the day or month of the meeting. Nor was he able to attest to hearing Dr. Weiss's name mentioned.

(In 1941, Herbert Christenberry, one of the two men claiming to have monitored the conference, told a U.S. Senate Judiciary Committee, "My report of these statements was absolutely correct." The Committee had convened in Washington to consider confirmation of Christenberry's nomination as U.S. Attorney at New Orleans. Sam Ballard, President of the Louisiana Association for Clean Government, and James J. Morrison, the Association's attorney, had cited the DeSoto report as one basis for disqualifying Christenberry. O. John Rogge, former assistant U.S. Attorney General, who prosecuted the Louisiana Scandals in 1939–40, had said that he could not recommend Christenberry. Rogge said that Christenberry's loyalty to a political faction [the Long machine] exceeded his loyalty to the Department of Justice. Nevertheless, Christenberry got Senate approval for the District Attorney's post and later became a Federal judge at New Orleans, a post that he held into the 1960s.)

In the cold light of over a half-century, it seems improbable that any real plot to assassinate Long came

[1] Both Christenberrys declined interviews with the author.

out of the DeSoto meeting. The conference was a political caucus called, first, to reach accord on a ticket to oppose Huey in the January primary, and, second, to try to bring Federal money into Louisiana. (There is evidence that Roosevelt gave assurances that he would back the group with Federal patronage and campaign funds.) Among the several hundred Democrats were five Louisiana Congressmen (Numa Montet, Third District; John N. Sandlin, Fourth District; Riley J. Wilson, Fifth District; Jared Y. Sanders, Jr., Sixth District; and Cleveland Dear, Eighth District), two former governors, five sheriffs, and District Attorney Odom.

Odom had this to say about the meeting:

"I heard not one word that would in any way indicate a plot was afoot to murder Long. It is possible, however—and persons who are familiar with the situation will realize that there is no particular significance to the words—that someone in there may have said that 'the only way to get rid of Long is to kill him.' The remark has been made on every street corner in Louisiana since the late Senator came into his full power. And it is grossly unfair to attach particular significance to it simply because it may have been voiced at this particular anti-Long meeting."

The caucus had occupied an entire floor. There had been no attempt to conceal either the purpose or the nature of the proceedings. Groups had met not in any single but in several rooms. The meetings had run for two days and two nights. There had been a steady flux of delegates and no guards posted. Anyone who had wanted to learn what was going on had had only to hang around and listen.

Every man that had been there denied the concoction of a murder plot or the presence of Weiss. Some tried to get a State or a Federal investigation of Long's charges. Uncle Sam said that it was none of his business. The State said that it couldn't be bothered.

The paucity of evidence didn't prevent the Long machine, spearheaded by gubernatorial candidate Leche, from using Huey's slaying to the utmost in the political campaign. It branded the opposition the "Party of Murder," the "Assassination Party." Representative Cleveland Dear, Democrat, Louisiana, Leche's opponent, was a blood-stained conspirator. Huey's voice returned from the grave on phonograph records played at hundreds of stump gatherings. Rural crowds saw his likeness looking down at them from platforms. The platforms were painted bright red to symbolize the blood of the martyred Kingfish. Long candidates called Dr. Weiss a tool of the Dear anti-Long faction whose leader, they charged, was now trying to profit by the killing he had master-minded.

For months the elder Dr. Weiss said nothing while his son's name was dragged through the bitter campaign. On January 9, 1936, he broke his silence. He told newsmen that he had written to Governor Allen, asking him to take his son's name out of the campaign. Governor Allen had made no reply. So now Dr. Weiss was making his appeal public. Perhaps he could shame

Allen into silence. In the letter to Allen, the elder Weiss had affirmed his belief in Carl's innocence. He had suggested that Huey's killers were his own bodyguards. "In the name of common decency and the humane feelings of his (Carl's) family," Dr. Weiss had implored the Governor to respect the dead and stop exploiting the tragedy for political advantage. The appeal had been fruitless.

Here follows the text of Dr. Weiss's letter:

"Gov. O. K. Allen
State Capitol
Baton Rouge, La.
Dear Sir:

"You and your political associates are daily making charges in your political speeches that my deceased son was associated or connected with a sinister plot to kill Huey P. Long.

"Through insinuations and innuendo, you and your political associates have tried to convey to the public that my deceased son was a party to a plot or conspiracy held in the DeSoto Hotel at the city of New Orleans which resulted in his selection to kill Huey Long.

"You know there exists conclusive evidence that my son attended no meeting in the city of New Orleans; that he never attended political meetings or conferences, but that his whole time was devoted to his profession and his family.

"These are serious charges.

"You know as well as every honest thinking man and woman knows, that these charges are without any foundation of fact, and are but political lies and propaganda, uttered for political purposes and to add suffering to the family and friends of the dead.

"You well know that you and your political associates are deliberately falsifying when you make such statements.

"You know and the public knows that you with the aid of your bureau of criminal identification have made every effort to connect my deceased son with a plot or conspiracy and to show that Long was killed as a result of a plot or conspiracy.

"You no doubt well know, and all fair-minded persons believe, as indicated by the facts so far as they have been permitted to be disclosed, that Huey Long was shot as a result of a personal difficulty, and that in all probability, he was not shot by my own (sic) son but by one of his own bodyguards.

"There is no doubt of the fact, however, that my son was ruthlessly assassinated by hirelings of the bureau of criminal identification after being overpowered and disarmed by them.

"I wish to suggest, sir, that as governor of this state, if you have any evidence to support your charges, that it is your duty to present those facts to a grand jury for investigation and punishment of the guilty.

"Your failure to do this is convincing proof that you and those associated with you are deliberately and willfully slandering the dead for political gain, a dastardly thing of which no honorable or decent man or woman should care to be guilty.

"In the name of common decency and the humane feelings of his family, I demand that you and those associated with you discontinue such public slander of the dead.

"I shall expect a reply from you at an early date as to your intentions.

> "Respectfully,
> Carl Adam Weiss"

Allen made no reply. But newsmen, dogging his footsteps on the campaign trail, confronted him with the letter. Allen said that he would pay no attention to it and make no references to it in his speeches.

"Everybody knows Huey Long was assassinated," Allen said. "Every newspaper in the country published pictures of Huey Long with the assassin by his side. Everybody knows that the assassination was the result of a plot. Any attempt to obscure the facts is purely for political effect."

"Every father and mother wants to shield their children, even to the gallows," Allen added later. "That is natural. Further than that, I have nothing to say."

Despite Dr. Weiss's appeal, the slaying stayed very much in the news. It was on everybody's lips in Louisiana. Spectators popped up at political gatherings to shout questions.

On January 10, at a rally in rural southeastern Louisiana, white-bearded Thomas Buller, an 88-year-old Elton man, leaned forward from his front-row seat. In a voice ringing with indignation that could be heard outside, he cried:

"If you have got such good witnesses and such good evidence that they plotted the death of Senator Long, why don't you prosecute them?"

Shirley Wimberly, pro-Long New Orleans attorney, paused on the platform. The eyes of the crowd shifted from Buller to Wimberly. Silence hung over the audience.

"I am going to tell you why we don't prosecute them," said Wimberly. "I'm going to tell you that right now. You are entitled to an answer and I am going to give it to you. If we were going to prosecute them while this campaign is in progress, every damn newspaper in the State would say we were persecuting them. After the election, we are going to prosecute them. We are going to prosecute them like hell. You wait and see."

Those who took stock in Wimberly's words are still waiting.

On January 15, Dear, the standard-bearer of the "Home Rule" ticket, said that he had been informed that one of Huey's bodyguards was now stating that he had slain his best friend. The story was going around the State at the time.

"Instead of poisoning the minds of the unthinking and scattering the teeth of hate throughout the State," Dear said in a radio speech, "why doesn't the machine tell the truth and tell the people that one of the chief bodyguards who was present and participating in this unfortunate affair (Long's slaying) is now in an asylum for the insane? And I am informed that he constantly cries, 'I killed my best friend.' "

Four nights later, Governor Allen called on each of the six bodyguards to come forward and "prove what a damnable lie Cleveland Dear uttered."

Thousands attended the New Orleans rally beneath the covered shed of the Bienville Street wharf on the Mississippi River. Joe Messina advanced from beneath a picture of Huey framed with red and white lights to lead off the parade of bodyguards.

"Ladies and gentlemen. This is Joe Messina talking. What Dear said is the blackest lie a coward ever utter—" Here Messina's voice was lost in the roar of applause. "I'll lick him the best day he ever saw and meet him anywheres."

Louis Heard said that Dear's statement was "a no-good lie, the biggest lie ever uttered. If Cleveland Dear were to tell me that face to face, I'd punch him in the nose so fast he wouldn't know what happened."

Voitier, Roden and McQuiston all branded Dear's statement "false."

"My testimony on trial has never been impeached," Coleman said. "Senator Long was shot in cold blood by an assassin named Dr. Carl Weiss. One man had a foreign gun and one bullet killed Senator Long. We couldn't have shot him because we used .45's and .38's and a man don't walk far with those bullets in him."

Immediately after the bodyguards' speeches, Leche leaped to his feet, took the microphone and said, "No matter what the newspapers say about these men, they are true friends and excellent peace officers. And during the next four years when I am elected, none of them will ever be without a job."

Leche, who referred to himself as "232 pounds of Huey P. Long candidate," challenged Dear to "shoot it out with him with .44 caliber pistols." Failure to return Leche and the Long machine to office, he told the electorate, would "not only be a reflection on Huey's memory but an act of ingratitude."

Huey's faithful were not ungrateful. Leche won by more than a 2–1 margin, rolling up an unprecedented 67 percent of the vote. He polled a record 363,000 votes to 176,000 for Dear. Virtually the entire machine ticket swept in on his coattails.

The election campaign marked the zenith, the highpoint of interest in Huey's death. As soon as the ballots were counted, the fervor to get to the bottom of the slaying suddenly faded.

The final effort came on May 31, 1936. The Louisiana House adopted without dissent a proposal by Representative Ben R. Simpson for a six-member commission to investigate the Long slaying. Simpson, a pro-Long lawmaker from Caddo Parish in northwest Louisiana, proposed that the commission have authority to summon witnesses at hearings, punish for contempt, and render a transcript report to the State Attorney General. The resolution carried a $100,000 appropriation. The official journal of the House records that on the following day the slaying probe resolution was withdrawn from the House files on Simpson's motion.

It eventually came out that Governor Leche, who had made a campaign promise to investigate the slaying, had had the bill killed. His reason, Leche later said, had been that the primary responsibility for investigation rested with the widow, Mrs. Rose Long, who was serving the final year of Huey's unexpired term in the U.S. Senate. Leche also said that, since both Long and Weiss were dead, he didn't feel that it would help either Huey or the State to go into a long-drawn-out investigation "that probably would have wound up as an inquisition." In an interview at his New Orleans home in 1961, nearly two decades after he had served 5 years of a 10-year Federal sentence handed down during the "scandals," Leche conceded that a third reason "may possibly have been" the fact that the State administration had been wooing FDR for Federal funds. (Some Long quarters had even accused Roosevelt of having a part in masterminding the shooting; and dragging in FDR's name, however far-fetched it may have been, would have crippled the peace-making appeal to Washington.)

Aftermath (Part Two)

"I still have an idea that the true facts surrounding this tragedy, which rocked the nation, have not been brought out. I probably know more about the facts than any other person, except those who know the *actual facts,* and I am not now prepared to say whether Huey Long was killed by Dr. Weiss or by one of his bodyguards."

—John Fred Odom, former District Attorney of East Baton Rouge Parish

Though official interest in the slaying was allowed to die, it continued unofficially through the years. Like all famous crimes in which the pieces don't fit together, the Long shooting drew its share of armchair sleuths. Their theories covered the spectrum.

One of the most unorthodox was advanced by Dr. J. D. Moreno, a psychiatrist internationally known for his "Sociometry" (a new method of tracing the effects of emotions in communities.) Long's killing, said Dr. Moreno, was not due to the actions of a single individual. Rather, it stemmed from a network of emotions in society. Long's slayer was a "sensitive agent" caught in an onrushing tide.

A few days after the shooting, Dr. Moreno analyzed Long's death like this:

Certain crimes, like political crimes, are not individual acts. Before they happen, they travel like a current through the minds of a thousand individuals "sensitized" for the particular form of crime. The "sensitized" spread the seed through the community's psychological network. It travels like a psychological infection. The crime is committed many times in fantasy and in many forms before it actually occurs.

In Louisiana, said Moreno, we have to visualize a state of mind of individuals in emotional turmoil. These emotions separate groups according to their partisanship for or against the dictator. From these groups, every possible emotion—jealousy, fear, hatred, anger, sympathy—travels through the psychological network. They affect the more sensitive individuals more, the less sensitive ones less, and some not at all.

It is from the Huey Long "sensitive agents" that the actor may one day arise. He is caught by an anti-Long current. He is more a symbol than an individual at the time.

Moreno concerned himself with the question, "Why?" As the years passed, interest shifted from the motive to the crime itself. One by one, reporters and columnists began to question the public story of the slaying.

The now-defunct magazine *Ken,* edited by Arnold Gingrich, later of *Esquire* fame, came out with the flat statement that Weiss was not Huey's killer. In a May 19, 1938, article entitled, "Who Killed Huey Long," *Ken* said that when Weiss stepped from behind a pillar he probably intended to kill Huey. But the doctor, an amateur facing trained gunmen, was cut down before firing a shot. At the same time, none of Long's bodyguards had to move his gun more than a few inches to have hit Huey. Persistent whispers had it, said *Ken,* that "someone in the excited group surrounding Long either thought very quickly—or didn't think at all, but simply moved in a reflex action, thought of for many years."

"Dr. Weiss didn't kill him," *Ken* said, "but in the young doctor's almost unmarked grave in Baton Rouge lies much of the reason for the power of Long's successors. Although they invoke Long's name as Communists invoke Lenin's and Catholics invoke Christ's, it is a cynical evocation, and their power would undoubtedly die the day it could be proved to the voters in the naive backwood parishes of Louisiana that Long was not hit by a .32 caliber bullet, such as those carried in the gun Dr. Weiss waved, but by a .45, such as those carried and fired by his bodyguards."

A June 26, 1939, issue of *Life* reviewed the shooting and asked, "Why have neither friends nor foes of Huey Long seemed anxious to clear up the mystery once and for all?"

"A fog of mystery still surrounds Huey Long's death," blared Walter Winchell.

Allan A. Michie and Frank Rhylick put forth this query in their book *Dixie Demagogues:*

How, within six minutes of the shooting, they asked, 18 minutes before anybody in Baton Rouge knew who the assassin was, did a Washington newspaperman know his full name? Michie and Rhylick attributed this allegation to Colonel Robert Brothers. Brothers was a hanger-on of the Long machine and one of Huey's devoted in Washington. The colonel, who styled himself "the personification of retributive justice and the avowed Nemesis in the Long case," charged that Washington had had advance information of the shooting. Weiss, killed at 9:26 p.m.,[1] was not identified by the Coroner until 9:49 p.m., Brothers claimed; but at 9:31 p.m. a Washington newspaperman telephoned to Baton Rouge for confirmation of the shooting and was able to give the Louisiana officials the slayer's full name and identity. Brothers did not say how he established the

---

[1] There is disagreement over the precise time of the shooting. The *Times-Picayune* reported it as 9:22 p.m., and that's the time the author has used.

three times, nor did he identify the newsman allegedly placing the mysterious call.

(Some official action apparently stemmed from Brothers' charges. But not much. On September 30, 1935, pro-Long Judge Womack of Baton Rouge ordered the Southern Bell Telephone and Telegraph Company to permit the State BCI to investigate the records of long-distance calls from Baton Rouge on the night of the shooting. BCI chief Louis Guerre, when asked what he expected to show, told newsmen:

"Plenty."

He declined to elaborate. Nothing ever came of the probe.)

Westbrook Pegler, who regularly blasted the Long machine and the easy corruption in Louisiana politics, rejected the conclusion that Weiss had assassinated Long.

Pegler interviewed Weiss's widow and visited Louisiana many times. In his "Fair Enough" columns of July 19 and 24, 1941, Pegler maintained that the bodyguards' testimony should be disqualified because they were interested parties. Their statements were self-serving. There was no other version they could tell without incriminating themselves.

". . . The words of Long's bodyguards obviously must be discounted," Pegler wrote, "for if Weiss did not shoot Long, then the assumption becomes very inviting that he was killed by a wild shot meant for a citizen who had merely punched him in the mouth. Deliberate treachery is also possible."

Pegler was doubtful that Weiss had fired his gun. Any one of Long's bodyguards could have fired Weiss's

pistol later, after removing it from his clothing or dis-
covering it in his car.

"The truth probably never will be known," Pegler
said.

Perhaps the most intriguing of all post-mortem pieces
came from Drew Pearson. Pearson met former District
Attorney Odom in Washington during World War II.
Odom, at that time, was chairman of the Louisiana
Democratic State Committee. They got to talking about
the case, and Pearson said that his column had recently
mentioned that Odom had not seen that an autopsy
was completed on Long. The autopsy couldn't have
determined the caliber of bullet that had killed Huey,
Odom replied, since the slug had passed through
Long's body. Odom added that he felt that the
true facts surrounding the shooting had still not been
brought out.

Even nine years after the slaying, Odom said he still
was not prepared to say that Dr. Weiss was Huey's
killer.

Odom prepared a statement setting down his theory,
and it appeared in Pearson's syndicated "Washington
Merry-Go-Round" column on November 21, 1944.
Pearson predicted that Odom's report might one day
prove to be an "historic document." Time hasn't fulfilled that forecast. But the column remains a remark-
able statement, in light of the fact that its views are
those of the most informed official connected with the
case who was not aligned with Huey in any way. It
follows herewith nearly in its entirely:

> "It was developed by unimpeachable testimony that
> only one bullet entered Long's body, and it entered from

the front and made its exit through the back. An autopsy could have thrown no light on the caliber of the bullet which entered his body, since it was not in the body, and the bullet could not be secured or identified. I think the statement will be borne out by any ballistics expert that the caliber of a bullet cannot be determined by the bullet hole alone.

"The spot where the encounter occurred was sequestered and guarded by the then 'State Police,' locally known as 'Cossacks.' They secured all the bullets that were found at the scene, and refused to surrender them. It was positively established that the dozens of bullet holes in the body of Dr. Weiss were made from bullets by pistols in the hands of Long's bodyguards. I have never heard that fact disputed.

"All the witnesses to the actual shooting were either members of Long's bodyguard, or were his active partisans. Their testimony followed the same identical pattern— that is, that Dr. Weiss was the aggressor, attacked Long, and fired the first shot.

"I then decided not to use all of the available witnesses, for the reason that if the facts developed were not true, it would be easier to have some of the witnesses who did not testify, testify to the true facts at a later date, if the facts were different.

"My experience has always been that if a witness swears to one state of facts, he will never, or seldom, change his statement.

"I saw that the only chance to get at the real facts, if they were different from those testified to, was by personal interviews. I conducted my investigation on my own until my term of office expired. I might add that my investigations, both at the inquest and subsequently, were done in close cooperation with the family of Dr. Weiss, and they heartily approved of the manner in which the case was handled.

"I still have an idea that the true facts surrounding this

tragedy, which rocked the nation, have not been brought out. I probably know more about the facts than any other person, except those who know the *actual facts,* and I am not now prepared to say whether Huey Long was killed by Dr. Weiss or by one of his bodyguards.

"Long was a very quick and active man on his feet, and I can visualize his frantic efforts to get away from the weapon of Dr. Weiss when he might have run into the fire of one of his guards.

"I am convinced, however, that even if Dr. Weiss killed Huey Long, it was not an assassination, or a murder. I base this conclusion on the fact that Dr. Weiss led a normal life the entire day preceding the night of the shooting. . . .

"Twenty minutes after his departure from home, he was dead in the Capitol building where he had never set his foot before.

"Why he went there will always remain a mystery. The theory of some members of his family is that he dropped by to see Mrs. Weiss's uncle, who was a member of the legislature.

"The weapon carried by Dr. Weiss was of small caliber, and looked more like a toy than a dangerous weapon. Had Dr. Weiss intended to kill Huey Long, he must have known that his body would have been riddled by the swarm of bodyguards who always accompanied Long.

"It was generally understood that Long wore a steel jacket—whether true or not, I do not know, but everyone in Baton Rouge believed it. Surely, if this man was bent on killing Long, he would have armed himself with a weapon which he felt could accomplish his purpose.

"Again, Long's lip was split, and he stated to the surgeon, 'That's where he hit me.' This indicates something of a scuffle before the shooting began.

"It occurs to me that had Dr. Weiss been bent on mischief, he would have reconnoitered the scene previously and laid his plans accordingly.

"But above and beyond all these reasons, the one im-
pelling reason why I believe that the facts were not developed is that there was a desperate effort on the part
of Long's friends to prevent the holding of the inquest.
I therefore concluded that Long's friends must have
thought that I was in possession of facts bearing on the
case, which I did not have, and they were determined
that they should not be brought out. . . ."

In Louisiana, C. P. Liter of the Baton Rouge *Morning Advocate* wrote an article on the tenth anniversary
of the slaying. Liter, who covered the shooting, said
reporters were skeptical of the version that had been
made public.

"Newsmen, at first, accepted the story of the assassination," Liter, later the paper's general manager, said,
"but before Long died . . . they were raising their
eyebrows in doubt. And the events of the next few days
led some to express belief that Dr. Weiss did not shoot
Long, but that Long received a shot intended for
Weiss."

Why did the powers refuse to let Huey's bodyguards
testify at an inquest for nearly a week? Why did State
officials never mention an abrasion on Long's lip? If
Weiss killed Long, Liter asked, what was the motive?

Margaret Dixon, of the same paper, one of Louisiana's veteran political writers, called attention to
Huey's cut lip in a fifteenth-anniversary story. She
developed her article around the theory that Weiss,
insulted by the Kingfish, may have struck Huey. This
is a version that many of Weiss's intimates believe.
According to this theory, a bullet fired by one of the

bodyguards may have struck the fast-moving Huey as he darted into the path of fire.

"They (Weiss's friends) say that, as Weiss hit Long, a bodyguard fired at the doctor," Mrs. Dixon wrote. "They believe Huey, turning away, stepped into the path of the bullet and was shot in the abdomen. Then, they hold, Dr. Weiss pulled out his pistol, a small one of German (sic) make, fired one shot which struck Roden in the thumb. Only one shot was fired from Weiss's pistol. The second one jammed."

Not all newsmen shared Liter's and Mrs. Dixon's view. A number who were present in the Capitol on the night of the shooting, including the AP's Ed Desobry and Quincy Ewing and the UP's J. Alan Coogan, believed that Weiss shot Long because of the alleged Pavy insult.

Most of Long's biographers raised questions about the slaying. Harnett Kane, for one, was unwilling to say without qualification that Weiss shot Long. Many in the State shared his skepticism.

In *Louisiana Hayride,* Kane said that one-third of Louisiana think that Long's panicky guards may have killed the Kingfish in the scuffle.

"Some believe that if, at a future date, the proper persons may be persuaded to speak," Kane said, "a sensation may result. This much can be said now: No evidence has yet been offered to connect Carl Austin Weiss with a plot of any kind; and there has been no disclosure of the full circumstances leading up to the moment when the young doctor stepped from behind the pillar, nor of the immediate events that followed."

Thomas O. Harris's biography, *The Kingfish,* is even more bold in its skepticism. "Today," Harris wrote in 1938, "the tragedy of September 8, 1935, is shrouded in seemingly impenetrable mystery. But, some day the truth will be revealed; and when it is, it is our thought that it will prove startling to those who now believe they know the facts."

In *Huey Long: A Candid Biography,* Forrest Davis made the flat statement that Weiss shot Long. But in the next paragraph he cast doubt on his own conclusion by conceding that Weiss had "only a casual, inconsiderable family grudge against the dictator."

Carleton Beals, author of *The Story of Huey P. Long,* said that Weiss "pressed a gun into the Senator's side and fired a bullet." But Beals was puzzled by the motive, which, he judged, was revenge for Long's gerrymander action against Judge Pavy. "Whether this or deeper motives were involved," Beals wrote, "may never be cleared up."

Allan P. Sindler called attention to the stifled probe of the slaying in his scholarly *Huey Long's Louisiana.* "While no supporting evidence was offered," said Sindler, a political-science professor at Duke University who did research in Louisiana for his book, "the subsequent behavior of Long's lieutenants indicated that the unproven plot version was preferred to whatever might be uncovered by thorough investigation into the assassination."

In *The Longs of Louisiana* Stan Opotowsky said that politics determined many people's opinions of the slaying.

"If you were for Long, then Dr. Weiss was the gunman in an organized plot," said Opotowsky, a native of New Orleans and later a *New York Post* reporter. "If you were against Long, then you could pass on the whispers that—despite the dozens of eyewitnesses and their remarkably consistent stories—Dr. Weiss didn't kill Long at all; some of the bodyguards did the deed by hysteria in one version, by design in another."

There were two strange bits of irony connected with the published writings on Huey's career. First, a surprisingly large number of people learned the details of Huey's life and death not from one of these biographies but from fiction or the cinema. Robert Penn Warren's widely-read Pulitzer-Prize-winning novel *All The King's Men,* published in 1946 and later made into an Oscar-winning movie, idealized Huey. The romantic-philosophic work also transformed the facts of his slaying into an entirely different set of circumstances—which, as a novel, it had every right to do. But—and this is the second ironic point—many outside Louisiana, who were not of Long's generation, came to accept the novel's story as the real version of the shooting.

In Warren's book, Adam Stanton (Carl Weiss) assassinates Willie Stark (Huey) in the Capitol after he learns that Stark has seduced Stanton's sister. Stark also attempts to blackmail a Judge Irwin (Judge Pavy) when Stark's aide uncovers a shady corner of the judge's life. Judge Irwin will not be blackmailed, and commits suicide. Warren, a professor of English at Louisiana State University in Baton Rouge when Huey was killed, claims that he did not write about Long. But his hero's career so closely parallels Long's life that it is hard to see how Willie Stark could be anyone else. (Three other novels built around the Long story were *A Lion Is in the Streets,* by Adria Locke Langley; *Number One,* by John Dos Passos, and *Sun in Capricorn,* by Hamilton Basso. "The facts of Huey Long's life," wrote Basso, "have been gradually transmuted, book by book, into the stuff that legends are made of.")

What do public records show?

Strangely, there are virtually none available. State Police Major Billy Joe Booth, supervisor of the Louisiana Bureau of Criminal Identification and Investigation in Baton Rouge, said that State Police files do not contain any record of the slaying, since, although Huey's BCI existed in 1935, the State Police had not yet come into existence. It was not until 1936 that the Legislature created the State Police (in place of the Highway Patrol) and made the BCI one of its divisions.

The assumption is that the file was not turned over then. Or, if it was, it became lost in the interim. The only records of the case in the East Baton Rouge Parish court, where the Weiss inquest was held, are the single-sentence death verdicts of the coroner's juries. The court has no transcript of the Weiss inquest in its files. Nor do the offices of the Parish District Attorney, Coroner or Sheriff.

Neither is there a Federal record of the slaying. Although Long was a U.S. Senator shot in a public building, J. Edgar Hoover, Director of the Federal Bureau of Investigation, said that the FBI "conducted no investigation of the matter . . . inasmuch as it did not constitute a violation of Federal law within the jurisdiction of this bureau."

What became of the gun that police identified as Weiss's automatic?

On November 24, 1936, District Attorney Odom wrote BCI chief Guerre, asking him to give back Weiss's gun so that it could be returned to the court's custody. Odom, defeated in the 1936 election, was leaving office. "I am sorry to advise you," Guerre replied, "that we wish to make further ballistic investigation of the .32 caliber Belgian Browning pistol, no. 319446, and it will be necessary for us to retain it for that purpose." That was more than a year after the shooting. Asked in 1961 what he had done with the gun, General Guerre said that it had remained behind at State Police Headquarters after he left. At State Police Headquarters, police officials said that they had no record of the weapon.

More than twenty-five years after the shooting, these questions remained unanswered:

1. What was the opinion of Huey's successor, Senator Russell Long, about the mysterious events of his father's shooting?

2. After a quarter-century and free from the emotion of the day, would Justice Fournet and Huey's bodyguards—in the twilight of their lives—tell the same story of the slaying?

3. Finally, what was the feeling of the Weiss family —silent through all the years—about what had happened in the Capitol?

I interviewed Senator Russell Long at his Baton Rouge home in October 1961. In his mid-forties, Russell is a dead ringer for his father. Elected in 1948, and in office continually since then, he rode his father's memory to the Senate but dismounted when he got there. He has none of Huey's bombast or maverick tendencies. Instead, Russell has shown a willingness to work within the Democratic harness, leaning to what people in Louisiana consider the liberal line but to what the rest of the country considers a more moderate position. "I was regarded as a wild liberal in Louisiana," Russell said, "but here (in Washington) I am barely over the line."

We sat in his massive den, and I asked him who he believed shot his father. Twice the Senator replied by launching into an extended appraisal of the political accomplishments of the Kingfish—"the greatest man I have ever known."

"The difference between Huey Long and me is this: When I campaign for election, say, in Vernon Parish, I have to hit all the outlying towns before I wind up in Leesville, the Parish seat. When Daddy campaigned, his people would put up handbills all over the Parish saying that Huey Long was speaking at Leesville. A few hours before Daddy was to speak, from all over the Parish they'd start comin' on horseback, in buggies, walkin'. Thousands of people from every town in Vernon Parish. And they'd listen to him for hours. And when he went away, you'd better be for Huey Long or you had a fight on your hands.

"If you read the daily papers those days," said Senator Long, "you'd think he was a pretty bad character. This fellow was uprooting a lot of old advantage and tradition that a powerful oligarchy had held on to for a hundred years. They didn't like it. When Daddy was

murdered, I felt a crying need for a man of that ideal-
ism to take his place. . . ."

"Senator, let me ask you point-blank," I asked. "Do
you believe Carl Weiss shot your father?"

"Yes," he replied.

"Those stories about the bodyguards were meant
to cast doubt on our candidates," Long said, "to get the
people to regard them as the murderers. . . . They
(the anti-Longs) got this murder wrapped around them
all over the State. The American Progress (Huey's
newspaper) has it all, including the 'One Man, One
Gun, One Bullet' speech. It was the Long ticket against
the 'Assassination Ticket.' They (anti-Longs) were
trying to get some way of getting some votes. You can't
win by assassinating a man and asking the people to
vote for you. That's what that suggestion was that the
bodyguards killed him (Huey)."

Russell was 16 and in New Orleans when his father
was shot. After the slaying, he campaigned for the
Leche ticket. To this day, Russell has kept on friendly
terms with many of his father's close associates. In the
summer of 1962 he endorsed Louisiana Chief Justice
John Fournet for re-election, recalling that it was Fournet who "struck at the assassin's pistol and deflected
it from its chosen mark. . . ."

I asked Senator Long if he would mind if I interviewed some of the surviving physicians who assisted
in the operation on his father and if I went over the
hospital records of the case. He said that he had no
objections. As we shook hands at his door near a sitting
room where a large oil painting of his father hung, he
said that he would be in touch with the doctors to give

his permission. To my knowledge, the Senator never did. Nor did he ever reply to any further correspondence from me.

Twenty-five years after the slaying, I traced the key surviving eyewitnesses to the shooting.

Justice John Baptiste Fournet had been elevated to Chief Justice of the State Supreme Court in 1949, a post assigned on the basis of seniority. At the time of the interview that I am about to describe, Fournet was finishing out a remarkably enduring career in State politics. After a modest start as a high-school teacher and principal, he had become a lawyer and joined the Long machine as the State Representative from south Louisiana's Jefferson Davis Parish. His unswerving loyalty had impressed Long, and Huey had made him one of his legislative chiefs. That had launched Fournet's career. In his lifetime, he has been one of the few men in the country to reach the pinnacle of all three branches of State government. He was House Speaker (1928–32); Lieutenant Governor (1932–35), and, for a short time, acting Governor; and Supreme Court Justice (1935–present).[1] In 1960, Fournet, 65, was a bald,

[1] In 1962, after 28 years on the high court, Fournet ran for re-election for his third 14-year term—the first State Supreme Court Justice to face opposition for re-election in 30 years. The race, Fournet said, would be a test "of the people's confidence in me." A political unknown, City Judge James Nelson Lee, 38, of Bunkie, showed surprising strength. He trailed Fournet by only 1,500 votes in the first primary. A third candidate drew enough votes to prevent Fournet from getting a clear majority, forcing a runoff between Fournet and Lee. Though he was now 67, Fournet got out and stumped in the terrific summer heat. Taking no chances, he called on some of the State's biggest political names to campaign for him, including Senator Russell Long, who rushed in from Washington. In the September 1 runoff, Fournet got 44,817 votes to Lee's 42,109. Fournet, in his victory statement, hailed the "wonderful vote of confidence." His victory margin was 2,709 votes of 86,926 cast.

tall, formidable figure, beginning to bow with age. He walked with a cane—the result of an operation to correct a ruptured disc which he traced to the movement after the shooting. ("I was about to grab Weiss when I twisted a muscle or got a crick. I couldn't move.")

Fournet was, at first, reluctant to talk about the shooting because of some gratuitous remarks that A. J. Liebling had tossed in about him in a *New Yorker* article on Earl Long and Louisiana politics. (Liebling had called attention to Fournet's silk summer suit, a diamond the size of a "colossal ripe olive" on his left hand, and a triangle of flat diamonds "as big as a trowel" in his tie. Said Liebling: All these gave Fournet what might be considered in another state the appearance of "a highly successful book-maker.") But Fournet finally consented to the interview. Sitting behind his desk in his office in the State Supreme Court in New Orleans, he recounted the story about the same way as he had presented it at the inquest. At one point, he got down on the floor to illustrate Weiss's position. He told his story with a quiet, easy manner that broke only once during the one-hour interview. That was when I asked how Huey got a cut lip.

"It wasn't a cut," Fournet snapped. "It was a fever blister."

At State Police Headquarters in Baton Rouge, Murphy Roden, who had become Public Safety Director (head of State Police and firemen) gave the same answer as Fournet. "The mark on Long's lip was a fever blister," Roden said. Roden, addressed as "Colonel Roden" (an honorary Louisiana title), went on to tell the story of the shooting that appears in Chapter Six.

Though only 57, the former bodyguard was beginning to be punished by age, too. He complained of a sore shoulder troubled by bursitis. A year after the shooting Roden had been made Assistant Superintendent of State Police. After serving in the Navy in World War II, he had resumed police work and become State Police Chief under Governor Earl Long, Huey's brother, in 1948. Roden had stepped out of public life from 1951–60 to become director of plant protection at an ordnance plant in Shreveport, Louisiana. He had returned to Baton Rouge briefly when ballad-singing Governor Jimmie Davis made him Public Safety Director in 1960. Roden had resigned in 1962, citing reasons of health.

After the shooting, BCI agent Elliot Coleman had gone back to his Tensas Parish home in the hardwood delta along the Mississippi. He had run for election as Parish Sheriff in 1936. He had won and been re-elected for 24 years. When Coleman retired at 79 (after one of his deputies had defeated him), he was the oldest sheriff in Louisiana. He had worn a badge since 1898, when, as a 17-year-old deputy, he had got a bullet in his leg after he had ridden out on horseback to bring in a Negro charged with murder. Coleman still carries the slug. What happened to the man who shot him?

"He was killed," Coleman said. He did not elaborate.

I interviewed Coleman on March 28, 1961, in his plantation home outside the little town of Waterproof in northeast Louisiana. He and his wife are both descendents of ante-bellum Louisiana families. Coleman was now nearly deaf and living with an oxygen tank in his remotely situated home because he has a heart condition. After spinning some colorful tales of the prohibition era, when he regularly cracked down on bootleggers, he slipped into an account of Huey's slaying.

Coleman said that BCI chief Guerre had telephoned him on the fatal weekend, asking Coleman to come to Baton Rouge while the Legislature was meeting. Guerre was uneasy about things, Coleman said.

"When the session ended Sunday, I was standing outside the House railing with Jimmy Noe," Coleman recalled. "Noe wanted me to talk to Huey and ask him to back Noe for Governor. Huey left the House after talking to Mason Spencer, and I turned around and started to walk to the back corridor.

"All of a sudden, a man walked past Huey, pulled out a gun and pulled the trigger.

"Roden jumped on the feller to hold him. Then, Huey grabbed his stomach and said, 'I'm shot,' and bumped against me. Roden grabbed Weiss's gun. There were several shots fired. And then there was pandemonium. People were running everywhere and suddenly a crowd gathered in the corridor. Louis Heard came up with a submachine gun. And someone yelled, 'Clear the hall, clear that hall. Shoot up and down that hall.' I grabbed that gun. I saw right away it was a one-man job."

Some months later, I saw a report of the inquest, and read that bodyguard Voitier had testified that he thought that Coleman had struck Huey, causing the "cut lip." I wrote Coleman, asking if he did strike Weiss in the face and then swung again and hit Huey with a wild punch.

"I hit Weiss on the jaw, not in the face," Coleman

replied, "and he staggered back against the marble column. He still held on to the pistol in an effort to shoot Roden. There was one shot fired and Weiss dropped to the floor. No one hit Long in the face that I know of. I certainly did not. Had it not been for the fact that Weiss's automatic gun jammed he would probably have fired more shots."

George McQuiston, who lives near Shreveport, and Paul Voitier, a supermarket employee in New Orleans, both declined to discuss the shooting. McQuiston was the bodyguard who refused to testify at the Weiss inquest.

Voitier did answer one question. He said that he did not believe that Huey had made the "nigger blood" remark about Judge Pavy. Voitier, one of the "inner" bodyguards who accompanied Long on trips to Washington, said that he had been with Huey all day on the day he was shot.

Bodyguards Louis Heard, Jos Messina, and Joe Bates are dead.

C. E. Frampton, the New Orleans *Item-Tribune* reporter who stumbled onto the shooting scene as he left the Governor's office, later became manager of the Cabildo museum (site of the Louisiana Purchase) in New Orleans' French Quarter. Going over the scene, Frampton recalled that when he opened the door he saw Weiss walk a couple of paces toward Huey and fire. Frampton went on to give an account of the shooting similar to his inquest testimony—but with the addition of a description of Weiss shooting Long. I reminded Frampton that his inquest testimony indicated that he had been inside the Governor's office and hadn't seen the first shot fired. Which account did he want to go by? I asked Frampton. His memory had been freshest then, Frampton said. He would go by what he had said in 1935.

Frampton went on to say that he had always believed that Weiss had assassinated Long. It had been said, Frampton related, that some of Huey's foes had played on Weiss's feelings. They had told Weiss of the tar-brush insult. A thing like that, said Frampton, is calculated to produce murder.

"Psychologically, the line between sanity and insanity is very narrow," Frampton continued. "I think it preyed on his mind and he became imbued with one idea—imagined or otherwise—to avenge that insult."

Could a fight in the hall have precipitated the shooting?

"No," Frampton said. "If Weiss had asked Huey about Pavy, then Long would have never said, 'I wonder why he shot me?'"

How did members of the Weiss family fare through the years?

After the excitement died down, they faded quickly from the limelight and slipped back into their normal routine of living. So far as national publicity was concerned, they were forgotten. In 1961, when the author approached the family for its side of the shooting, Thomas Edward Weiss, Carl's younger brother, said that it was the first time a writer had contacted him in the quarter-century that had gone by.

Yvonne Weiss, Carl's widow, had gone East and faded into anonymity. She had got her master's degree in French, eventually re-married, worked as a librarian. She had had no more children. She visits her family in Opelousas each year, keeping her ties with her native Louisiana. Her memories of Carl Weiss are still vivid. She likes to talk about him—though not about the shooting.

"He (Carl) was very quiet, very calm, and nobody could rush him or hurry him. And I remember Daddy (the elder Weiss) coming for him for operations, and he'd (Carl) sit down, and I'd say, 'Oh come on, Carl, hurry. Your father's waiting.' He'd say, 'Oh, Dad's so impatient.' And he'd always take his time. He was very calm, very deliberate, not excitable at all. He had a great sense of humor, quiet, and I never saw Carl angry in my life."

Carl's son went to medical school at Columbia University. He did his residency at St. Vincent's Hospital in New York City and trained to be an orthopedist at Bellevue Hospital, where his father had been a resident. After an Air Force tour to fulfill his military obligation, he opened a practice in Garden City, one of Long Island's wealthiest communities. Carl Jr., who is married and has three children, learned about the circumstances of his father's death when, as a boy, he read about the slaying in an old issue of *Life* magazine. "My mother glazed over the story," he said, "saying he was accidentally killed in a shooting. But she never gave any details."

Carl's father never got over the loss of his eldest son. For years, he had looked forward to turning over his practice to Carl. He continued on alone. Inwardly, he was a man broken in spirit. Outwardly, he tried to appear the same, but he was not always successful. Mer-

chants said that you could still set your watch by Dr.
Weiss in the morning. But his military bearing began
to slump. And he didn't always see you when he passed.
Nurses said that his hand began to shake during surgery. He stopped operating after a while. He never
gave up trying to vindicate Carl's name. He sought
to have a private detective organization probe the
slaying. It refused. There was too much politics mixed
in, it said. Scores of letters came to him from all over
the country. They purported to have inside information on the shooting. Most of them were crank letters.
Dr. Weiss ran down every one. All led to dead ends.

He kept on. He wrote to every publication which,
without qualification, branded Carl as Huey's assassin.

"On page 1133 of your Oct. 5, 1935 copy . . . you
have printed the notice of my son's death," Dr. Weiss
wrote to the *Journal of the American Medical Association.* "Would that you had not printed the notice of
his death at all, since you so unnecessarily used the
word 'assassin'. . . . You know but one side of this
gruesome affair. . . ."

To *The Reader's Digest,* Dr. Weiss wrote on September 25, 1939:

"Annually, on the anniversary of his (Carl's) death,
obituary notices are printed in the daily papers of
Louisiana proclaiming him a martyr. There have been
at various times, movements started to erect a public
monument to his memory which we have promptly
discouraged. The church which he and his wife attended the very morning of that fatal day was crowded
to overflowing with kneeling communicants, friends
and patients with heads bowed with sorrow and not

with a morbid crowd actuated by curiosity. Equally large was the gathering at his grave who stood around in a pelting rain until long after the last burial rites were pronounced. You, unfortunately, term my son, Dr. C. Austin Weiss, an assassin. You must admit an assassin would hardly be shown such respect and homage. . . . You are constantly striving to bring sunshine and happiness into the lives of the blind. Be a bit more magnanimous and extend that virtue into lives of the seeing who must bear the burden of unjust persecution."

Kenneth W. Payne, *The Reader's Digest* managing editor, replied that the magazine's motive was to call attention to the fact that the public accounts of Long's death do not represent the whole truth. "Perhaps the article will serve a real purpose in forcing an investigation," Payne said. It didn't.

Dr. Weiss believed his son innocent until his dying day, in 1947. He was 71.

Carl's mother, still alive in 1962, and Olga Weiss, his sister, share the elder Weiss's belief in Carl's innocence. The family have never referred to the tragedy as an "assassination." They use the word "shooting" or "slaying." "Assassination," they say, presupposes Carl's guilt.

What then is the Weiss family theory today of what happened in the Capitol the night of the slaying? I asked Dr. Thomas E. Weiss that question. Here, in his own words, is his full answer. It appears in print for the first time:

Q. — Do you recall your father's theory, or what is your theory as to what actually happened that night?

Dr. Weiss: "Well, it was our impression that Carl

was headed for the hospital to turn in his instruments
to be sterilized for surgery scheduled the next morning.
We felt this was his reason for leaving his home. What
caused him to stop, what caused him to go, or to be
brought or led into the Capitol, we don't know. To
gain information he was not beyond talking to anyone,
or trying to talk to anyone. It seems a little odd that he
should stop on the way to the hospital to try to talk to
someone like Long. Along those lines we wondered if
word had reached him of Long's supposed insult to
the family. I personally feel that if it had, he was man
enough to approach Long and ask him if such were
so.

"First, it must be appreciated that my family was
suddenly swept into a confused and frustrating period.
We learned of Carl's death from a radio report, a newspaper reporter and a remark from a stranger. It was
unrealistic for our family to suddenly become involved
in this shooting. Because of the family sorrow, the
accusations and threats of bodily harm, and because
we were isolated from satisfactory information, we had
no idea what transpired after Carl left home that night.
Of course, my father was the strongest force trying to
learn as much as possible about the shooting. He felt,
because all the primary witnesses in the shooting were
either in the hire of the State Department, or deeply
indebted to it, and because some of these men had used
physical force on others who stood in their way, he
could not accept their version of the shooting as the
whole story.

"Dad's doubt of the published version of the affair
grew stronger as time passed. The behavior of the bodyguards in repeatedly shooting a body on the floor, the

failure of a bodyguard to testify at the inquest, the statement by Long himself that he was hit in the mouth, the lack of a complete investigation, the feeling of numerous fair-minded citizens of Baton Rouge that Carl was innocent, and the utterly false stand by the State Administration that Carl attended the DeSoto Hotel plot gave support to Dad's theory that Carl did not walk up to Long to shoot him. He felt some unobserved or unreported events preceded the shooting, during which Long was struck in the mouth and the bodyguards fired innumerable times, during a matter of seconds, in close quarters, and this was when Long was shot.

"Now people have asked, and you mentioned in an earlier question, how Carl may have heard Long cast aspersions on the Pavy family. I've thought about this many times and I've wondered how he could have found out. I'm not sure just who would have said this to him, and I don't think things like that were being put in writing. I don't think anybody—we're not aware of anyone—could have been listening in the gallery or on the floor of the Legislature that night and heard this and then rushed over and told Carl that this is what Long said. Now, maybe someone did hear him say that, thought that Carl ought to know this, and waited for Carl to come out of his home and told him; and Carl went to the Capitol, with that in mind, to verify it. We know of no one who contacted him. The only time he was away from Yvonne was (1) when he went out to feed the dog, and (2) when he left to go to the hospital; otherwise, he was with Yvonne the whole time. It's conceivable that someone said that Long had insulted his family and Carl thought—'This won't be. I'll just go up and give him a punch in the mouth.' Now, this he would be capable of. This he would be man enough to do. I recall once Father Gassler, our old German pastor, who used to be adverse to people standing up in the rear of the church. He would stand on the altar, or in the pulpit, and see someone standing in the back and say, in a blaring voice, 'You, get a seat.' Apparently one day Father Gassler did just that when Carl was in church and, after, Carl got up and ran back to the rectory and told Father Gassler off. They were great friends, but you don't usually call the Pastor down.

"So, if I had to give a theory, one is that somebody got to him and maybe passed this insult on to him; however, I would think he would really have passed it over because he would have considered the source. But maybe he didn't, and Carl approached Long, wanting to talk to him but, in the rush in the corridor, where there was pushing of strangers about, unrecorded but heated words followed, and then Carl quickly struck Long in the mouth; shooting followed and Long was wounded. I also think there's a good possibility that after Carl was killed, a gun was found in his car and removed.

"During our earlier investigation, Dad interviewed a student nurse, Jewel O'Neal, who attended Long after he was admitted to Our Lady of the Lake Hospital. She overheard Long explain the cut on his lip, stating, 'That's where he hit me.' From all reports, no one else in the group definitely did strike Long in the face. I can't understand how Carl could have thrown a blow and then fired a gun. Both would have probably been with the right hand and, with the numerous bodyguards about Long, Carl would have not had a chance to do more than strike Long with his fist. Also, Long would probably have attempted to get away from the scuffle and not hesitated to remain a further target. I have also felt that there was no need for bodyguards to fire unduly at a body on the floor—unless some mistake had been made.

"Knowing Carl's moral makeup, respect for life, love of his family, the events of the day, his disinterest in petty local politics, and the facts we accept for truth, I am convinced he didn't, with purpose or malice, walk into the Capitol corridor to shoot Long."

Conclusion

"U.S. Senator Huey P. Long died on September 10, 1935, in the 42nd year of his life from the effects of a bullet wound inflicted at this place on September 8, 1935."

    —Plaque outside the Governor's office, Louisiana State Capitol

When this book was first published in 1963, you could trigger lively discussions in any part of Louisiana by raising the question, "Who shot Huey Long?"

For those who accepted the story that Long's bodyguards and State machine officials told, there was only one answer: It was Dr. Weiss. Testimony of a dozen eyewitnesses established this beyond reproach, they said. It was a crime of compulsion, madness, or design.

But others asked if the bodyguards could be accepted as objective witnesses.

Weren't they themselves deeply involved in the shooting? If Weiss did not shoot Huey, if Huey were hit in the general gunplay, wouldn't the bodyguards have an obvious motive for confusing the facts? The same holds true for Long officials on the scene. If Weiss did not shoot Huey and they testified to that, wouldn't they (a) have, in effect, indicted Huey's own bodyguards and (b) have stripped the Kingfish of his martyr's mantle four months before a primary in which every State official's post was on the block?

Similarly, if, seconds before the firing, Huey and Weiss had been in a fight in which a racial insult had been hurled, wouldn't that incident, brandished in headlines, have tarnished the shining halo of martyrdom?

Eight days and four postponements passed before the bodyguards appeared at the inquest. It is known that a meeting had taken place in Attorney General Porterie's office, and Porterie himself appeared at the inquest to protect the interests of Long machine officials.

This much is undisputed. The science of ballistics was not used to determine Long's killer. The slug that hit Huey passed entirely through his body. History records Dr. Weiss as Long's assassin on the words of men who, by so stating, vindicated themselves.

But, for the moment, let's look beyond the controversial version of the slaying. If Weiss assassinated Long, there has to be a motive.

There are three possibilities:

(1) Weiss picked the short straw in a death conference.

(2) Weiss acted out of personal interest to avenge a racial slur against Judge Pavy, his father-in-law, and, hence, indirectly, against his own wife and son.

(3) Weiss, sorely distressed at the state of affairs in Louisiana and Huey's ever-widening dictatorship, was finally stirred to violent action by the Pavy gerrymander bill.

Let's look at each more closely

The Death Conference. The inadequacy of this version has been discussed in Chapter Ten. The DeSoto conference was a political caucus to choose a ticket to oppose Long. If words were uttered about Huey's death, according to all indications they were spoken wishfully by frustrated foes. The evidence points to the fact that efforts to link Weiss to this meeting were politically motivated. They came to naught. But that wasn't established until the election was over. Meanwhile, the Long machine had a key campaign issue.

If Long leaders seriously believed that Weiss had taken part in a murder plot, they would have moved heaven and earth to bring the conspirators to trial. They had all the weapons. Long officials possessed the names of all the DeSoto participants. Pro-Long judges sat in virtually every parish in the State. Yet, there was no attempt at prosecution. Not a single man was brought to trial before or after the Leche election. Finally, if Weiss had really been chosen as an assassin, it seems logical that he would have been armed for such a dangerous mission with a better weapon than a small-caliber souvenir European pistol several years old.

The Racial Slur. If this remark had ever been made, it had never reached the ears of the Pavy family (for whom it would have been intended), the Weisses, and such Long "insiders" as Senator Allen Ellender, Seymour Weiss, Richard Leche, Chief Justice John Fournet, Louis F. Guerre, James O'Connor, and bodyguards Roden, Voitier and Coleman. The author interviewed all these persons. All gave similar answers.

Judge Pavy's son, attorney A. Veazie Pavy, said in a 1961 interview in his Opelousas law office, that he did not believe that the remark had ever been made.

Q. — Was there ever a racial slur to your knowledge made against Judge Pavy by Long?

A. — I have no knowledge of that. I had seen at the time an editorial from some newspaper . . . to the effect that such a slur had been made. But I have no knowledge of that, and I don't believe that ever took place.

The Weiss family also doubted that the slur had been

uttered. Mrs. Weiss said that the story first came out after the shooting. "It was a trumped-up thing just to give an excuse to Carl," she said.

None of the Long insiders questioned could say that he had personally *heard* Huey make the remark or that he believed that the "nigger blood" story was true.

Still, some people insist that Long originated the insult in the Capitol on the very day of the shooting. It is a fact—and Senator Russell Long himself corroborated this when I interviewed him—that Huey sometimes called political opponents "kinky" or "shinola." Assuming that the Pavys and the Weisses are wrong, assuming Long's intimates are wrong or just won't say, and Huey did make the remark, could the insult have gotten to Dr. Weiss without reaching his wife? She had been with him virtually his entire last day. For argument's sake, let's assume that the remark was passed and that somehow it got to Weiss and not his wife. Could a man of Weiss's intelligence, sophistication, and demeanor be stirred to cold-blooded murder on the strength of a *rumored* remark—a remark which he, himself, had not even heard? Weiss had a temper. Conceding that a report of the slur moved him to confront Long, would Weiss have shot Long without even asking Huey if the Pavy insult had actually been uttered? Suppose the rumor, if it existed then, had been false —like so many stories being told around Louisiana then. Could Weiss have taken Long's life, and sacrificed his own in the process, without even bothering to confirm that Long had actually made the charge? The hasty intemperateness of the action is inconsistent with everything in the careful, deliberate, studious young doctor's habits and life history.

The Pavy Bill. There is no doubt that the gerrymander maneuver had troubled Weiss. Since he was a political outsider—unschooled in the give-and-take of hip-shooting politics—the ouster bill might have bothered him even more than its intended victim. Judge Pavy was said to have joked about it. It is hard to believe that this bill, by itself, could have brought Weiss to commit murder.

But perhaps there is a fourth motive. Perhaps the combination of all these factors—Weiss's dislike for Long, the alleged racial slur, the gerrymander—had all festered inside him. As ex-newsman Frampton theorized, perhaps, beneath his calm exterior these thoughts had haunted him, unbalanced him, and imbued him with one idea—vengeance—his mind had driven him to the suicidal act. If this had happened, it is certain that Carl Weiss had reached the moment of truth when he weighed life against death, when he asked himself what life meant, what he was sacrificing.

This is what the balance sheet shows:

He was a young doctor who had spent over five years of his adult life—five years beyond medical school—in preparation for a career as an ear, nose and throat specialist. He had had the opportunity for more advanced training than perhaps any other Louisiana doctor in those days. He was highly regarded, skilled in the operating room. His father, a former president of the State medical association, was turning over a flourishing practice to him. And he seemed certain to surpass the elder Weiss's accomplishments. He was a man who had never taken any outward interest in politics, not even enough to attend a single precinct meeting. He was on the very threshold of life, happily married, normal, devoutly religious, blessed with a newborn son. He was 29.

Would the slaying of a politician whom he considered a petty tyrant have been worth casting away his life and career?

The day before the shooting, Weiss had bought new furniture for his home, including a large china closet, a dining room table and chairs. It was to be delivered the next week. His mother said that he had ordered a costly gas-heating floor unit installed in his home. He had said that he expected to be there for the next ten years. The very night of the shooting he had telephoned a colleague to confirm the site of an operation scheduled for the next morning.

Medical studies on suicide point out that most potential victims plant clues, consciously or unconsciously, before the ultimate fatal step. According to his family's account of his last days, Carl Weiss left no death clues. There were plenty of life clues. The pattern of his actions points wholly the other way— that when Carl Austin Weiss left his house on the night of September 8, 1935, he had every intention of returning.

Finally, let's explore the other side of the coin. Let's have a look at some of the details that do not fit the assassination pattern and argue against the slaying story as it has been told.

(1) If Weiss shot Long without provocation, why did Huey order that no statements be made, as he went under anesthesia?

(2) The motives attributed to Weiss point to a premeditated shooting; but if the slaying had been premeditated, why had Weiss *driven* to the Capitol? Consider the situation: Weiss lived two blocks from the Statehouse—two-tenths of a mile—a three-minute walk. Hundreds of autos were parked in front, behind, and around the Capitol that night. A Legislative session was underway. Big doings in little Baton Rouge on a Sunday night. There were so many cars that Carl's younger brother hadn't been able to find a space earlier that night after driving around and around the building. Tom Ed Weiss had eventually given up. The chances of Carl's finding a parking space while the session was on were slim. And, living in Baton Rouge most of his life, he certainly knew this. Would Carl, bent on assassination, knowing the deed was suicidal, have taken his car to drive the two blocks? Would he have risked being stuck without a parking place? It seems so logical for him to have simply walked over. Yet, his Buick was found parked *directly* in front of the building. Isn't it possible that he was actually going to Our Lady of the Lake Sanitarium, as his wife believed? And, on the way, as he drove along the Capitol front (a route he would have taken to get to the hospital), he suddenly decided to stop? Perhaps someone backed out of a parking place in front of the Statehouse. And, on impulse, and attracted by the lights and the crowds, Weiss took the vacated place and went inside.

(3) If Weiss came to assassinate Long, why didn't he shoot when Huey passed him the first time—all alone? Long's witnesses said that Huey had walked from the House down the Governor's corridor well ahead of his entourage. Then, he turned into the Governor's anteroom, stayed inside a second or two, and walked out to the center of the corridor to converse with some cronies. Weiss, according to the inquest testimony, stepped from behind a pillar and shot Long in the midst of his bodyguards. Why would Weiss have turned down the golden opportunity presented only a few moments earlier when Huey marched down the hall alone and unprotected?

(4) The mysterious cut on Huey's lip—Jewel O'Neal, the student nurse who reported Huey's saying, "That's where he hit me," stood by her account when questioned in 1961. "I did sign the affidavit at the request of Dr. Carl Weiss's father with the permission of Sister Henrietta, administrator of Our Lady of the Lake at the time," she said. "As I recall, there was no other conversation in my presence as to what happened. Dr. Vidrine may not have been aware of my presence when the question was asked as I was preparing a hypodermic at his back and there was no one else in the room. Huey Long gave no indication as to who 'he' might be." She added: "The cut was on Long's lower lip and I believe it was the right side."

Why didn't any State official mention the cut? In separate interviews, Justice Fournet and Roden each replied it was not a cut—it was actually a fever blister. This does not explain how blood poured forth as Huey reached the Capitol basement and ran into O'Connor.

There are a number of other explanations for that small injury. Dr. William Cook, one of the attending physicians, testified that it was "an abrasion or brush burn." State Attorney General Porterie raised the possibility that the wounded Huey could have bumped his face on a hard surface while going downstairs. (But not a single witness verified this at the inquest.) Bodyguard Paul Voitier said that Elliot Coleman may have clipped Huey while going after Weiss—despite the fact that witnesses said that Huey bolted from the scene right after he was wounded. Coleman said that he struck Weiss but never touched Huey. The one explanation that the pro-Long theories do not espouse is that Weiss hit Huey. Nurse O'Neal quoted Huey as saying, "That's where *he* hit me." Long did not know Weiss's name. He could only refer to Weiss as "he." But Huey knew his bodyguards. If a bodyguard had struck Long, Huey could have named him. Moreover, if Weiss and Huey brawled, there would have been precedent. Huey's brash, steamroller tactics sparked many fights. Only the night before Long had had a run-in on the House floor with old T. O. Harris of Shreveport. One of Long's bodyguards slapped him, Harris charged. Years back, Huey had been punched in the face at a party at Sands Point, L.I. Earl Long, Huey's own brother, often remarked about the Kingfish's fear of being struck. It was to prevent a repetition of the Sands Point incident that Huey surrounded himself with armed guards.

(5) If Weiss had silently walked up to Long and shot

him, wouldn't that have brought Huey's police swarming to his and his family's home as soon as Weiss's body
was identified? Some Long officials were tracing the
slaying to a death conference. Yet, the Weiss and Pavy
families said that they were never questioned or even
notified of Weiss's death by State law-enforcement
authorities. On the other hand, if Weiss and Huey
were involved in an argument that led to the shooting,
then the reason for the slaying would have been self-
evident and there would have been no need for questioning his family.

My own theories are:

(1) Weiss's background and actions of the day on the
slaying do not support the widely accepted story that
he was a *premeditated* murderer.

(2) The evidence indicates that Weiss did not go to
the Capitol with the intention of shooting Long—
though he may have gone inside with the idea of
buttonholing Huey.

(3) Long's witnesses did not make a consistent, and
therefore satisfactory, accounting for Huey's cut lip.

(4) Finally, there is at least as much reason to believe
that Weiss and Long engaged in an altercation that
precipitated the shooting as there is to believe that
Weiss murdered Huey in cold blood without a word
and without provocation.

In 1963, I went to Baton Rouge to visit the graves of
Huey and of Dr. Weiss. It's an 80-mile arrow-straight
drive from New Orleans. You go up U.S. Highway 10
along still bayous and flat, lush swampland. Here and

there industrial sites rise among old-time sugar plantations.

In the Capitol, the State of Louisiana has closed off that part of the corridor where the shooting took place. They have made it into a reception room outside the Governor's office. A plaque on the wall approximates the spot of the slaying. It says:

"U.S. Senator Huey P. Long died on September 10, 1935, in the 42nd year of his life from the effects of a bullet wound inflicted at this place on September 8, 1935."

When it was open to the public, the corridor was a "must" for tourists. The Duke and Duchess of Windsor were among hundreds of thousands to see it and look at the scars in the marble. Then as now, no one seems certain which are bullet holes and which are simply defects in the marble.

Outside, Long's tomb stands in the center of the sunken garden in the shadow of the Capitol tower. He is still a kind of demigod in his bailiwick. His birthday is a legal holiday in Louisiana, and his tomb a kind of shrine. If you're there on a Sunday, you'll see rustic pilgrims come with their wives and children. There is a reverential hush. They take off their hats and look up at the Kingfish's 12-foot bronze statue, which Louisiana erected in 1940. A heroic bronze figure of Huey stands on a 20-foot granite base. He faces the Statehouse in a double-breasted jacket pulled tight over his bulging stomach, the garment already faded to the dated vestment of another era. His shoulders are thrown back. He stands among melancholy Southern trees with his hands open, outstretched, pleading the cause of poor men among the magnificence of the plush Capitol and the majestic splendor of the exquisitely manicured garden.

Carved in granite at the base of the statue are the words:

"Here lies Louisiana's great son, Huey Pierce Long, unconquered friend of the poor who dreamed of the day when the wealth of the land would be spread among all the people."

On one side of Huey's monument is a relief of the log cabin in which he, like Lincoln, was born. On another side, Long places free school books in the hands of children. On a third, Huey grasps the hands of laborers in their soiled overalls and crumpled caps. On a fourth is the Kingfish's famous slogan: "Share our wealth—every man a King but no man wears a crown."

When the sun sets, a floodlight from the Capitol's 24th story blazes down on the statue. The light illuminates it all night. Except for a period during an anti-Long administration, the Kingfish has never been in darkness.

Dr. Weiss lies buried in a large cemetery about two miles east of the Capitol. As he was obscure to the general public in life before the shooting, so has he become in death. The caretaker at Roselawn Cemetery had to look up Dr. Weiss's name on a master plan before he could locate the grave. The caretaker had lived through the Long era, but he wasn't able to place the name.

"Weiss, Weiss," he mumbled. "Seems to me I know

a Dr. Weiss in New Orleans. Yessir, a Dr. Thomas Weiss. Treated me for arthritis. He a relative?"

I knew that Thomas Weiss was Carl's brother. But I didn't tell the man, and if he really knew who Carl was he didn't tell me as he escorted me to the grave.

It was a dreary day, a day like the gray one on which Weiss was buried. A fine, misty rain was beginning to put droplets on the plain, granite family headstone. Nearby, there were two markers embedded in the ground. One was for the younger Weiss, the other for his father. It was difficult to believe that a quarter-century had passed since the slaying. In a few years, every man who had been there would be dead.

Overhead, the moss of an old oak swayed in the wind. Leaves dropped to the ground and all but covered the grave marker under which lies all that is mortal of Carl Austin Weiss—his lips sealed in death.

Fifty-Six Years Later

The Exhumation	October 20, 1991
The Scientists' Report	February 21, 1992
The State Police Report	June 5, 1992

"All we are relying on as to what happened is the slippery slope of eye witness testimony."
—Professor James E. Starrs
George Washington University

"They're digging up the wrong body."
—Professor Glen Jeansonne
University of Wisconsin

Burials went on quietly in Roselawn Cemetery for the next three decades, and, for the most part, there were few visitors to the Weiss family plot. That scenario changed radically one fall Sunday in 1991. On October 20 of that year, workmen broke ground over Carl Weiss's grave as the sun's first rays climbed over the horizon.

About three hours later, with television cameras rolling, the laborers raised a rusted galvanized steel vault. A team of scientists and family members walked up to inspect the 900-pound vault. Inside was a partially decayed cypress coffin. It had a crucifix on top bearing the name "Carl Austin Weiss." The scientists would later open the coffin and examine Weiss's remains for evidence they hoped would shed light on the assassination. The exhumation was the idea of Professor James E. Starrs, a forensic expert at George Washington University in Washington, D.C. He had won the confidence of the Weiss family and gotten them to approve the project. The 61-year-old Starrs had gained a national reputation for reexamining old mysteries. Three facts piqued his interest in the Long case: an unlikely assailant, a weak motive, and a lack of scientific evidence. Starrs was surprised to find there had been no autopsies, no ballistics tests, no detailed medical records. Even the physical evidence—the murder weapon, the bullet it fired, and the victim's blood-stained clothes—were missing. So was the investigatory file.

"All we are relying upon as to what happened is the

slippery slope of eye witness testimony," said Starrs. "What we are trying to do is take the scientific evidence and put it against the eye witness testimony. The more it supports it, the more it proves Weiss did it. The more it weakens it, the more it shows there was a different scenario than the one that was portrayed."

Using modern scientific methods, Starrs's studies of skeletal remains had produced new findings—sometimes provable, sometimes not. His reopened investigations included the famous Sacco-Vanzetti case. Now, he brought his deductive talent to Louisiana.

Despite his credentials, some were skeptical of the project. "They're digging up the wrong body," said Glen Jeansonne, a history professor at the University of Wisconsin who wrote a biography of Long. "I don't see how they can conclude whether Weiss shot Long by looking at his (Weiss's) body. . . . They might find something from Long."

Starrs had not overlooked that angle. But the possibility of examining Huey's remains was infinitely more formidable. For one thing, he lay buried beneath tons of concrete. For another, the Long children—Russell, Rose, and Palmer—remained unalterably opposed to an exhumation.

Access to Weiss's remains was less of a problem. The Weisses had nothing to lose. Tom Ed, now in his 70s, continued to hope that evidence would eventually be found to clear the family name. And Carl Weiss's son, now in his 50s, began taking an interest in the case. As it turned out, results of the exhumation would be a disappointment.

But the project would have unexpected fallout. It

would lead to the discovery of evidence missing for 56 years. A key find was Weiss's long-lost gun along with seven .32 caliber bullets—one of which had been fired. Also uncovered was a voluminous state police file that included photographs of what was said to have been the clothes that Long wore on the fateful night. The state police announced they were reopening their investigation—even though the shooting occurred more than five decades earlier and the major suspect was dead.

There was more. Some people, including the funeral director who embalmed Long, began disputing the story that the bullet that killed Huey went through him. Others said the two holes in Long were both entry wounds and neither came from Weiss's gun.

All of a sudden, the Kingfish seemed to be resurrected—if not in body then in spirit. His name blazed again in headlines. The struggle over the newfound evidence became front-page news all over Louisiana. News media in other states found the story fascinating. Major newspapers like the New York *Times* and the Washington *Post* ran extensive special articles. National Public Radio aired a report as did the NBC network television show, "Unsolved Mysteries."

But before taking a closer look at the dramatic events triggered by the exhumation, it is important to put the new data in perspective.

In 1985, the 50th anniversary of the assassination, *Newsday*, the Long Island newspaper where I worked, assigned me to do a story on the shooting. A half-century after the fact, the editors wondered what people in Huey's home state thought really happened? Did they accept the official version?

What I learned surprised me. As I went around the state, I found that the same kind of divided opinion prevailed not only about how Long died but about how he lived.

Many in the Bayou State, particularly working people, farmers and those dependent on welfare, still cherished his memory. "Everybody loved him," said Alcide Verret of St. Martinville, who was shown on Ken Burns's 1985 documentary film *Huey Long*.

A very different attitude existed among the middle-class.

Huey's name still brought up harsh words. Many said his dictatorial reign left a legacy the state has yet to overcome. Those who were alive in Huey's era vividly recall how deeply passions ran and how widespread they were. The first report of the shooting set off panic in scores of homes. "A lot of people immediately thought he (the gunman) was somebody in their family," said Betty Carter of New Orleans. She is the widow of Hodding Carter, then the editor of a staunchly anti-Long newspaper in Hammond.

"When the report came over the radio, I said, 'Oh, my God. Where's Hodding?' I ran downstairs and found him. Then, the phone rang. It was my Mother from New Orleans. I said, 'It's all right. Hodding's here. But hang up, Mother. Now, I have to find Mr. Carter (Hodding's father).'"

As for a consensus about who killed Huey, many Louisianians—both those who lived in the Kingfish's times and those born later—still questioned the official version.

In 1985, after a speech on the assassination I gave to

the public in the House Chamber of the capitol, I asked how many believed Carl Weiss did not shoot Huey Long. The audience of about three hundred sat only steps from the corridor where Long met his doom. About half raised their hands.

"How many believe there is still some doubt?" I asked.

Almost all the hands shot up.

When I asked Gov. Edwin W. Edwards what his feelings were, he said he was not in the capitol that night. In fact, he was only eight years old. Nevertheless, Edwards volunteered an opinion. Like the consummate politican he is—Edwards is the only Louisiana governor to be elected four times—he managed to put himself on both sides of the issue.

Edwards said he felt that Weiss's bullet had killed Long. At the same time, he said he thought it was possible that Weiss just took the gun "as a protection." Weiss may have gotten in an argument with Long, Edwards said, and "just hit him in the face. I would guess if he did that, in those days, the guards would have probably ended up shooting."

Perhaps, the most equivocal position came from the late T. Harry Williams, whose biography of Huey won the Pulitzer Prize in 1970. In his book, Williams dismissed the notion that Weiss did not kill Long, calling it a "myth." Yet, in a 1965 review of this book and another supporting the official version of the slaying, Williams hedged. "On the basis of present knowledge," he wrote, "I would cast my vote for the (official) thesis—but with the qualification that it might have happened another way."

The piece I wrote for *Newsday* ran in its Sunday maga-

zine on August 4, 1985. A few days later, Larry K. Starkey, then the public relations director of the Mutual Life
Insurance Company, called me. He said he had been
rummaging through the company's archives and found
an investigator's report on the slaying. Mutual, now
called MONY Financial Services, held $20,000 worth of
life insurance on Long. The company was obligated to
pay double indemnity—twice the value of the policies—
to Mrs. Long and her children if Huey's death was
caused by "external, violent and accidental means."

In fact, the firm did pay double indemnity. Those
who believe Weiss was innocent cite this fact to bolster
their case. They say the payment means the firm concluded that a wild bullet from the bodyguards had accidentally killed Long. But that is a false notion that has
assumed credibility over the years simply because no
one bothered to check with the insurance company.

Richard E. Mulvey, MONY's chief counsel, said that
the firm considers death by accidental means to include
death by assassination. That was the company's policy in
1935, Mulvey said, and it remains the same today. So,
Mutual Life Insurance would have paid double the
value of the policy no matter who shot Long.

Even so, the records show that H. P. Gallaher, chief of
the company's bureau of investigation, wanted more information on Long's slaying. In October 1936, he asked
one of its investigators, K. B. Ponder, to verify the facts.
Ponder's report, which had gathered dust in the company's archives for almost fifty years, ended with an
unexpected conclusion. "There is no doubt that his
(Long's) death was an accident," Ponder said, "but the
consensus of more informed opinion is that he was killed

by his own bodyguards and not by Weiss." Although the seven-page report, written in November 1936, contains some errors of fact and essentially restates what is known about the slaying, it is of interest because it comes from a source outside the state, someone removed from the strong partisan politics of Louisiana.

The company could not provide background on Ponder because its officials said records were no longer available from the 1930s. But Stephen Beach of Jackson, Miss., an attorney who worked for Mutual at the same time that Ponder did, readily vouched for him. Beach said Ponder was "absolutely tops as an investigator . . . He knew his way around, and he was aggressive. If he signed a report, it would be a first-class investigation in my opinion."

In his report, Ponder said "there is no doubt that Weiss attacked Long, but there is considerable doubt that Weiss ever fired a gun." The evidence, Ponder said, was set up "to represent conditions in the light most favorable to the insured (Long) and to those who expected to profit by the political control the insured had established in the state of Louisiana."

Ponder's report did not expand on this. Nor did it go into detail about another hypothesis it raised—the so-called two-bullet theory. There was "considerable talk," Ponder said, that Long was hit not by one bullet but by two—one entering from the front, the other from the back.

Ed Reed, a Baton Rouge public relations man and author of a 1986 book on the Long shooting called *Requiem for a Kingfish,* became champion of the two-bullet theory. In his book, Reed said the holes in Long were really entry wounds made by different bullets. Dr. Vidrine found one in surgery, Reed said. Another physician who assisted in the operation, Dr. Clarence Lorio, discovered the other at the Rabenhorst Funeral Home.

According to Reed, Lorio came to the mortuary at night after all had left except the undertakers. The doctor undid the sutures and donned a rubber glove. After probing inside Huey's body, he extracted the second bullet. Reed said neither the bullet Vidrine retrieved nor the one Lorio found was a .32 caliber, the type that would have come from Weiss's gun.

The story was potentially dynamite. If it could be proved, it could blow the case wide open. The problem was its source. It was not the two doctors, who were dead, but one of their distant relatives and Merle Welsh, the undertaker.

Reed said L. Coleman Vidrine Jr., the son of a cousin of Dr. Vidrine, told Reed that the surgeon gave his father a .38 caliber bullet that Dr. Vidrine said he removed from Long. Dr. Vidrine supposedly did not disclose finding it because its larger size would have pointed to the bodyguards as Long's killer. The guards said they were armed with .38 and .45 caliber guns. How Vidrine would have known what size weapons they were all carrying so soon after the shooting is not clear. The bullet has since disappeared.

Welsh, who lived above the funeral home with his wife, waited almost 50 years to tell his story. By then, he was in his eighties and his memory less than razor-sharp. Welsh died in September 1991, at the age of 89. When I talked to him in 1985—two years after he was interviewed by Reed—Welsh repeated the main points of his account in a rambling narrative. He said he embalmed both Weiss and Long. But his recollection of names and details often blurred. "My memory goes bad," he said in a weak voice.

At one point, Welsh said Vidrine took out a bullet from Long's abdomen and Lorio from the back wall of the chest. At another point, the funeral director said Lorio extracted the bullet from the front of Long's body.

When this inconsistency was called to his attention, Welsh seemed confused. "Pardon me," he said. "My story was inaccurate. My mind is clearing up a little bit. I've been having some (memory) problems. . . . A bullet (that Lorio found) was somewhere in the neighborhood of the seventh or eighth cervical vertebrae, a tiny entrance-type bullet hole." "Cervical" refers to the neck area. Welsh probably meant to say "lumbar" which refers to the lower back. Nevertheless, Welsh was convinced that what he reported was correct. "I know I saw it done," Welsh said. He recalled that he had to restitch Long when the doctor left. "I know it was removed."

Lt. Don Moreau of the Louisiana State Police, a homicide detective assigned to investigate the Long assassination in 1991, said flatly he did not believe Welsh's story. "If you ever go to an autopsy, you would find bullets do not just lie around in a body cavity. They really have to be looked for. Pathologists will tell you stories about how they have to cut a body wide open trying to find some bullet. I have been to dozens of autopsies searching for bullets in homicide investigations.

"The idea that a doctor later comes in the funeral home, unbuttons Huey's shirt, tears open the stitches, rolls his shirtsleeve up, sticks his hand in Huey's body, and 'pop' comes out with the magic bullet is just not credible. It's nonsense."[1]

[1] Supporting his belief in the two-bullet theory, author Reed said, was the fact that the bullet hole in Long's back was smaller than the entrance wound. Reed said if the bullet entered from the front and exited from the back, logic would dictate that the exit wound would be larger. However, firearm experts say an exit wound is not always bigger. It is not unusual, they say, for a jacketed bullet (like the one Weiss allegedly fired) that does not strike bone to make a clean, smaller hole on exit. Patrick Lane, forensic scientist for the Louisiana State Police, said the jacket around the bullet keeps it from expanding and so "an exit hole may very closely approximate the bullet diameter or appear slightly smaller."

Professor James E. Starrs is a Renaissance man. A lawyer as well as a forensic scientist, he bicycled across the country three times and often pedals the 30-mile round-trip from his home to his classes at George Washington University. He has also edited a book on bicycling.

But scientific sleuthing is his passion. The professor publishes a magazine devoted to the use of forensic science in law enforcement. And he is a member of a small but growing group of historical detectives who use scanning electron microscopes, spectrographs, and other high-tech equipment to try to resolve lingering mysteries.

To some observers, the graveyard detective seems as much a showman as a scientist. An impish man with a snow-white beard and the vibrant voice of a Shakespearean actor, Starrs has appeared on national television and become the subject of scores of articles. His multi-faceted personality makes him a feature writer's delight. He is bright, colorful, irreverent, witty, sometimes arrogant, occasionally flamboyant, often egotistical. He has read the complete stories of Sherlock Holmes four times and seems to take them to heart. Some colleagues say he fashions himself as a latter-day Holmes.

Starrs wants to dig up the skulls of the father and stepmother of Lizzie Borden to see if she really did them in with a hatchet. Also on his list are the remains of Meriwether Lewis of the 1804 Lewis and Clark expedition that blazed a trial to the Pacific Northwest. Five years later, Lewis' gunshot body was found at an inn in Tennessee. It remains a mystery as to whether the legendary explorer was murdered or committed suicide.

The most famous crime that Starrs has investigated is the Sacco-Vanzetti case, the robbery-killing of a paymaster and his guard in Massachusetts. Many thought the two Italian anarchists were executed in 1927 not because they were guilty but because of their radical beliefs. Starrs said the scientific evidence indicated that Sacco's .32 caliber gun fired the fatal bullets. Vanzetti's gun was never found.

Starrs was not the only scientist intrigued with the idea of unearthing historic remains. Exhumations were proliferating. On June 26, 1991, even as Starrs announced plans to look at Weiss's remains, scientists in Kentucky disclosed results of their examination of Zachary Taylor, the nation's 12th president. After all the fuss, the high-tech research showed he probably died from a severe stomach ailment—just as doctors in the 1850s had said.

The Taylor case ignited a brushfire of criticism. The idea of using modern forensic science to re-examine history was exciting. But people began objecting to what appeared to be a stampede to unearth public figures. "They're digging up our people," said Ralph Miller, a member of the Louisiana State Legislature. "First, it was Zachary Taylor. Now, they're talking about Dr. Weiss. Who knows who's next? Maybe your grandfather or mine."

The exhumations, which got widespread publicity whether they were successful or not, were disturbing even within the coterie of graveyard sleuths. "People seem to be jumping on a bandwagon," said Carl Snow, a forensic anthropologist at the University of Oklahoma. "But a lot of solid scholarship and research must first be done to see if there are reasonable grounds to believe that science can straighten things out."

At the University of Minnesota, ethicist Arthur Caplan said forensic sleuths were becoming the "Peeping Toms of Science." He suggested establishing panels of experts to set guidelines. "If we don't want to devalue the past, then we're going to have to restrict the access of those who can rummage through it."

If such guidelines had existed, Starrs might have been asked some hard questions. For starters, how could looking at Weiss's body explain how Long was killed? Starrs was not clear about this. He said examination of Weiss's remains might show the trajectory of the bullets. Comparing their course with the eyewitness accounts might verify or discredit those statements.

Starrs also said scientists would look for traces of a drug or opiate that might have influenced Weiss's actions or a brain tumor that might have unbalanced him. But that notion appeared to come out of thin air. No one—neither the Weiss family, nor the police, nor the Long faction—ever made those charges.

As it turned out, Starrs did not have to defend his project. In September 1991, a few weeks before his team was to break ground for the exhumation, he made a surprising discovery. It was not the smoking gun, but it was as close to it as one could come after 56 years.

The professor located Carl Weiss's pistol as well as a 600-page police investigation report that contained photographs of Huey's bullet-torn clothing. The two long-missing pieces of evidence held the potential of divulging more about the assassination than anything uncovered in all the years that had passed since the shooting.

Starrs said he made his dramatic find because he believes physical evidence is rarely lost. He thinks it is usually out there somewhere waiting to reappear at the right moment. So he acted on a hunch.

"It came from experience in the Sacco-Vanzetti case and others," he said. "Vital physical evidence was often missing. It usually turned up in the family of one of the investigating police officers. In one instance, the officer in charge of the case had passed it on to a son. I suspected the same thing might have happened here. So I made a list of police officers and investigators. Starting with the top man, I tried to find out when they died."

Starrs learned that Gen. Louis P. Guerre, who headed the state police investigation into Long's slaying, died in 1966. Starrs hired a private investigator to look at Guerre's will. Sure enough, there it was. There was no mistaking it. The general listed the gun not only by its distinctive make but also by its serial number.

In his will, Guerre, a retired Army brigadier general, described Weiss's weapon this way: "One 7.65 Calibre Browning Automatic manufactured by 'Fabrique Nationale D'Armes de Guerre, Herstal, Belgium' Serial 319466." He put the value of the gun, a 1910 model, at $25.00. In addition, Guerre listed 14 individual files of investigative documents under the catch-all title of "Miscellaneous papers and documents."

The will removed all doubt about what happened to the gun and the case files. When he resigned from his state post, Guerre took them with him—although he told this writer in 1961 that he had left them behind at state police headquarters. He treated this vital evidence as "booty to lay claim to," Starrs said. Others say Guerre took them because he did not want them to get into the hands of an incoming anti-Long administration. In 1940, Sam Jones, a reform candidate, defeated Huey's brother, Earl, for the governorship.

If there is no precise answer to explain why Guerre kept the evidence, it is clear that Starrs's detective work made them accessible for the first time. Guerre's will showed he left the gun and the documents to his three daughters. Eventually, they ended up with his last surviving child, Mabel Guerre Binnings.

Finding the gun and files turned out to be the easy part. Now Starrs had to get Binnings to release them, or, at the very least, to allow him to examine them. The professor could not have imagined the Byzantine scenario that would follow.

When Starrs sent his investigator to Binnings' home, she was less than cordial. She bombarded him with questions. "What are you doing here? How do you know I have the gun? Who told you I had it?" She would neither admit nor deny she owned the weapon.

Her admission soon became irrelevant. Starrs knew he was on the right track. He learned that Binnings had been trying to sell the gun.

"I found out that through an intermediary she had asked Sen. Russell Long if he wanted to buy it or knew someone who did," Starrs said. "His response was, 'No.' He suggested she give it to Louisiana State University."

Binnings had attempted to sell the gun to others as

well, Starrs said. In 1985, a prospective buyer came to examine it. The visit did not result in a sale. Nor did Starrs learn the asking price. But it was reported that the gun that Jack Ruby used to kill Lee Harvey Oswald sold for $220,000.

When Starrs told Carl Weiss Jr. about the gun, Weiss hired an attorney to try to get the weapon. At the same time, Binnings got her own lawyer. A court struggle began before Orleans Parish Civil District Judge Revius Ortigue Jr. The judge acted immediately to be sure the gun would not disappear again. He ordered the sheriff to hold it in protective custody.

When the sheriff showed up at her house with a court order, Binnings reluctantly led lawmen to a safety deposit box in her bank. There, she turned over the weapon along with six unfired bullets and one spent cartridge. She also gave them her father's file that included photographs purporting to be of Long's clothing. She had kept the file in her home.

As word of the litigation got out, the dispute grew. The state police and the secretary of state joined the suit. The police said they were reopening the case "due to many unanswered questions regarding the shooting." They said they needed the gun for ballistics tests. The secretary of state argued that the weapon had historic value. It belonged in the state archives, he said.

Meanwhile, another tug-of-war began over the case files. The press said the public had a right to see them. The state police said they needed the papers for their investigation.

Louisianians had not seen a court struggle quite like it. Newspapers and television stations reported every turn of events.[2] While the suit dragged on through the summer and fall of 1991, the material remained sequestered in the sheriff's office.

All this delay frustrated Starrs. He was under pressure to report his findings. He planned to present them at the annual meeting of the American Academy of Forensic Sciences. It was to be held in February 1992, less than four months away, and he needed to have his firearms expert examine the gun.

Judge Ortique would not speed up the court proceedings. But in December 1991, he granted a request from the state police to run ballistics tests to see if the expended bullet came from Weiss's gun. He also allowed police investigators to read the Guerre files. In turn, they agreed not to release any findings until they presented them to the judge.

So, in a conference room in the courthouse, a state police team—a lawyer, a forensics specialist, and a homicide investigator—began cataloging and examining the voluminous files. While the slow work proceeded, police firearms experts began ballistics tests at the state crime lab in Baton Rouge. To do this, police loaded Weiss's gun with a .32 caliber round of the same vintage as the spent bullet that Guerre had saved. They fired it and compared the rifling impressions on its surface to those on the preserved bullet.

The science of forensic ballistics is based on the fact that each gun leaves behind its own signature on the

---

[2] The court eventually ruled Mrs. Binnings could not claim legal ownership since her father had taken the gun illegally. In a settlement, all parties to the suit acknowledged Carl Weiss, Jr. as the owner with the understanding he donate it to the state. Before doing so, he had it appraised—it was valued at $265,000—and took a tax write-off. The gun is now displayed in the Old State Capital in Baton Rouge.

bullets it fires. Gun barrels are made with rifling, or spiraling grooves, that impart a spin to each bullet. It is the spin that stabilizes the projectile in flight and gives the bullet its accuracy. Rifling in every gun barrel is slightly different because the machine tools that make the barrel create tiny imperfections. As the bullet passes down the barrel, these imperfections are etched into its surface. Under a microscope, the markings look like hills and valleys (or, as ballistic specialists call them, "lands" and "grooves"). They give each fired bullet its distinctive characteristics.

When the day came to test the spent bullet found with Weiss's gun, ballistics experts put the preserved bullet under a comparison microscope next to one just fired from the gun. Silence fell over the crime lab. The markings failed to match.

Lucien C. Haag, a ballistics specialist from Arizona who was at the lab as an observer for the Starrs team, remembers the moment. "As a firearms expert, I would have put big bucks on the test showing the bullet came from Weiss's gun. You could have heard the proverbial pin hit the floor." Haag looked at Lt. Don Moreau, the state police homicide detective. "Well, Lieutenant," Haag said. "you know what this means." Obviously, it meant the spent round in the Guerre file could not have come from Weiss's pistol.

Moreau said nothing. He looked at his own examiner at the microscope. Then, one of the state investigators said, "Well, it (the projectile) has nothing to do with the case." In fact, the state police's position would be that there was no "chain of custody" and, therefore, no way of knowing if the bullet was related to the Long slaying.

Haag felt whatever claim the state police had for objectivity vanished at this point. "I could see it wasn't going to be science (that motivated the state police) but political criminalistics," said Haag. "They didn't want that bullet to have anything to do with the case because it tarnishes the historical account of what happened."

While the police investigation was going on, Starrs's team was busy examining the remains of Weiss, such as they could find. Starrs had chosen to start the exhumation at dawn, an hour when there would be no visitors at the graveyard. After Weiss's vault was raised, scientists took X-rays of the coffin to establish the position of any remaining bullets. The casket was then taken to a forensic laboratory one hour away in Lafayette where Starrs's four-man team began their examination. On the team were:

(1) Douglas H. Ubelaker, curator of physical anthropology at the Smithsonian Institution and a consultant to the FBI. His job was to evaluate the bones and any fractures or marks made by the bullets.

(2) Dr. Irving M. Sopher, chief medical examiner of the state of West Virginia. He had exhumed Lee Harvey Oswald to prove it was his body that was buried in a Dallas cemetery and not the remains of a stand-in Russian agent. Sopher's assignment was to perform an autopsy.

(3) Alphonse Poklis, director of the toxicology laboratory at the Medical College of Virginia in Richmond. He was to screen tissue and bone marrow for toxic substances.

(4) Haag, the weapons expert from Phoenix, Ariz. A former president of the Association of Firearms and

Toolmark Examiners, he was there to assess the fire-arms evidence and make trajectory analysis.

Results of the first examination were not promising. At a press conference the day after the exhumation, scientists said X-rays had revealed the location of some of the bullets, including one that apparently entered the skull. But there was little else to report except bad news. Moisture had seeped into the vault. It caused the decomposition of much of the cypress casket as well as Weiss's body.

In their preliminary report, scientists reported nothing to alter the historical account.

But Starrs said the search for clues had just begun. The team had more work to do. The bones, especially, had a story to tell. They would be moved to the Smithsonian. Results of their analysis, as well as the full team's report, would be presented at the 44th annual meeting of Academy of Forensic Sciences. By a coincidence, the meeting was being held in Louisiana.

Every seat was taken in the conference room at the Hyatt-Regency Hotel in New Orleans when the Starrs team presented its long-awaited report. Several hundred forensic scientists, pathologists, and medical examiners were in the audience. About two dozen reporters and television newsmen sat scattered among them.

Starrs began by making it clear that he neither sought nor received any money from the Weiss family for its cooperation. He said he had also asked Russell Long for permission to exhume his father's remains, but Long declined to give it.[3]

Nevertheless, Starrs said there was much to be learned from the Weiss exhumation. He told the audience there had never been any scientific investigation. His project was trying to fill a 56 year-old void with whatever data it could uncover.

The next speaker, medical examiner Sopher, described the autopsy on Weiss who, he said, was buried in a black suit coat with matching vest. Beyond that, Sopher had little to report. Because of the body's deteriorated condition, no tissue remained to be analysed.

The bones were something else. The task of Ubelaker, the forensic anthropologist, was to document the trajectory of the bullets. After X-rays were taken of all

[3] "There are still some people who refuse to believe that John Wilkes Booth shot Abraham Lincoln," Russell Long told Starrs in a letter. "And I suppose there will always be some who would want to argue about the identity of the person who shot my father. I am fully satisfied that I know what happened."

the bones, he hand-carried them in boxes and paper bags to Washington.

On a wooden table in his office on the third floor of the Smithsonian's National Museum of Natural History, he reconstructed the skeleton, showing all the points of impact. "Under the microscope," said Ubelaker, "you can tell the direction the bullet came from by looking at how the bone is splintered and repositioned." Not all the projectiles hit bone, but Ubelaker found evidence indicating that 24 gunshot wounds did. In the unrelenting barrage, bullets poured into Weiss from all directions.

"He was shot many times from many different angles," said Ubelaker. "That doesn't prove Long was caught in the crossfire. But it's certainly possible." Most disturbing of all was Ubelaker's finding that 12 of the bullets, half of those accounted for by the skeletal remains, came from the rear.

But Ubelaker could not tell how many times the bodyguards fired into Weiss's back when he was down. Starrs would later say the guards never disclosed where their bullets struck Weiss and that information "might have made Dr. Weiss appear as less an aggressor."

As to the lingering question about Weiss punching Long, Ubelaker said an examination of his hands yielded no conclusive evidence. Up to 16 percent of all broken fingerbones can be traced to fights. Blows from the hand, if they result in fractures, usually damage the fourth or fifth knuckle. Nothing was found other than some hairline fractures that appeared in both hands and in his feet as well. They must have resulted from changes after death, Ubelaker said.

Poklis, the toxicologist, came up empty handed. In 1935, the number of pyschoactive drugs were relatively limited, he said. His examination found no identifiable drugs that would have affected Weiss's behavior.

But Haag, the ballistics expert, turned up some new data. It centered around a hollow point .38 caliber bullet that Ubelaker found lodged in the brain case. Hollow point bullets are designed to break up on entry, thus wreaking more damage. This one did not work right and remained intact. The bullet, which appeared to have entered under Weiss's left eye, should have had enough energy to pass through his skull unless it lost force by hitting something else first.

Haag said he found a tuft of light tan cotton fibers in the slug's hollow point, fibers that appeared to come from the white cotton shirt that Weiss wore. "How would you get fibers in a bullet that goes under the eye and into the head? Could Weiss have raised his arms to shield his face during the shooting?" Answering his own questions, Haag said the slug could have gone through his sleeve before hitting his face, picking up fibers that would become discolored in Weiss's brain. In fact, Ubelaker found skeletal damage to fit this theory: one bullet wound to Weiss's left wrist and two to the right arm.

Starrs would later use Haag's report to underscore what he considered to be a significant finding. "This indicates Dr. Weiss was not in an attacking posture. He had gone to a defensive posture and yet they continued shooting him." None of the bodyguards talked about Weiss throwing up his hands. If Weiss had done that,

Starrs would say, it would not have proven his innocence, but "it would have at least added to the element
of reasonable doubt."[4]

The scientists' detailed presentations, accompanied
by slides, lasted almost three hours. Finally, it was Starrs'
turn. A hush fell over the room as he stepped to the
podium.

"Who shot Long?" Starrs asked. A ripple of electricity
coursed through the crowd. "Either it was Weiss or the
bodyguards or a combination. . . . To answer that question it becomes relevant to look at evidence found not
only in the grave of Dr. Weiss but above ground. . . .
Materials found in possession of Mabel Guerre Binnings must be interwoven with previously known evi-
dentiary details in order to do justice to this inquiry."

Starrs said that the state police examination of the
Guerre files found photographs of garments presum-
ably worn by Long. The bullet-torn coat jacket showed
"clear evidence" of powder-staining from a point blank
entrance wound to the right abdomen. Another picture
showed what looked like an exit wound, probably in the
left back. "None of these pictures give support to the

---

[4] Some observers took exception to Starrs's conclusion. They noted that
Weiss still could have shot Long, then thrown his hands up moments later
when he encountered gunfire from all sides. Ubelaker later said he would
"hesitate to make too much out of the defensive position . . . We cannot sequence the shots. One can easily imagine an assailant (after shooting someone) recoiling into a natural defensive posture after he himself gets hit."

Lt. Don Moreau, who investigated the case for the Louisiana State Police,
said the fact that the bodyguards did not mention Weiss's defensive stance—
if he did assume one—should not undercut their credibility. Given the
crowded hallway, the suddenness of the shooting, the ricocheting bullets, the
deafening explosions, "it doesn't surprise me that they didn't notice he raised
his hands."

two-shots-into-Long theory . . . ," Starrs said. "All of which makes the statement of mortician Merle Welsh, so heavily relied upon, to be so much wool-gathering."

Starrs paused for a moment. He was ready to put forward the strongest evidence—the expended .32 caliber bullet. He told the audience there was a spent round found with the gun in Binnings safety deposit box and it "had all the indicia of being involved in the tragedy." It was retained with other items whose common thread was that they were all apparently traceable to the Long slaying.

The expended bullet bore two marks indicating it had traversed a person and rebounded off a solid object like the marble lining the corridor. First, under a scanning microscope, a tissue-like material—never identified—could be seen adhering to the bullet, supporting the view the round had passed through a person. (The state police would dispute this point, saying it was impossible to tell what the material was or where it came from. They noted that many persons in the crime lab and at Louisiana State University had handled the bullet.)

But the main reason Starrs said he believed the bullet hit someone was its slightly blunted nose, an imperfection that apparently resulted from contact with the corridor wall. Because the damage was relatively minor, Starrs believed the bullet had to pass through a person. If its flight had not been slowed, it would have smashed into the marble surface at full speed and been totally bent out of shape.

The discovery of the expended bullet—which was the identical caliber as those in Weiss's gun—at first appeared to strenghten the case against Weiss. However,

Starrs said, the "greatest surprise of all" came when police test-fired Weiss's gun with another .32 caliber bullet and compared it to the "enigmatic" bullet. Markings on the bullets did not match.

"And so," Starrs said, "the enigmatic bullet with all the trappings of a bullet that had pierced the abdomen of Huey Long, exiting from his back and then caroming into the marble of the hallway could not have been fired by the weapon carried by Carl Weiss. . . . What weapon then did fire the enigmatic bullet? And whose finger was on the trigger? These are questions beyond the purview of our scientific investigation."

Starrs ended his speech by drawing two conclusions, which he emphasized were his own. They were: (1) "There is clear evidence of a pattern of silence and inaction and concealment over many years involving materials and information highly relevant to a proper investigation of the deaths of Long and Weiss." (2) "It is submitted there is significant scientific and other evidence establishing grave and persuasive doubts that Carl Austin Weiss was the person who killed Huey Long."

In a press conference afterward, Starrs appeared to back away somewhat from the strong tone of his conclusion. He conceded the data did not prove conclusively whether Long was shot by Weiss or his bodyguards. Nor could he say with certainty that the enigmatic bullet was the bullet that killed Long. "But," he asked, "why else squirrel it away with the evidence? Why save it?" Starrs added he was convinced there was more evidence still available somewhere—such as the original statements the bodyguards made to police investigators—that had a material bearing on the case.

Reaction to Starrs's presentation was mixed even on his own scientific team. A poll by the author showed that Haag, the firearms expert, supported Starrs's statements. Poklis, the toxicologist, said he had formed no opinion. But Sopher, the medical examiner, and Ubelaker, the forensic anthropologist, both felt Starrs's conclusion was an overreaction.

"It was a strong statement," Sopher said, "stronger than the actual evidence represented." Ubelaker, while generally deferring to Starrs's greater knowledge of the case, said he himself would have been more conservative. Instead of using the words "grave and persuasive doubts," Ubelaker said he would have simply said there are "continued concerns" about whether Weiss shot Long.

A number of forensic experts who heard the team's presentation said they felt that Starrs's presentation fell short of proving his theory. "It was interesting speculation but not conclusive," said Dr. Michael M. Baden, executive director of the Forensic Sciences Unit for the New York State Police.

Unhappiest of all were two state troopers. The lawmen came to see whether Starrs would abide by the court's gag rule prohibiting the police from disclosing their findings. They stormed out of the meeting and called the judge. State Police Capt. Ronnie Jones told reporters that Starrs had displayed and discussed materials in police possession that were supposed to be confidential pending a final court ruling on their ownership.

There was a report that Judge Ortigue was fuming when he heard the news and was considering issuing a contempt of court order—though, in the end, he did not do so.

The news of the judge's displeasure quickly spread. Starrs insisted that he was not bound by the confidentiality ruling because he had neither consented to the order nor signed it. But he appeared shaken.

Nevertheless, Starrs had made his point. In Baton Rouge, the *Advocate*'s front-page, typical of headlines across the country, read: "Probe Raises Doubt Weiss Killed Long." There would be television news interviews, a stint on the NBC network show "Unsolved Mysteries," plus pictures and articles in *Time* and several other publications.

Four months later, the state police held a press conference and reported the results of its investigation. It was based on the very same two pieces of evidence that formed the centerpiece of Starrs's report: the spent bullet and the photos of Long's blood-stained clothing. The police conclusion was 180 degrees different.

Lt. Don Moreau, who headed the eight-month investigation, told reporters in New Orleans the probe had corroborated the findings of his brother officers, albeit of another era. The state police concluded that Weiss, not the bodyguards, assassinated Long.

"Nothing we found was in conflict with the original historical theory," Moreau said. "If Weiss were alive, he would be arrested, indicted, and convicted. Absolutely. There's enough evidence to convict." State Police Superintendent Paul Fontenot said the original murder investigation would never formally be ended. But he said police now considered the case "officially closed."

Moreau, discussing the Guerre files, said they were of no help in the investigation. They consisted of the general's notes and correspondence about the unproven conspiracy theory. (When this book went to press, the court had still not opened the files to the public.)

Turning to the enigmatic bullet, Moreau confirmed that ballistics tests had proved that Weiss's gun could not have fired it. Police firearm experts agreed with the conclusion of Starrs's team that the bullet's slightly blunted nose indicated it had struck a hard surface like the corridor's marble walls. Judging from the moderate damage it sustained, the experts thought it may well have been slowed by passing through the soft tissue of a person.

Police experts also found embedded in the bullet grains of calcium, a mineral found in marble. But Moreau said there was no evidence that the bullet hit Long or had anything to do with the assassination. The microscopic examination showed no trace of blood, and the calcium grains could have come from concrete or other substances as well as marble.

However, the major reason that Moreau said no one could link the bullet to the assassination with any kind of certainty was the lack of a "chain of custody." No one knew who had handled the weapon and the bullets in the half century that passed since the slaying. So Moreau, unlike Starrs, did not feel the bullet carried any weight in supporting Weiss's possible innocence.

On the other hand, he said the photographs of the

garments were the "most significant pieces of evidence" obtained from Mrs. Binnings. They consisted of pictures of a double-breasted suit, a white sleeveless garment believed to be an undershirt, and a long-sleeved shirt. Moreau said all indications were that Long wore them when he was shot.

He gave these reasons: (1) Long's clothes were custom-made by Godchaux, a New Orleans clothier, and the white sleeveless garment and long-sleeved shirt had Godchaux labels. (2) The sleeveless garment bore the initials "HPL." (3) The bullet holes—a jagged one in front and a smaller rounded one in back—were consistent with the sites of the wound reported by Huey's doctors.

"The places where the surgeons say the bullet went line up with where the holes in the clothes were," Moreau said. But the key evidence was the hole in the front of the jacket. A bullet shot from two or three feet away or farther makes a clean, round hole. A bullet from a gun in contact with the victim's clothes leaves an irregular tear surrounded with black debris, commonly called "powder burns."

Long's coat jacket showed an irregular tear—the hole had the shape of a four-sided star—and it had a sooty residue around it. Only a bullet fired at point blank range could have left such a tear, Moreau said. Weiss was the only person with a weapon who got that close to Long, according to testimony of the bodyguards and Judge Fournet.

Slow-motion movies showing the sequence of a contact shot would look something like this: when the trigger is pulled, hot gases explode and propel the bullet down the spiraling grooves of the barrel. The gases follow the bullet out of the gun and expand into a cloud. As the bullet pierces the material, the red hot gases rip the cloth. Burning residue collects around the bullet hole, making a distinctive blackened stain. Such telltale markings are easily spotted by a firearms expert even in a photograph. Moreau said Long's wound was made from "loose contact" distance, probably less than an inch away.

If Starrs and Moreau disagreed on the significance of the enigmatic bullet, they were even farther apart on the importance of the photographs. In his speech, Starrs used the bullet holes in Long's clothes to discredit the two-bullet theory. Moreau saw this evidence another way. More importantly, he said, the powder burns made a strong case against Weiss.[5]

Patrick A. Lane, forensic scientist in the State Police Laboratory, summed up the implication of the clothing: "Theories about the bodyguard's ricocheting bullet striking Huey as he fled down the hall are disproved by the presence of contact testing and residue around the hole in his coat."

Why, Moreau was asked, did Starrs not draw the same conclusion from the clothes? "As a police officer, I can just call it like I see it," Moreau said. "I'm not going to say Professor Starrs distorted things. Let's just say he drew some awful good conclusions from very little evidence."

---

[5] The powder burns also argue against the theory that Long was struck by a bodyguard's bullet that had gone through Weiss first. If that were the case, Long's clothes would not have had the sooty residue. Nor, assuming the photographs are accepted as genuine, could the fatal bullet have been a ricocheted shot.

Starrs did not answer repeated telephone calls to get his response. But some observers were skeptical about the credibility of the state police probing the actions of their fellow officers even though they were from an earlier time. "It (the findings) was exactly what we expected," said Edmond G. Miranne Jr., a New Orleans attorney whose grandfather handled the probate proceedings of Huey Long's estate. "When you investigate yourself, you don't find yourself guilty."

In addition, the same argument about the lack of a chain of custody in the case of the gun could apply as well to Long's clothes. The coat jacket could have originally had a clean round hole in the front. The irregular tear and powder burns could have been made later when someone, bent on changing its appearance to implicate Weiss, pressed a gun directly over the hole and fired into it.

There are other weaknesses to the photographs as evidence. The markings on the coat appear to be consistent with those made by a contact gunshot wound. But they are pictures. Only a chemical test of the coat itself could prove the stain came from powder burns, not blood. Also, since the police had Long's clothing and made photographs of them, it is hard to understand why they did not produce the bullet-scarred garments and photographs at the time.

Moreau could not answer that. Nor could he say conclusively that the clothes were Huey's. Or, if they were, that he wore them the night he was shot. Moreau also conceded he was assuming that the garments had not been doctored. Still, he said the weight of the evidence supports that assumption. "The wound the surgeon describes lines up with the holes in the coat," the lieutenant said. "The shirt wounds look the same and someone has bled into it. Based on all that, it is probably Huey's coat although, because there is no chain of custody, I couldn't possibly introduce it (in court) as conclusive evidence. It would never survive a motion to suppress."

In a telephone interview a few days after the press conference, Moreau talked candidly about some of the issues his controversial investigation raised.

The 43-year-old officer, a member of the state police since 1974, said he could take a fresh view of the assassination because he was not alive when Long was shot. "Someone said the first thing people will ask you is if your family was pro-Long or anti-Long," said Moreau. "I didn't know. So I called my father and he said, 'Your great-grandfather was anti-Long but your grandfather was pro-Long.' On my mother's side, they were anti-Longs. So I guess I'm okay."

Moreau thought it was likely that the .32 caliber bullet Weiss fired was found in the hall after the shooting. "If they made any attempt to collect it, they would have found it." But he added that this is not to say the spent bullet in the Guerre file is the same bullet that came from Weiss's gun.

What, then, is it doing with the six other bullets found with the gun? There is no proof, Moreau said, that any of those bullets were the original ones. "There is a 56-year gap in the history of that gun. Between the shooting and when it was recovered in 1991, we don't know what became of it. Mrs. Binnings said it was offered for sale at least twice. It may have been test-fired. Mrs. Binnings' attorney indicated to me that it had, in fact, been fired.

"The (enigmatic) bullet is perplexing. The first question that comes to mind is: why is it in there if it is not related to the case? I asked myself that many times. On cross examination, it is the same type and caliber as the other bullets. When I first examined it, I said, 'This is the fatal bullet.' However, the ballistics comparison found that the bullet did not come from Weiss's gun. The only .32 automatic I could find anyone firing was Weiss's automatic. All the bodyguards were armed with much heavier guns—.38s and .45s. So where did the bullet come from? It remains a mystery. I can only say it wasn't fired by Weiss's gun."

Moreau suggested an alternative scenario. Someone inspecting the gun for sale test-fires it at a pistol range. The person walks to a backstop and looks on the ground. All kinds of bullets are scattered around. "Someone saw that bullet and picked it up," Moreau said. "That's a possibility."

As to the conspiracy theory, Moreau said he did not think Weiss was involved in a plot to kill Long. Nor does he think that Weiss was deranged.[6] Neither does he fit the mould of the loner like John Hinckley and Lee Harvey Oswald.

If he had to give a theory, Moreau said he thought the racial slur had upset Weiss. He brooded over it. The re-

---

[6] Notes of Long's biographer, T. Harry Williams, quote bodyguard Murphy Roden as saying that Weiss was mentally unbalanced. Roden said Weiss had suffered a nervous breakdown while in Paris. The Weiss family denies this.

mark, whether spoken or intended to be made later, riled him to the point of no return.

"I think he was driven to desperation by his thought of the attack on his father-in-law (Judge Pavy). The thing that broke the camel's back came from a rumor started years before in St. Landry Parish that Judge Pavy's family was part black. Louisiana had a 1/32nd law then and did even in my lifetime.

"The law said if a person had 1/32nd black blood, he was racially classed a Negro. The reason it stayed on the books so long is because black legislators fought to keep it there. And the reason they did is there are a number of prominent families in New Orleans—a city that is 60 percent black—who ran as blacks to get black support. They were probably as close to being black as I am."

Actually, the 1/32nd law was not enacted until 1970. The Legislature repealed it in 1983 after an unsuccessful court challenge brought much negative publicity.

However, prior to 1970, an even stricter state racial standard applied. Court decisions upheld a rule dating from the state's French and Spanish colonial days that said that a person with "any traceable amount" of black ancestry was considered black. That definition covered a lot of ground. Genealogists say intermingling between the races in south Louisiana was not uncommon and it was said that many white families had at least one ancestor who "became white" when he joined the family. Huey Long reportedly contended that if you sliced a loaf of bread and gave it to only pure-white people in Louisiana, it would take a year to pass it out.

Despite their considerable numbers, those with mixed blood had no real place in Louisiana society. These residents, called "people of color," had to fit into a rigidly controlled two-caste system. They had to live as either blacks or whites. Segregation affected every phase of life and those classified as black—no matter how light their skin—were forever members of the "out" group. That was the situation in the state in 1935 and the context in which Huey Long's alleged racial remark would have been considered.[7]

"Anyway," Moreau continued, "Huey was going to say, in his own style, that the Pavys had 'a little too much coffee in their cream.' In other words, he was going to allege they were Negroes. Understand that would have made Dr. Weiss's wife a Negro and his newborn son a Negro.

"That was the key. If Huey could make the charge stick, it meant the whole future of Weiss's son was in jeopardy. It meant he might not go to school with white kids. He might not go to medical school. He might not be able to mingle in white society.

"Nobody knows whether this would have happened. But it was potentially there and Weiss might have thought about it. Being a Negro in Louisiana in 1935 was a hell of a lot different than 1992. I think that when the rumor came out that Huey was going to say that, it was the straw that broke the camel's back."

[7] In fact, race was such a charged issue then that alleging there was "nigger" blood in a white family could have provoked reprisals. "If that slur had been used publicly, it would have been almost a shooting matter," said A. Veazie Pavy, an Opelousas attorney who was Judge Pavy's son. In an interview in 1961, he said many juries would have acted leniently toward a man who assaulted another for making such a charge. "I can't recall a jury having acquited a man for killing someone over such a remark. But it could certainly have been taken as an insult to impugn the purity of that person's race. It was the supreme insult."

So, after all is said and done, have the exhumation and the discovery of the gun and the photographs of Long's clothes made a difference? Have they changed opinion?

Not that of the Weiss family. Dr. Tom Ed Weiss's conviction that his brother was innocent remains the same. Today, he leans toward the belief that his brother entered the capitol without a gun. Weiss recalled how he found Carl's car in front of the building after the shooting. He said his brother's canvas-wrapped medical instruments appeared to have been rummaged through and the flannel sock that held his gun lay on the floor. After Tom Ed went home and came back with the keys, he said he found the car on the east side of the capitol grounds. "It was very likely that someone else had keys and had moved the car. I contend that not only were the keys removed earlier from Carl's pocket, but the car was entered. And it is quite possible that the gun was removed from the glove compartment, and he could have even entered the capitol without a firearm."

A recent statement by Col. Francis Grevemberg, who was state police chief from 1952 to 1955, lends support to Tom Ed's theory. Returning in his car after a gambling raid in the 1950s, Grevemberg said he listened as Trooper John DeArmond and two others talked about being assigned to the capitol on the night Long was shot. Grevemberg said this was the story they told:

When Weiss approached Long, he started shouting at Huey, then tried to punch him. Bodyguards Roden and Messina rushed over and opened fire. Other guards joined in, and pandemonium broke out. After the smoke cleared, Messina was distraught, convinced that a richocheted bullet or bullets from his gun had hit Long. When the guards searched Weiss's body, they found he had no weapon. One of the troopers planted in Weiss's hand a .25 caliber gun that the trooper had confiscated in a barroom raid.

Guerre came on the scene. When he was told Long had been hit with a .38 caliber bullet, he said the .25 caliber gun was too small. He had it replaced it with a .32 caliber pistol. (Grevemberg, asked where the gun came from, said he does not know.)

The day after hearing this story, Grevemberg called the troopers into his office and told them to repeat their narrative before the state police attorney. They had a sudden memory lapse. Grevemberg said Martin Fritcher, his driver and bodyguard, also would not substantiate it. Later, Fritcher apologized but told him it was an "unwritten law" among state troopers not to talk about the Long slaying.

Both DeArmond and Fritcher are dead. Grevemberg, who was 78 and clear-headed when I interviewed him in 1992, said he never made the story public because police officials had little interest in the assassination until the Guerre evidence surfaced. Grevemberg wrote his recollection of the incident in 1989—more than 30 years after he said it took place. When asked to sign the four-page statement before a notary, Grevemberg did so.

Nevertheless, Lt. Moreau, the Louisiana State Police investigator, said the Grevemberg account was only hearsay. The bulk of the credible evidence clearly points to Dr. Weiss, Moreau said. Any other scenario is speculation.

But, he was asked, would a person of Weiss's intellect

and background and potential commit murder—an act he must have known would have been suicidal—to settle a score with a politician?

Moreau thought for a moment. Then, he said: "If you make a man scared enough or mad enough, he will do something. Unlike animals, man has the ability to fight for abstract causes—whether they be Confederate soldiers charging the Union lines at Gettysburg or American soldiers going over the top in World War I or the Marines landing at Guadalcanal. People who are emotionally charged or desperate do not fear death.

"Weiss may not have gone into the capitol as a rational man or planned this out. If he had, he almost certainly would have used a better weapon than a .32 caliber pistol. But maybe he went there with the goal of at least seeing this demon who was haunting his family. And he stood there and suddenly he saw Huey Long walking toward him in all his power and all his arrogance.

"There are many instances in history of men attacking suicidally in defense of their family. I think that's how Dr. Weiss saw it. He was going to shut Huey Long's mouth once and for all. And shut it, he did."

As for myself, I still feel as I did when I wrote this book in 1963. I think the results of the Starrs probe and the state police investigation, in effect, amount to a wash. The enigmatic bullet points to Weiss's innocence. The photographs of Long's clothing tilt toward his guilt. Both pieces of evidence are suspect because no one knows where they have been over the years. Without them, we are back where we were 30 years ago. Then, as now, I believe that Weiss did not go into the capitol intending to kill Long. The inquest testimony notwithstanding, it is likely that the two exchanged words. And there is just as much reason to think that Weiss only punched the Kingfish as there is to believe that he shot Long.

And what of the sons of the victims?

In commenting on the assassination just before the Weiss exhumation, Russell Long, who was 16 when his father died, revealed how deeply he felt his loss over a lifetime. "For many years after my father's death, I had dreams that he was still with me on earth; that he had somehow survived the assassination attempt and that I was working with him to carry on the work he had been doing. Many mornings I woke up thinking my father was still living."

Russell Long said he has never been able to totally eliminate the shooting from his thoughts. Whenever he discusses the case, he said "dark and disturbing" memories return. There is one consolation. If the tragedy lingers, he said he bears no bitterness now.

"Nothing can be done to bring back my father. And nothing can be done to bring back Dr. Carl Weiss. The case of Huey Long and Carl Weiss has been decided by a judge who knows everything there is to know. We would like the matter to rest at that."

What of Carl Weiss's son? When I talked to him in 1992, he was 57 years old, living on Long Island, still making occasional visits to Louisiana to keep his ties to his native state. He was too young to remember his father, but he said he thought about him often. One day, he found a diary his father kept about his travels through Europe. Years later, Carl Weiss Jr. made the same trip, following his father's footsteps through Paris, Vienna, and Italy.

At first, Weiss Jr. kept out of the debate on the shooting, letting his uncle, Tom Ed, carry the burden of trying to clear the family name. But as Weiss Jr. matured, he became more involved. He, too, became convinced of his father's innocence and stated his view publicly. It was he who gave permission for the exhumation.[8]

What are his feelings about the assassination? At first, he declined to comment. But a few weeks later, he sent me a letter. It ended like this:

"No one will ever know exactly why my father stopped at the State Capitol in Baton Rouge that night. . . . (But) if we look to history, there has never been a political assassination carried out by a physician. My father surely was not the first. Everything about him, his background as a religious man, his sensitivity as a musician and sculptor, and his devotion to his family suggest otherwise."

Weiss said he had neither the facts nor the witnesses to buttress his convictions. But he said his life in many ways has paralleled that of his father's—in education, in

---

[8] In an unusual development, Russell Long and Carl Weiss Jr. met privately a month before the 50th anniversary of the shooting. It was Long's idea and it came during an interview I was doing. I happened to mention that Carl Weiss Jr. practiced on Long Island. Long said he always wanted to meet him. They shared a common bond, he said. Both lost their fathers in the same tragedy. The senator asked me to convey that.

In July, 1985, the sons of the Kingfish and his alleged assassin had breakfast together in a New York City hotel. Long asked that details of that meeting remain private. But both said they spent a cordial two hours together.

travel, and in his work. All of it, he says, gives him insight and inferential evidence about the kind of man his father was.

"It, therefore, makes no sense either in the historical or personal perspective for me to believe my father fired a shot at Senator Huey P. Long.

"Alas," Carl Weiss Jr. said, "the mystery continues and probably always will."[9]

[9] Indeed, the dispute stayed intact through the end of the century. At a 1999 symposium on the Long family at Louisiana College, speakers on the assassination panel differed sharply. Donald R. Moreau, the state police detective who reinvestigated the case in 1992, said he was satisfied that Weiss shot Long. But James E. Starrs, the law professor who discovered Weiss's long-missing gun and bullets, said Moreau had formed his conclusion in advance. "On a credibility basis, I give you a zero," Starrs said. "There is no doubt in my mind that Weiss did not kill Long." Moreau fired back, calling Starrs's opinion "ludicrous. . . . Nothing in the (newly found) evidence rules out the historical theory of how this occurred." Panel chairman David Culbert, history professor at Louisiana State University, had the last word. There are some events in life, Culbert said, whose absolute truth will always remain clouded.

Appendixes

A. Report of K. B. Ponder to Mutual Life Insurance Company of New York

B. State of Louisiana Department of Public Safety and Corrections Final Investigative Report

C. Statement of Russell B. Long

D. Statement of Carl Austin Weiss, Jr., M.D.

Report of K. B. Ponder to Mutual Life Insurance Company of New York

Excerpts from Inspector's Report
11-9-36

Mr. H. P. Gallaher, Supt.,
Bureau of Investigation,
1936
The Mutual Life Insurance
Company of New York
New York, NY

RE: Your letter October 23—
Huey P. Long . . . Paid
Death Claim.
Pol. Nos. 3473640 et al
$20,000

Dear Sir:

In connection with the above-mentioned instructions, I submit the following report. The information contained herein has been obtained from various sources, is considered reliable, and I believe represents the true background, causes and facts surrounding the death of the insured. For reasons which will be fully explained in the report, some of the circumstances herein set out cannot be proved, for to prove anything in connection with the life and death of the insured would necessitate involving people associated with the insured in his political and personal life. Naturally there have been any number of rumors in connection with this case, documentary evidence has been destroyed, or else it was set up in the beginning to represent conditions in the light most favorable to the insured and to those who expected to profit most by the political control the insured had established over the State of Louisiana.

. . . .

St. Landry Parish (County) Louisiana, of which Opelousas, La., is the Parish Seat, is situated in about the South Central Part of the State. It is, or was until recent oil developments occurred, strictly an agricultural section. It has been controlled in politics and other ways for several generations by a few wealthy families, among them the Pavy family. The population of the Parish, predominantly white, is composed for the most part of French people, small farmers, who have followed the lead of these outstanding families for several generations. From the beginning of Long's political career, (he was nominally a Protestant and came from the northern or hill-country section, while St. Landry Parish is 90% Catholic), he was bitterly opposed by the politicians and voters of St. Landry Parish, chief among them the families in control. The Pavy family possibly exercised more control, politically, than any other family in the Parish, and this family came in for considerable amount of trouble at Long's hands. Naturally they were not without political, (and other), sins of their own so he had plenty of ways in which to trouble them. The man, Dr. C. A. Weiss, Jr., of Baton Rouge, La., alleged to have shot Long, was married to the daughter of Judge Pavy of Opelousas, St. Landry Parish, La. and was the father of a small child. Long, in one of his political speeches, had at one time broadly intimated, or asserted, that there was Negro blood in the Pavy family.

It was Long's custom to call an extra session of the legislature whenever the occasion arose where certain laws were necessary to protect him or to provide ways and means of achieving some political or personal end. This custom continued after he went to the U. S. Senate, he using the Governor Allen for whatever purpose he had in mind. On the night of September 8, 1935, (Sunday) one of such extra sessions was being held, the fifth or sixth such session in 1935.

Long, then U. S. Senator, was in Baton Rouge, La., at this special session of the legislature, was on and off the floors of the House and Senate, putting through such legislation as he had called the legislature to pass. It was as he was leaving the House of Representatives chamber that he was approached by Dr. C. A. Weiss, Jr., a Baton Rouge, La., physician, and accosted. It was here that Dr. Weiss, Jr. is alleged to have shot him.

Dr. C. A. Weiss, Jr., a young physician, practiced in Baton Rouge, La., with his father, Dr. C. A. Weiss, Sr. Dr. Weiss, Jr., was educated at Tulane University, New Orleans, La., and upon his graduation did the required amount of interne work, then went abroad and continued to study medicine for a year or two. Classmates at Tulane state that when there he was of a quiet, studious type, intensely interested in his work, intelligent. Upon establishing himself at Baton Rouge, La., Dr. Weiss, Jr., married a daughter of Judge Pavy of Opelousas, La. Dr. Weiss, Sr., father of the alleged murderer, has been a prominent physician of Baton Rouge, La., for years. He is successful, considered a competent, ethical practitioner. For a time, immediately prior to the Long regime, Dr. Weiss had been receiving certain favors in the way of medical practice from the State. When Long offered for Governor he opposed Long and continued to fight him politically and for this reason gained Long's ill-will. Thus, in the opinion of informants, the environment in which Dr. Weiss, Jr., lived was one of intense dislike and opposition to Long, and without doubt he was constantly subjected to hearing his own father and his wife's people dwell at length on their injustices suffered by them at Long's hands. Long was without a doubt, with every means available, fighting and persecuting the Pavy family (Weiss, Jr.'s wife's people) and plans then being formulated called for certain avenues to be built, leading from the State Capitol, that would pass through Weiss, Sr.'s property and it was the intention of the administration to condemn (by Court action in controlled Courts) the property which would involve considerable financial loss on the part of Weiss, Sr.

340   APPENDIX A

It was about this time that Long is quoted as charging that
the Pavy family was tainted with Negro blood, and this is believed to have been taken by Dr. C. A. Weiss, Jr., as an insult
that could not be overlooked.

On the night of September 8, 1935, (Sunday) as Long was
leaving the House chamber, Dr. Weiss, Jr., was waiting for
him in the main portion of the first floor of the Capitol Building. As Long came out of the House chamber he was followed
at a short distance by Associate Justice John B. Fournet of the
State Supreme Court. (See report on this individual as an ap-
plicant for insurance.) Following Fournet were several members of Long's personal bodyguard, among them one Roden,
now Assistant Superintendent of State Police, and Joe Messina, a New Orleans thug who had been Long's bodyguard for
several years. What followed when Dr. Weiss accosted Long
has never been definitely established. When the action was
over Long was hurried to the hospital, shot through the stomach. Dr. Weiss had upwards to 30 bullets fired into his body,
practically all of them fired while he lay on the floor.
. . . .

From various sources comes the following information.
Weiss, when he approached Long in the Capitol Building,
spoke to him and when Long replied, Weiss struck him in the
mouth with his fist. It is an established fact that when he got to
the hospital Long's mouth was bruised and there was some
bleeding. There is nothing to show that it is possible for him
to have received this bruise any other way. Long's bodyguard
rushed Weiss and he attempted to draw a pistol. The bodyguard started firing their pistols and Long was killed by a bullet fired by one of his own bodyguard. One of the bodyguard,
Joe Messina was later sent out of the State for a time, following a drunken remark to the effect that "I killed my only
friend." There was some rumor at the time that he was being
confined to the State Insane Asylum but this cannot be verified. This version of the affair is believed to be true by most
unbiased informants. There have been remarks made by

those close to the situation that bear this out. There is no doubt that Weiss attacked Long, but there is considerable doubt that Weiss ever fired a gun. Witnesses stated that there were forty or fifty shots fired by the bodyguard and there was evidence that some of the guard were firing blindly and wildly.

. . . .

Long was buried on the grounds of the new State Capitol Building. His is buried deep, with tons of concrete in the underground vault. His political friends said that this was done to insure that he would never be moved. Others said that it was done so that none might ever have a chance to examine the body.

There is no doubt that his death was accidental, but the consensus of more informed opinion is that he was killed by his own guard and not by Weiss.

Yours very truly,
K. B. Ponder

State of Louisiana
Department of Public Safety and Corrections
Final Investigative Report
Senator Huey P. Long
5 June 1992

SYNOPSIS: United States Senator Huey Pierce Long was shot at the Louisiana State Capitol on September 8, 1935. He expired as a result of this wound on September 10, 1935. Files pertaining to the shooting and subsequent investigation were discovered in possession of heirs of the late General L. F. Guerre. In 1935, General Guerre was head of the Louisiana Bureau of Criminal Identification and Investigation. Due to many unanswered questions regarding the shooting, the Louisiana State Police reopened the case.

NARRATIVE: On September 30, 1991, I [Lt. Don Moreau] was assigned by Lt. Col. Kenneth D. Norris to investigate the shooting and subsequent death of U. S. Senator Huey P. Long. This investigation was prompted by the discovery of the alleged murder weapon and investigative reports. These items were located among the memorabilia in the possession of Mabel G. Bennings*. Ms. Bennings is the daughter of General L. F. Guerre. General Guerre was the Commander of the Louisiana State Bureau of Criminal Investigation at the time of the assassination.

Colonel Norris informed me that the investigative team would consist of myself and Pat Lane from the Louisiana State Police Crime Laboratory. Civil Sheriff Paul Valteau of

Orleans Parish was charged by the court in New Orleans with maintaining custody of the Guerre papers and the weapon. Dr. Donald Lemieux, an archivist with the Louisiana State Archives, was assigned to assure the proper handling and preservation of all documents and objects.

On October 3, 1991, the files were opened and an initial reading and cataloging of the documents took place. It became apparent almost immediately that we were not in possession of the assassination case file. What we had were notes and correspondence regarding the possibility of a conspiracy to assassinate Senator Long. These documents, while undoubtedly of value from a historical standpoint, shed little light on the shooting of Senator Long.

The handgun was examined and shown to be functional. Also found with the handgun were six (6) .32 auto cartridges and one fired .32 calibre projectile. The fired projectile appeared to be of the same type as the unfired cartridges found with it. All projectiles, both the fired and the six unfired, were tin plated, copper jacketed .32 auto calibre. The fired projectile had visible rifling impressions on its surface and the nose of the projectile was deformed. Scientific analysis of the fired projectile by the Louisiana State Police Crime Laboratory proved that the fired projectile could not have been fired from the .32 calibre pistol identified as the weapon used to shoot Senator Long.

Due to the complete lack of any chain of custody or information as to the history of the weapon, or its possible use since the assassination, it was not possible to draw any conclusions regarding the origins of the fired projectile.

The most significant pieces of evidence in the documents obtained from Ms. Billings* were a series of photographs. The first of these photographs depicted a man's double-breasted suit coat marked with a label "C. Napolitana New Orleans" and the handwritten marking "Long-34." The second photograph depicts a white sleeveless garment, possibly an undershirt, marked with a label "Godchaux's New Orleans Custom Made," and handwritten markings "L-34," and "HPL." The third photograph depicted a long sleeve shirt labeled "Made for Godchaux's By The _____ Guild," and a handwritten marking "L-34." The coat, undershirt, and long sleeve shirt had all been cut open and tacked to a display board. All the garments displayed what appeared to be bullet entry and exit holes. There was obvious tearing and sooty residue on the front of the suit coat.

The photographs were examined by the Louisiana State Police Crime Laboratory and comparison test firings were done with the alleged murder weapon. The Crime Laboratory interpreted the hole in the front of the coat to be a "loose contact bullet entry." There is another hole slightly lower in the back of the coat. This hole is interpreted as a bullet exit. The holes in the white sleeveless garment and in the long sleeve shirt are in conformity with the damage done to the coat. All evidence available indicated that these items of clothing were worn by Senator Huey P. Long when he was shot.

Over the years, there have been several books written on the subject of the assassination of Senator Huey Long. These books have advanced various theories on how Senator Long came to be shot. The historical or official theory is that Huey Long was shot in the abdomen at pointblank range by a "small man in a white suit." This man was shot in turn by bodyguards and later identified as Dr. Carl Weiss, M.D. The other most popular theory has been that a bullet from the bodyguard's gun passed through Weiss and struck Long or that a ricocheting bullet struck him. The damage to the coat speaks for the "official" theory. Huey Long was shot in front of numerous witnesses. Two of these witnesses, Murphy Roden and Judge John Fournet were very close to Senator Long at the time of the shooting. Both of these men testified at the coroner's inquest held on the death of Dr. Carl A. Weiss, the alleged assassin. Both of them identified Dr. Carl Weiss as the man they saw shoot Senator Long. Five other witnesses came forward to say the same thing. Senator Long himself lived for two days following the shooting, and at no time did Senator Long identify anyone other than Weiss as his assailant.

The other documents contained in the collection provided by Ms. Binnings revealed several other facts concerning the assassination and subsequent investigation. A series of what appeared to be coded reports were found. These proved to be the written reports of private detectives employed by the William J. Burns Detective Agency of New York. These detectives were apparently hired by the Louisiana Bureau of Criminal Identification and Investigation to conduct clandestine surveillances on members of the Weiss family following the assassination. Why private detectives were used for this purpose instead of the Bureau's own investigators remains a mystery.

One enigma in the events immediately following the shooting of Senator Long has been that Harry Costello, then Director of Sports Publications at Louisiana State University, reportedly received a call from Washington, D. C. identifying Carl Weiss as the assassin. The call was received at 9:33 P.M. September 8, 1935, approximately eleven minutes after the shooting. This has been cited by some as evidence of a conspiracy involving President Franklin Roosevelt, a political enemy of Senator Long. The Binnings documents provided a copy of a telegram from Allen Coogan, then employed by United Press International. Coogan revealed that a correspondent had obtained the identification of Weiss from Allen Ellender, the Speaker of the House, at Our Lady of the Lake Hospital minutes after the shooting and had telephoned the identity to the Washington, D. C. Bureau of United Press International.

It is significant that in none of the internal memos and correspondence between General Guerre, then head of the Louisiana Bureau of Criminal Identification and Investigation, and other investigators and members of the Long organizations, is there any mention of the possibility that someone other than Dr. Carl Weiss fired the fatal shot.

Huey Pierce Long was shot once by a small statued man in a

white suit. The shot was fired at "loose contact" distance. The projectile entering the upper right abdomen and exiting from the lower right back after traversing the body. The description of the wounds given by the attending surgeons coincide with the bullet hole locations observed in the photographs of Senator Long's garments.

All observations made of the photographic and other evidence was supportive of the official version of the shooting. A careful examination of literary sources and historical information provides no credible contradictions. The lack of any chain of custody on any of the evidence is distressing. But every effort was made by the investigators to be as thorough as possible while remaining professionally skeptical.

This report does not answer every possible question which could be raised concerning the shooting of Senator Long. It does, however, shed some light on what had previously been one of history's many mysteries.

The police report misspells Binnings as Bennings and Billings.

Statement of Russell B. Long
October 16, 1991

I have received requests from the news media for interviews concerning circumstances surrounding the assassination of my father, Huey P. Long. For many years after my father's death I had dreams that he was still with me on earth, that he had somehow survived the assassination attempt and that I was working with him to carry on the work he had been doing. Many mornings I woke up thinking my father was still living.

Even though I have discussed this subject many times over the past five decades, each time I do so brings back dark and disturbing memories. For this reason, I have chosen to respond to inquiries through this statement which will be issued to members of the media who request it.

I was 16 years old and living in New Orleans when I received news that my father had been shot. Following Huey Long's death, I spoke with Murphy Roden and Louisiana Supreme Court Justice John Fournet, who were both eyewitnesses to the shooting. I also read the transcript of the coroner's inquest and numerous other data concerning my father's assassination. Based on my own interviews and research, there is no doubt whatsoever in my mind that Dr. Carl Austin Weiss went to the Capitol with the intention of assassinating Huey Long and that he fired the shot that killed my father.

In the 1960s, Dr. T. Harry Williams—a renowned historian—conducted considerable research of his own into the assassination for his book, *Huey Long*. I suggest that anyone interested in this subject read pages 858–876 of Dr. Williams' book. Dr. Williams was awarded the Pulitzer Prize in Biography and the National Book Award in History and Biography for his book.

In my personal interview with State Trooper Murphy Roden—shortly after my father's death—he recounted the following: He was close to my father and Dr. Weiss when Dr. Weiss fired his gun. After the shot, Murphy grabbed for Dr. Weiss' pistol. He showed me a flesh wound between the thumb and forefinger where the recoil mechanism had pinched his flesh. Murphy said that he was struggling with Dr. Weiss for possession of the gun, which Weiss was trying to fire again—and that the two of them slipped and fell onto the slick marble floor. Murphy was beneath Dr. Weiss at this point. Murphy looked up into the barrel of another state patrolman's pistol. He told me he fully expected to die at that moment. The gun went off and Dr. Weiss was shot in the head. Murphy said he felt the body go limp, at which point he jumped from beneath Weiss' body as more bullets started flying.

John Fournet told me the following: He saw Dr. Carl Weiss approach Huey Long with the gun in his hand. Justice Fournet reached out and struck at the gun, knocking the aim downward. At that point the gun went off, shooting Huey Long in the abdomen. Huey shouted, "I'm shot" and ran from the room.

I do not believe that anyone could ever convince me that those two brave men (Fournet and Roden)—who tried to save Huey Long's life—would not be telling the truth. John Fournet went on to become chief justice and Murphy Roden became a distinguished U. S. Naval officer during World War II.

About five to six years ago my office was contacted through a third party regarding the possible sale of the gun used to kill my father. This was the first time I had heard of the existence of the gun since its disappearance following the assassination. I sent back word that I had no interest in the gun and suggested that it could be donated to LSU.

I have nothing to say concerning the exhumation of Dr. Carl Weiss' body. If that is what his family wants, so be it. Others may wish to investigate the matter further, I personally do not feel the need for additional inquiry.

Prior to my father's death, I had been reading a book entitled, *Forgive us Our Trespasses*, by Lloyd C. Douglas. The book teaches me that we should forgive people for their mistakes, even those who do not ask for forgiveness. In my view there is nothing to be gained and a lot to be lost by Huey Long's loved-ones carrying unkind feelings in their hearts.

A question was raised regarding the possible exhumation of my father's body from its grave on the Capitol grounds. I have spoken with my brother, Palmer, and my sister, Rose, and they have authorized me to speak for the three of us on this matter. We are unalterably opposed to exhumation of our father's remains.

Nothing can be done to bring back my father. And nothing can be done to bring back Dr. Carl Weiss. The case of Huey Long and Carl Weiss has been decided by a Judge who knows everything there is to know. We would like the matter to rest at that.

Statement of Carl Austin Weiss, Jr., M.D.
September 1992

My father's death in September of 1935, and the subsequent demise of Sen. Huey Long, have understandably had a profound impact on my life. The events that led to this double tragedy are shrouded in mystery. These uncertainties have only been increased by recent inquiries.

I fully understand that Russell Long believes the simplistic "one man/one gun" explanation, since he was told this by the people at the scene from the first day. These participants had reason to perpetuate that version of the violence. However, we all know that history is regularly re-written, and that the passage of time frequently offers a more accurate perspective.

No one will ever know exactly why my father stopped at the State Capitol in Baton Rouge that night, but it should be understood that his house on Lakeland Drive was adjacent to the Capitol . . . almost on the very grounds. His drive home from the hospital that Sunday night would normally have taken him on the route he followed.

He probably wished to have a conversation with Sen. Long, unfortunate though this was in retrospect. There is absolutely no reason to believe that he had any malicious intent, subsequent events notwithstanding. For here we can look to circumstantial evidence. He bore no man any malice.

Dr. Carl Austin Weiss was a man of sound mind and body

(investigation into possible physical or mental defects was one reason for his exhumation by Prof. Starrs in September 1991), and there is abundant evidence that he was proceeding with his normal daily activities. He offered to drive a nurse home from the Baton Rouge General Hospital just a few minutes before the shooting. He had firm plans for surgery the following morning and for the activities of a young father and homeowner in the weeks ahead.

Thus, the man had NO MOTIVE for involvement with Huey Long, and he had no animus toward him. Even Judge B. H. Pavy, my grandfather, had no strong feelings towards Long other than those of political opposition. If we look to history, there has NEVER been a political assassination carried out by a physician. My father surely was not the first. Everything about him, his background as a religious man, his sensitivity as a musician and sculptor and his devotion to family suggest otherwise.

Only common sense and circumstantial evidence, not hard physical facts of credible witnesses, are available to buttress my convictions. My own life experiences as doctor and surgeon, with a liberal education and broadening travel much like my father's, gives me much inferential evidence of his makeup and his potential.

It therefore makes no sense either in the historical or personal perspective for me to believe that my father fired a shot at Sen. Huey P. Long. Alas, the mystery continues and probably always will.

Bibliography

1. *Louisiana Hayride,* Harnett Kane, Morrow, 1941.
2. *The Story of Huey Long,* Carleton Beals, Lippincott, 1935.
3. *The Kingfish,* Thomas O. Harris, Pelican, 1938.
4. *Dixie Demagogues,* Allan A. Michie and Frank Rhylick, Vanguard, 1939.
5. *Huey Long's Louisiana,* Allan P. Sindler, Johns Hopkins, 1956.
6. *Huey Long: A Candid Biography,* Forrest Davis, Dodge, 1935.
7. *The Longs of Louisiana,* Stan Opotowsky, Dutton, 1960.
8. *Dynasty,* Thomas Martin, Putnam, 1960.
9. *Surgery, Gynecology & Obstetrics:* the official scientific journal of the American College of Surgeons, Chicago. "Historical Aspects of Penetrating Wounds of the Abdomen" by Frank L. Loria, B.S., M.D., F.A.C.S. (December, 1948).
10. *The Politics of Upheaval,* Arthur M. Schlesinger, Jr., Houghton Mifflin, Vol. III of The Age of Roosevelt, 1960.
11. *New Yorker* Magazine, May 28, June 4, June 11, 1960, series on "The Great State," by A. J. Liebling.
12. *Life* Magazine, "The Huey Long Legend," article by Hamilton Basso. (December 9, 1946)

SELECTED SOURCES CONSULTED IN THE LAST CHAPTER

1. *The Huey Long Murder Case,* Hermann B. Deutsch, Doubleday, 1963.
2. *Huey Long,* T. Harry Williams, Knopf, 1969.
3. *Requiem for a Kingfish,* Ed Reed, Award, 1986.
4. *The Kingfish and his Realm,* William Ivy Hair, LSU, 1991.
5. *Messiah of the Masses,* Glen Jeansonne, HarperCollins, 1992.

Index

Abraham, Cal, 132–33
Allen, Governor Oscar Kelly
  (O. K.), 13, 30, 42–43, 98,
  119, 121, 153, 166, 170, 174,
  184, 185, 189, 225, 237–38,
  239–40, 241
American Progress, 181, 261
Anderson, Frank Hartley, 178

Ballard, Sam, 235
Basso, Hamilton, 258
Baden, Dr. Michael M., 319
Bates, Joe, 114, 127, 215–16,
  217, 219, 266
Baton Rouge *Advocate*, 320
Beach, Stephen, 299
Beals, Carleton, 256
Beasley, Opal, 166
Beven, J. L., 159
Binnings, Mabel Guerre,
  307–08, 316, 317, 322, 325
Bird, Dr. Thomas R., 129–30,
  183, 195, 196, 198, 210–11,
  219
Birmingham Age-Herald, 182
"Bloody Monday," 38–39
Boagnia, Kenneth, 234
Booth, Billy Joe, 258
Borah, W. E., 181
Bouanchaud, Hewitt, 33
Brian, G. C., 183, 195
Bridges, Burk A., 31
Brothers, Robert, 169, 249–50
Broussard, Dr. A. C., 74
Buller, Thomas, 240

Burke, Edmund G., 16, 18,
  19, 21
Burns, Ken, 296
Bushong, James, 168

Caillouet, Father Louis Abel,
  50–51
Cajun, definition of, 25 n
Caplan, Arthur, 305
Carter, Hodding, 296
Cason, B. W., 231–33
Christenberry, Earle, 153–54,
  165, 167–68, 169, 226, 227,
  233–34
Christenberry, Herbert, 231,
  235
Cleveland Plain Dealer, 182
Coad, George, 107–08
Cockerham, J. T., 205
Coleman, Elliot, 97, 114, 121,
  214–15, 217–18, 219–20,
  242, 264–66, 279, 285
Coogan, J. Alan, 100–01,
  125–26, 172, 255
Cook, Dr. William, 75, 140–41,
  146, 150–51, 199, 203–04,
  285
Cyr, Paul N., 38

D'Armond, John, 195–96
Darrow, Clarence, 180
D'Aunoy, Dr. Rigney, 142
Davis, Tom, 183, 195
Davis, Forrest, 256

Dear, Cleveland, 236, 237, 241, 242
Dempsey, Jack, 180
Dent, Fred C., 117, 150
Desobry, Ed, 97, 106, 122, 123–25, 255
DeSoto Conference, 278–79
Dick, Dr. William H., 65–67
Dixon, Margaret, 254, 255
Dore, Hugo, 113
Dos Passos, John, 258

Edson, Dr. W. L., 82, 159
Edwards, Edwin W., 297
Ellender, Allen J., 15, 97, 100, 117, 120, 170, 189, 215, 279
Ellender, Dr. Willard, 170
Ewing, Quincy, 100, 120–22, 165–66, 167, 168, 169, 255

Father Coughlin, 180
Femrite, I. I., 168, 172
Fitzgerald, Mary, 74–75
Fontenot, Paul, 320–21
Fournet, John, 38–39, 97, 112, 115–16, 118, 166, 189, 198, 200–03, 208, 215, 217, 218, 219, 259, 262–63, 279, 284, 322
Frampton, C. E., 101–02, 107–08, 119–20, 195–96, 266–67
Frederick, C. Sidney, 205
Fritcher, Martin, 330
Fuqua, Henry L., 33

Gallagher, Wes, 122
Gallaher, H. P., 298
Garland, Helen, 234
Gassler, Father Francis Leon, 15, 273

Gassler, Monsignor Leon, 156–57, 158, 160
Gilkison, Helen, 129
Gingrich, Arnold, 248
Goslinski, Jake, 183, 195
Grace, Lucille May, 117, 142
Green, William, 180
Grevemberg, Francis, 329–30
Guerre, Louis F., 102, 129, 198, 210, 212, 214, 217, 250, 259, 279, 306–07, 309, 316, 321, 325, 330
Guillory, Isom, 101

Haag, Lucien C., 310, 311–12, 315
Hardin, Fair, 230
Harper, John, 30–31
Harris, Thomas O., 103, 104, 256, 285
Heard, Louis, 114, 121, 216, 241–42, 265, 266
Heidelberg, Roy, 113
Heywood, W. Scott, 14–15
Hoffpauir, Smith, 184
Hoover, J. Edgar, 258

Jackson, Dr. Rufus, 142
Jean, Cooper, 205
Jeansonne, Glen, 294
Jones, Judge W. Carruth, 17
Jones, Ronnie, 319
Jones, Sam, 307
Jones, Tom (Spec), 159
Julias, Francis M., 107

Kahle, Dr. Jorda P., 142, 171
Kane, Harnett, 255
Kansas City Star, 181
Ken, 248–49
Knobloch, W. M., 183, 195

Kennedy, O. P., 210
Ku Klux Klan, 34

Lane, Patrick A., 323
Langley, Adria Locke, 258
Latham, Gordon, 210
Leche, Richard, 99, 225, 237, 242, 243, 279
Lesage, Louis, 113, 117, 214
Levy, Dr. Louis, 142
Liebling, A. J., 263
Life, 249
Lindsey, Coleman, 184
Liter, C. P., 167, 169, 254, 255
Long, Caledonia Tison, 26
Long, Earl, 40, 153, 167, 264, 285, 307
Long, George, 153
Long, Huey P., Jr., 14, 21–25, 66, 80–81, 86, 97, 98–108, 112, 133–34, 137, 147–48, 227, 277–89; actions in House Ways and Means Committee, 13, 15–21; assassination of, 114–26; assassination plots, 229–37; assassination theories, 247–59; ballistics test, 309–10; biographies of, 249–58; bodyguards for, 104–07; campaign for governor, 19–24, 33–35; childhood and youth, 26–28; emergency efforts for, 142–54; foreign response to assassination, 182–83; funeral of, 183–92; governor of Louisiana, 35–42; hospitalization of, 165–72; impeachment charges against, 39–40; inquest for, 195–221; insurance investigation, 297–99;

interviews about, 259–74; lawyer, career as, 29–31; newspapers, relationship with, 24–25, 37, 38; radio talks, 24; Railroad Commission, term on, 31–33; two-bullet theory, 299–302; U. S. Senator, 42–44
Long, Huey P., Sr., 26, 27, 28
Long, Julius, 105, 153
Long, Rose McConnell, 29, 171, 175, 183, 189, 243
Long, Russell B., 139–40, 171, 188, 190, 259–62, 280, 294, 295, 313, 332
Loria, Dr. Frank L., 151–52, 167, 175
Lorio, Dr. Clarence, 142, 145, 150–52, 175, 176, 300, 301
Louisiana Progress, 37

Maes, Dr. Urban, 142
Manship, Charles, 38
Marlow, James, 168, 169, 173–74
Matthews, M. W., 159
McGehee, Dr. Webb, 89, 204
McIntyre, Marvin, 138
McKowen, Dr. Henry, 142–43, 146, 150, 159, 203
McQuiston, George, 103, 209, 219, 242, 266
Messina, Joe, 98, 105, 114, 122, 126, 127, 200, 208–10, 216, 219, 229, 241, 266, 329
Michie, Allan A., 249
Milwaukee Sentinel, 182
Miranne, Edmond G., Jr., 324
Moley, Raymond, 21
Montet, Numa, 236
Moreau, Don, 301–02, 310,

320, 321, 322, 323, 324–28, 330–31
Moreno, J. D., 247–48
Morgan, Cecil, 38
Morrison, James J., 235
Mulligan, Hugh, 21
Mulvey, Richard E., 298

New Orleans *Item-Tribune,* 120
Newsday, 295, 297–98
New York Times, 35, 165
Noe, James A., 14, 126, 140, 144–45, 165–66, 168, 169, 170, 265
Norris, George, 225–26

O'Connor, James P., 107, 127–28, 174–75, 176–77, 220, 279
Odom, John Fred, 159, 195, 196, 197, 198, 199, 200–21, 236, 251–54, 259
O'Neal, Jewell, 144, 273, 284, 285
Opotowsky, Stan, 256–67
Ortigue, Judge Revius, Jr., 308, 309, 320

Parker, John M., 33, 58–59, 159, 198
Pavy, A. Veazie, 279
Pavy, Judge Benjamin Henry, 44, 76, 79–81, 155, 160, 234, 256, 266, 279, 327
Pavy, Dr. F. Octave, 93, 155
Pavy, Louise Yvonne, 76–79, 80
Pavy, Marie, 86
Pavy, Paul D., 86
Pearson, Drew, 251–54
Pegler, Westbrook, 250–51
Peltier, Harvey, 184

Perrault, W. C., 234–35
Philadelphia Record, 181
Pittsburgh Press, 179
Poklis, Alphonse, 311, 315, 319
Ponder, K. B., 298–99
Porterie, Gaston L., 197, 203, 204, 210, 220, 277–78, 285

Reader's Digest, 269–70
Reed, Ed, 299–302
Rhylick, Frank, 249–50
Riddle, C. A., 206–08
Rivers, Dr. James D., 142
Robicheaux, D. F., 235
Robins, Ashton, 159
Roden, Murphy, 98, 105, 114, 115, 116–17, 118–19, 196, 201, 202, 209, 210, 212, 215, 216, 219, 242, 255, 263–64, 265, 266, 279, 284, 329
Rogge, O. John, 235
Roosevelt, Franklin D., 43, 180, 231, 243
Roy, E. P., 117, 129, 168–69, 188
Rummel, Archbishop Joseph Francis, 156–57

Sabatier, Dr. Joseph, 119
Sanders, Jared Young, 59, 159, 230, 236
Sanderson, Dr. E. L., 142, 168, 175
Sandlin, John N., 236
Shushan, Abe, 170
Simpson, Ben R., 243
Sindler, Allan P., 256
Sissom, Dr. Nelson W., 67
Smith, Reverend Gerald L. K., 166, 189, 190–92, 198–99, 203
Snow, Carl, 304–05

Songy, Sidney, 228, 229, 230, 231
Sopher, Dr. Irving M., 311, 313
Spencer, Mason, 39, 44–45, 115, 213, 265
Standard Oil, 32, 33, 37–38, 40, 113, 227, 228
Starkey, Larry K., 298
Starrs, James E., 293–94, 303–19, 321, 323–24
Stitch, Frank J., 184
Stone, Dr. Russell, 142, 170
Straughn, Earl, 206

Taft, William Howard, 21
Thomas, A. J., 102
Thomas, Norman, 180

Unbehagan, Jack, 130, 183, 184, 186
Ubelaker, Douglas H., 311, 313–14, 319

Valedon, Oscar, 187
Vidrine, Dr. Arthur, 98, 133, 140, 143, 146, 150–53, 165, 168, 300
Vidrine, L. Coleman, Jr., 300
Voitier, Paul, 98, 114, 169, 216, 217, 218, 242, 265, 266, 279, 285

Wallace, George, 18
Warren, Robert Penn, 257–58
Weiss, Dr. Carl Adam, 51–53, 58–59, 148, 154–56, 159, 177, 210–12, 237–40, 268–70
Weiss, Dr. Carl Austin, 49–51, 71, 81–94, 115, 116, 131, 137, 144, 165, 183, 192, 196, 226, 233, 242, 248–49, 254–55, 259, 261, 277–89, 305, 322, 326; assassinates Huey Long, 115–19; assassination motives, 278–86; childhood and youth, 52–58; death of, 129–30; exhumation of, 311–12; forensics debate, 319–34; forensics investigation, 313–19; funeral of, 158–61; Huey Long inquest, 195–221; interviews about, 259–74; medical internships, 60–67; medical practice, 71–76; student, as, 59–60
Weiss, Dr. Carl Austin, Jr., 268, 332
Weiss, Olga Marie, 53, 67, 270
Weiss, Seymour, 141, 150, 166, 167, 170, 174, 184, 185, 186, 189, 192, 279
Weiss, Thomas Edward, 53, 67–68, 97–98, 131, 132, 147–48, 159, 160, 179, 267, 270–74, 283, 288–89, 294, 329, 333
Weiss, Yvonne, 81–82, 85–90, 131–34, 147, 155, 156, 159, 160, 250, 267–68, 280
Welsh, Merle, 130, 183, 195, 300–01, 317
Weller, D. R., 37–38
Wheatley, Ralph, 225
Williams, Lavinius, 38
Williams, T. Harry, 297
Williamson, Jack, 17, 18, 19–20
Wilson, Riley J., 236
Wimberly, Lorris, 184
Wimberly, Shirley, 240–41
Winchell, Walter, 249
Womack, J. D. (Red), 229, 250